GARDENS OF SAND

GARDENS OF SAND

Commercial Photography in the Middle East 1859 – 1905

Issam Nassar
Patricia Almárcegui
Clark Worswick

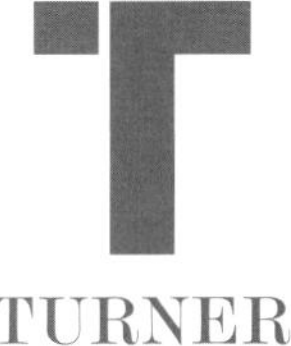

TURNER

Contents

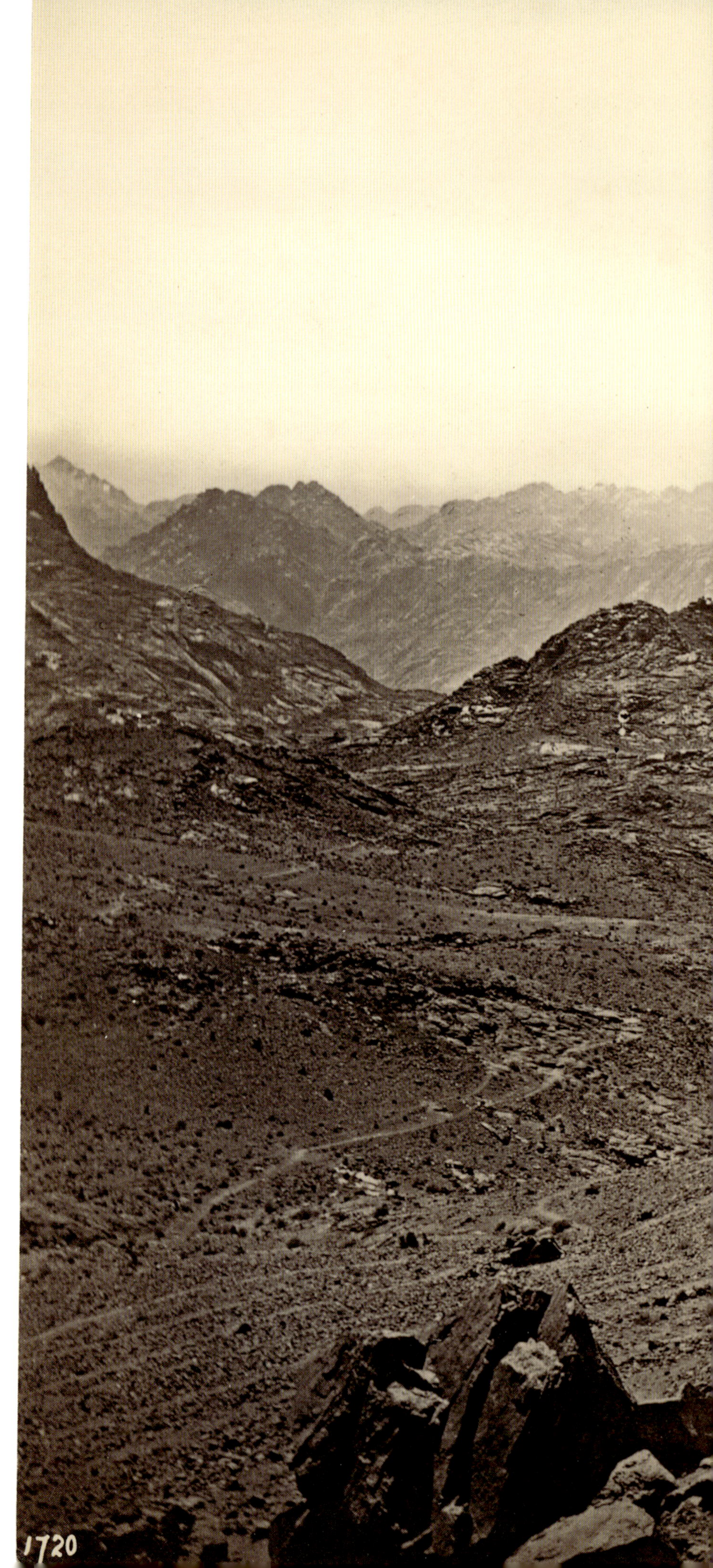

FRANK MASON GOOD
The Sinai Desert
1866

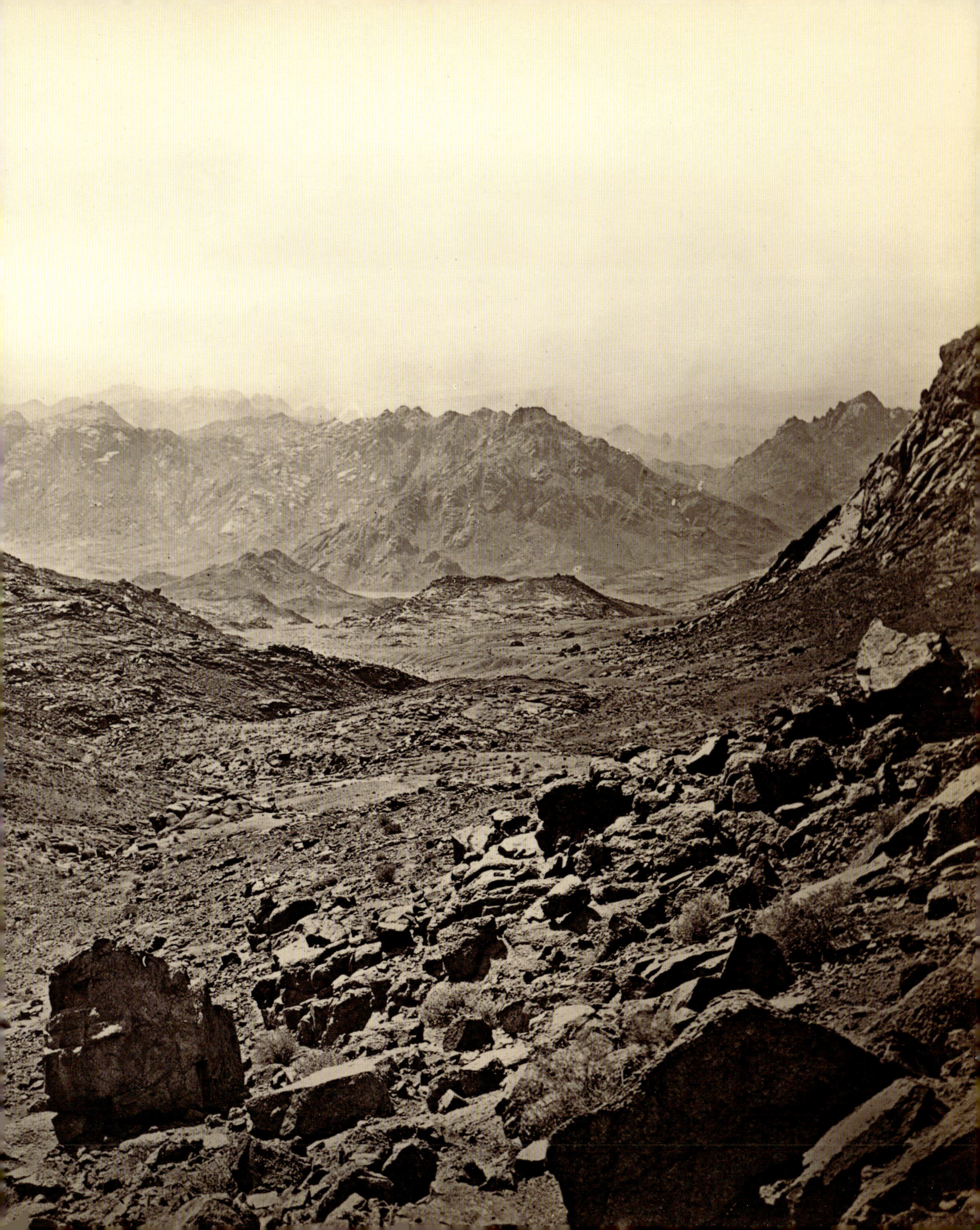

The Lure of the Orient: Early Photography of the Middle East

Issam Nassar

In the nineteenth century the Middle East was one of the world's most heavily photographed places. More than 280 photographers arrived in the region by the early 1880s according to one study.[1] Among them were many French, Britons, Germans, Italians and a few Americans. They include such renowned names as Francis Frith (1822–1898), Francis Bedford (1816–1894), Félix Teynard (1817–1892) and Wilhelm Hammerschmidt – who opened a shop in Cairo in the 1860s. Furthermore, photography was taken up as a career by a growing number of Ottoman subjects, some having learned their trade from the European photographers residing in the region. By the 1860s, the Ottoman Sultan had official court photographers and photographic establishments started to appear in various cities within the empire, most notably Istanbul, Beirut, Jerusalem and Jaffa.

In 1839, Louis-Jacques-Mandé Daguerre (1787–1851) announced to the French Academy of Sciences the invention of photography, which he and his partner Nicéphore Niépce (1765–1833) had been working on for several years. Commenting on the new invention, the secretary of the Academy, François Arago, highlighted its usefulness for recording of the hieroglyphs of Egypt and ancient monuments so that scholars could study them.[2] Three years after Arago's pronouncement, the antiquarian Joseph-Philibert Girault (1804–1892) conducted the first extensive archaeological and architectural survey of the region with about 250 Daguerreotype images of Greece, Anatolia, Syria, Palestine and Egypt, none of which survive. However, Girault was not the first photographer to arrive in the region. Two Frenchmen, the painter Emil-Jean-Horace Vernet and his nephew Frédéric Goupil-Fesquet, preceded him in photographing Palestine and Egypt, in fact, only months after the French Government announced on 19 August 1839 that the photographic invention was a gift 'free to the world'. It did not take long for many other photographers from Europe to arrive in the region and for some of them to settle and practice locally. Most, if not all, of these early photographers

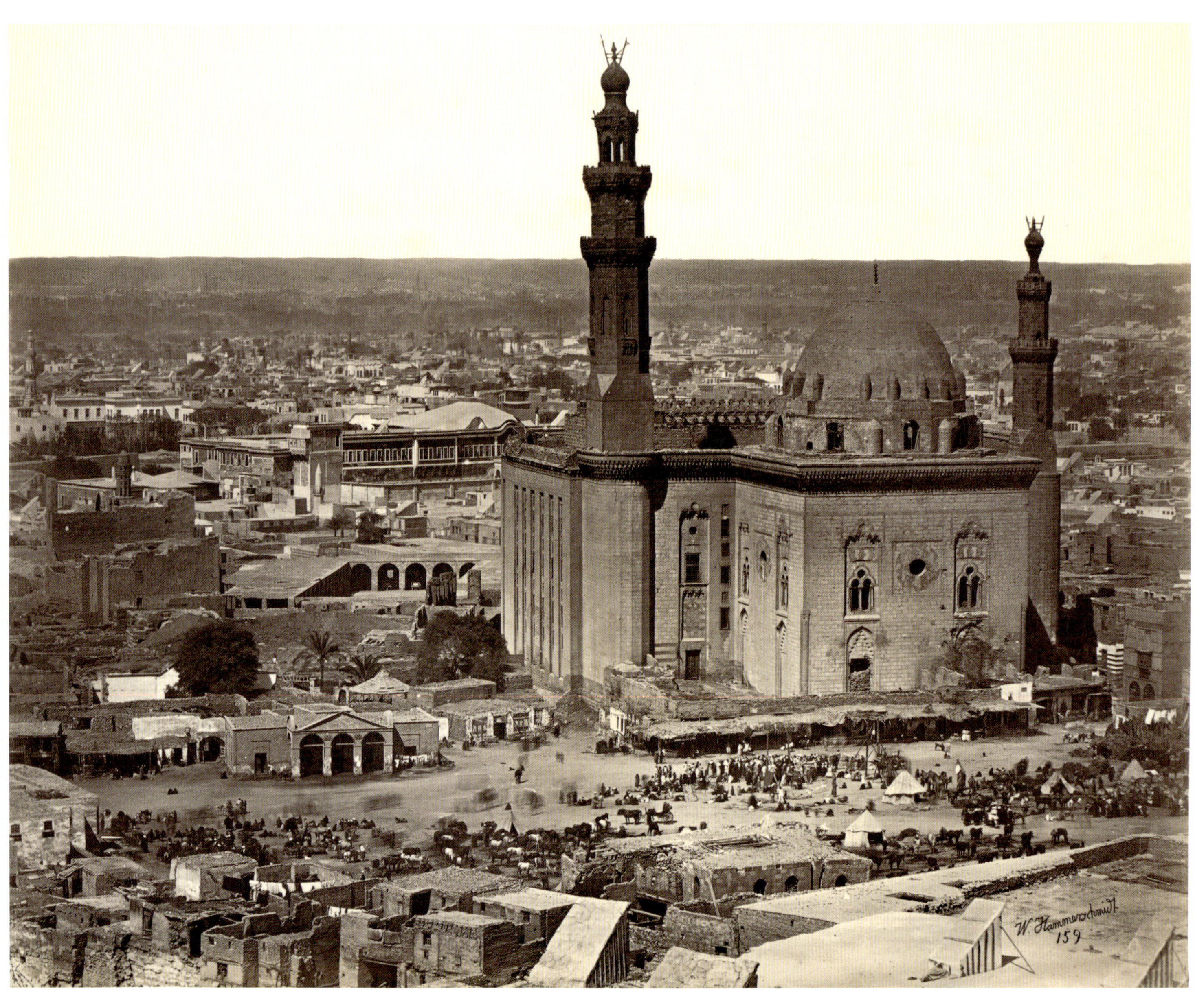

WILHELM HAMMERSCHMIDT
Mosque of Sultan Hasan
Cairo, 1862

of the East were sent on missions specifically to document previously chosen themes, locations or objects.

While archaeological, scientific or military missions dispatched some, other commissioned photographers were sent by biblical organisations in order to document the lands mentioned in the Bible. The few who travelled to the East motivated by the desire to see and photograph ancient lands and cultures did not produce images that were distinct from those on commissions. Their work was related more to the European imaginary of the East than to the region as it appeared to its own peoples. The Frenchman Maxime du Camp (1822–1894) was one such photographer. In 1849–50 he visited Egypt, Greece, the Levant and Istanbul in the company of his friend the writer Gustave Flaubert. Du Camp's photographs appeared in Gide and Baudry's album *Egypte, Nubie, Palestine et Syrie*.[3] Although this album is Du Camp's only known photographic work, it made him an incredibly famous photographer. His journeys in the region preceded, although only by a year or so, the arrival in Istanbul in 1851 of the British-Italian photographer Felice Beato (1832–1909), accompanied by the British photographer James Robertson (1813–1888). Robertson opened a photographic studio in Istanbul the same year. In 1863, the painter Jean-Léon Gérôme used their 1856 photograph of the Mamluk Tombs in Cairo in his painting *Napoleon in Egypt*. Apart from Napoleon's portrait – the main theme of the painting – the men on horses in the background and the tombs behind Napoleon appear to be identical in terms of perspective to those in the original photographed scene. In the same period two other French photographers also arrived in the region. Auguste Salzmann (1824–1872) – originally a painter – was sent by the French Ministry of Public Instruction to document Jerusalem and its environs in 1855 with the purpose of validating the theories of Louis Félicien de Saulcy on ancient cuneiform inscriptions. Later in the same decade, another French photographer named Louis de Clercq (1836–1901) arrived in the region in the company of a French archaeological expedition to the Near East headed by Emmanuel Guillaume Rey. He published a series of albums under the general title of *Voyage en Orient*.[4] Similarly, from the 1860s onwards several British expeditions, mostly organised by the Palestine Exploration Fund, included photographers as part of their teams, including Henry Phillips, James McDonald and Horatio Herbert Kitchener.

A number of the visiting photographers chose to reside in the region and to start up photographic establishments to serve the growing tourist demand for pictures. Félix (1831–1885) and Marie-Lydie (1837–1918) Bonfils moved from France to Beirut and established their own photographic studio in 1867. They, along with their son Adrien (1861–1929), photographed the Near East extensively from 1867 until the early part of the twentieth century.[5] Arriving at the same time, another European, Tancrède R. Dumas (1830–1905), set up a studio in Beirut in competition with the Bonfils.[6] Several other photographers established studios in Istanbul, the capital of the Ottoman Empire. Aside from James Robertson, they include Pascal Sebah, who established a large studio in 1868,[7] and the brothers Hovsep, Vichen and Kevork Abdullah, who in 1862 were appointed court photographers to Sultan Abdul Aziz and later to his successor Abdul Hamid.[8] Others settled in Egypt and established studios in Cairo, Alexandria, Port Said and other cities, including L. Fiorillo, an Italian who established himself in Alexandria in the 1870s. Fiorillo's business seems to have merged with that of another photographer in the 1880s. The signature 'Marquis and Fiorillo' appears on all of his later photographs.[9] The photographs signed by Zangaki also seem to belong together with this group, despite the fact that we are not certain whether or not he was a resident photographer. Two photographers of Greek origin, possibly brothers named H. Arnoux and

G. Zangaki, appear to have worked together under the name Zangaki and had their studio in Port Said.[10] The photographs taken by Zangaki cover an extensive part of the region over a period extending from the 1870s to the turn of the twentieth century. In around 1904, Ernst Heinrich Landrock (1878–1966) and Rudolf Franz Lehnert (1878–1948) opened up a photography shop on Avenue de France in Tunis, relocating their practice to Cairo shortly following the First World War.[11]

It did not take long for a native population to take up the craft and by the early 1860s there were already a few practicing photographers in the region. The Armenian Abdullah brothers, mentioned above, opened their photographic shop in Istanbul in 1862. Their work was extensive in nature and their collection of pictures of Ottoman officials, staff and soldiers is widely accessible from the Library of Congress in the US and the Ottoman archive in Istanbul. Two decades later, in the 1880s, they relocated to Cairo supported by a grant from Egypt's Khedive. They also participated in the Paris Universal Exhibition of 1867 as part of the Ottoman wing.

In the same period as the Abdullah brothers, another Armenian started to practice photography. Yessai Garabedian (1825–1885) had moved to Jerusalem from Istanbul to become the librarian at the main Armenian convent. From 1864 until his death, he was the Armenian Patriarch of Jerusalem, becoming known as Esayee of Talas, and founded a workshop within the St James Church compound that taught young Armenians photography. As a patriarch he was unable to practice photography, but his talents and energy were now diverted to teaching others. A number of his students became established and pioneering photographers in the region. Among them was Garabed Krikorian who, in the 1880s, opened Jerusalem's first photographic studio, located outside the Jaffa Gate of the Old City.[12] His apprentice, Khalil Raad (1854–1957), became Palestine's first Arab photographer, soon to be joined by Issa Sawabini and Dauod Sabonji in Jaffa in the 1890s.[13] Meanwhile, in Beirut, a photography 'renaissance' was taking place with a number of natives taking up the practice. Most famous among them was the Syrian doctor, Louis Sabounji, whose practice – both medical and photographic – was established in the 1850s. He trained his brother, George, who emerged out of that practice as one of the most important early photographers of Lebanon.[14]

In comparison with Asia Minor, Syria, Palestine and Egypt, photography was late to arrive in Hijaz in the Arabian Peninsula. An Egyptian engineer and officer named Muhammad Sadiq – also known as Sadic/Sadiq Bey – took the first known images of Arabia during his survey of the peninsula in 1861. Among other locations, Sadiq photographed Mecca and Medina for the first time. Those pictures are not part of this collection, but the holy shrines in Arabia appear in pictures taken by Pascal Sebah for the collection of Sultan Abdul Hamid II about two decades after Sadiq.

Photographs of Mecca in this collection include one taken by Sulayman al-Hakim from around 1900 and by a native of the region named Sayyid Abd al-Ghaffar dating from the 1880s.[15] While al-Hakim was a Damascus-based photographer who was active from the 1870s,[16] Abd al-Ghaffar was a Mecca-based physician who practiced photography from around 1884 and was most likely the first native Arabian photographer.[17]

In general terms, nineteenth-century photography of the Near East tended to be Orientalist in nature. Its themes, choice of subjects and settings, captions and general application at the time were more of a reflection of Europe's historical imaginary of the East. In terms of subject matter, photographs of the region pictured ancient landscapes, biblical and other archaeological sites related to ideas already popular in Europe and its worldview. They also included subjects that relate directly to the image of the Orient as an exotic and mystical place with harems, dancers and

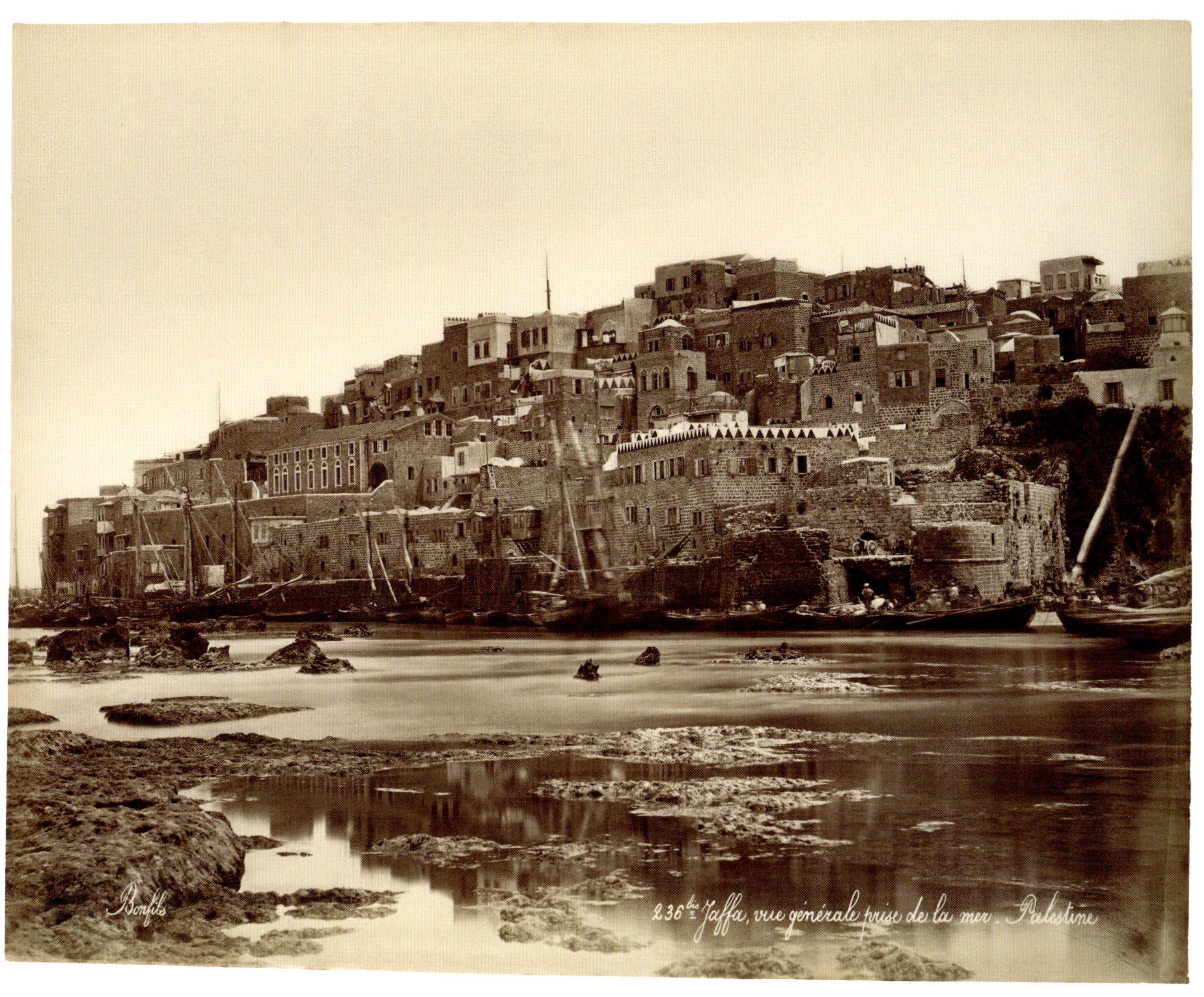

FÉLIX BONFILS
Jaffa
1870s

snake charmers. It appears that despite the 'objective' character of the photograph capturing an object in place in time, photographers of the region were not capable of seeing what was in front of their eyes. Choosing instead to present to their clients and customers images of a familiar Middle East that do very little to challenge the region's image in the Western imaginary. The problem of Orientalism in occidental photography and art has been thoroughly studied by historians and critics.[18] But that should not undermine the fact that the nineteenth-century photographs, such as those in this collection, are works of art in themselves.

Various photographers, many of them mentioned above, captured the photographs that appear in this book. The photographs, individually and as a collection, are fascinating and cover the span of half a century of early chemical images of the region. They are fascinating because of a combination of amazing skill and the themes they depict. They take the viewer on a journey to a world that is at once mysterious and exotic. A world that was only possible to see through the lens of the camera and a historically constructed imaginary about the Middle East. Indeed, the bulk of the photographs consists of archaeological, historical and architectural themes and thus leaves the people of the region and their lives out of the frame. More often than not, those photographed had their pictures taken in the studio in a carefully staged manner, mostly in order to illustrate the different types of Oriental peoples. This is how the East was represented in early photography, whose main customers were Europeans, at least during the first half a century following the invention of photography in 1839.

Granted, while the bulk consists of archaeological, historical, architectural and holy sites, several of these images show people in various settings. Aside from the usual man standing next to a monument to illustrate its height, quite a few portraits and group pictures appear. Some of the studio portraits and pictures are staged in a manner that clearly corresponds to the image of the Orient in European high art, literature and popular culture. A few images appear to have been captured on the spot, depicting a market, a Bedouin tent or village scene. The pictures that were never taken by the photographers of this collection are of social, economic or political life in the region at that time. The absence of any photographs documenting the war over Crimea, at least not on the Ottoman front, that engulfed the sultanate in the 1850s, or the British colonial occupation of Egypt starting in 1882 is conspicuous. Most of the photographs represented here were taken around the time when Egypt erupted in its first mass revolt that brought the nationalist leader Ahmad Urabi to power, but not a single one of them shows anything remotely connected with such an upheaval.[19] Similarly, the French intervention into Mount Lebanon and the civil war that preceded it are completely absent from the images.

The clear disinterest of early photography in the lives of the people of the region is evident. However, this apparent Orientalism of the photographs should not render them useless for social historians. Rather, it could further enhance our understanding today of how Europe viewed and imagined the East. Furthermore, the pictures are very powerful by themselves as they are the work of the great early photographers of the Ottoman world and beyond. With their remarkable details and carefully planned settings, those early photographs continue to have, as Walter Benjamin observed, 'an aura, an atmospheric medium that lends them a *phantasmic*, instantaneous, hallucinatory quality – a quality that is by no means the mere product of the primitive camera'. By 'aura' Benjamin was referring to that feeling that overcomes us when we 'follow with [our] eyes a mountain range on the horizon'.[20] The phenomenon of distance and awe that we experience is precisely what Benjamin described as the 'aura' of the mountains. The collection of images in this book certainly reveals an aura of a world that is grounded in history and in the exotic that belongs at once to the world of the Bible and the Arabian Nights. Still, to limit them only to those two would not only belittle their aesthetic qualities, but would also undermine the very fact that those images constitute a kind of visual archive from the period.

The photographs that appear here were taken by some of the most prominent photographers who worked in Egypt and the Levant in the second half of the nineteenth century and the first two decades of the twentieth. Together, they are among the early photographic images of what we call today the Middle East. While European photographers, visiting or resident, took the bulk of the photographs in this book, a number of images that were taken by some of the early native photographers of the region appear as well.

[1] Nissan N. Perez, *Focus East, Early Photography in the Near East (1839–1885)*, New York: Harry Abrams, 1988.

[2] On the history of photography see: Beaumont Newhall, *The History of Photography: From 1839 to the Present*, London: Martin Secker & Warburg, revised edition 1982.

[3] Nissan N. Perez, op. cit., p. 159.

[4] For more information on Louis de Clercq, see: Paul Chevedden, *The Photographic Heritage of the Middle East*, Lancaster, CA: Undena Publications, 1981, pp. 1–2.

[5] See: Carney E.S. Cavin, *The Image of the East*, Chicago and London: The University of Chicago Press, 1982, pp. 17–37.

[6] Perez described Tancrède R. Dumas as being of Italian origin: op. cit., p. 160.

[7] More information see: Michelle Woodward, 'Between Orientalist Clichés and Images of Modernization: Photographic Practice in the Late Ottoman Era', in *History of Photography*, vol. 27, no. 4 (Winter 2003), pp. 363–74.

[8] Ibid., p. 124.

[9] Ibid., p. 163.

[10] Chevedden, op. cit., p. 3.

[11] For early photography of Egypt, see: Colin Osman, *Creative Camera: Early Photography in Egypt*, London: Colin Osman, Coo Press, 1979.

[12] For more on early Armenian photographers, see: Badr el-Hage, *L'Orient des Photographes Armeniens*, Washington, D.C.: Cercle d'Art, 2007.

[13] For more on the early photographic pioneers in Palestine, see: Issam Nassar, 'Familial Snapshot: Representing Palestine in the Work of the First Local Photographer', in *History & Memory*, vol. 18, no. 2 (Autumn/Winter 2006), pp. 139–55.

[14] For more on early photography in Syria and Lebanon, see: Badr el-Hage, *Des Photographes à Damas, 1840–1918*, Grenoble, France: La Bouquinerie, 2001.

[15] For more on early photography of the Arabian Peninsula, see: William Facey, *Saudi Arabia by the First Photographers*, London: Stacey International Publishers, 1998; Badr el-Hage, *Saudi Arabia: Caught in Time*, Unknown publisher, 1997; and John de St. Jorre, 'Mohammed Sadek [sic.]: Pioneer Photographer of the Holy Cities', in *Saudi Aramco World*, vol. 50, no. 1 (January/February, 1999), pp. 36–47.

[16] See Perez, op. cit, p. 174.

[17] F.E. Peters, *The Hajj: The Muslim Pilgrimage to Mecca and the Holy Places*, Princeton: Princeton University Press, 1994, p. XIV.

[18] Issam Nassar, 'Biblification in the Service of Colonialism: Jerusalem in Nineteenth-century Photography', *in Third Text*, no. 20, 2006, pp. 317–26.

[19] Ahmad Urabi led the mass protests in Egypt following the establishment of the European financial commission that was to oversee Egypt's payment of its debt to the European Banks.

[20] Walter Benjamin, 'The Work of Art in the Age of Mechanical Reproduction' in *Illuminations*, New York: Schocken Books, 1968. Available on line in full at: http://www.marxists.org/reference/subject/philosophy/works/ge/benjamin.htm

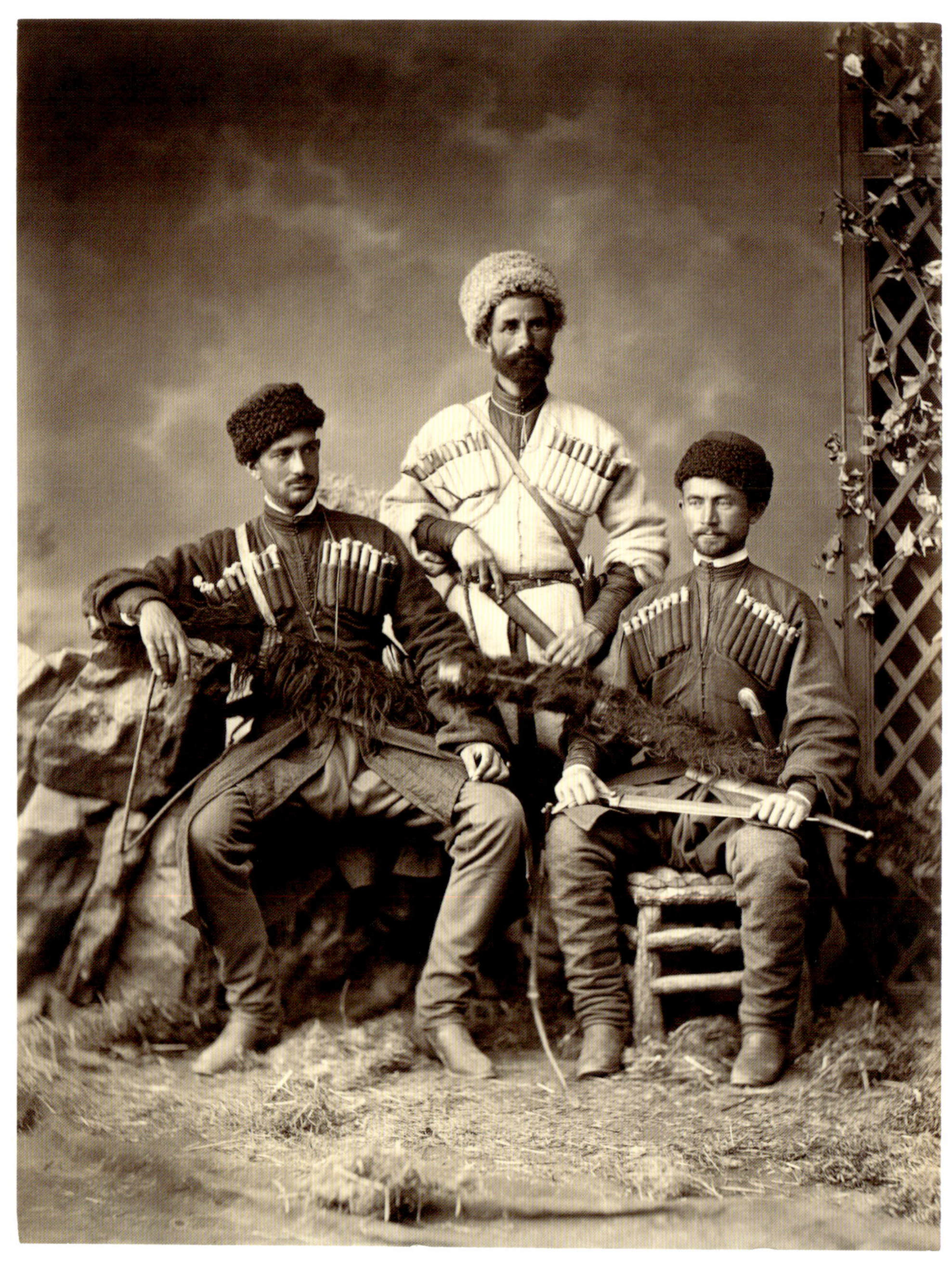

ABDULLAH FRÈRES
Circassian Bashi-Bazouks
1865

Orientalism and Photography

Patricia Almárcegui

In recent years, visual communication has become the main instrument for reciprocal knowledge and photography, as well as a new cultural form of research, due to the documentary capacity that has been attributed to it since its inception. And yet, despite its potential for evidence, the ambiguity of photography has long been recognised, for, while it documents, it can also lie: an interesting ambivalence that allows us to reflect on its role as a constructor of identities.

Photography's fragmentary and intensifying nature, its spatial and temporal ambiguity and, above all, the semiotic reading implicit in it, make it possible to de-narrativise the types, motifs, stereotypes and even the gestures that have been configured by different cultural visions. More than questioning these ways of seeing, we should look at the forms that have originated them and analyse them, with no specific aim in mind perhaps, but in order to show the new critical readings and tensions that they have produced.

The development of photography in the last third of the nineteenth century led to the creation of the photographic industry and, in turn, to photographers being sent to far-flung places to document the world and make a visual inventory of it. There was great demand for representations of exotic peoples and landscapes. The huge intercontinental mobility of colonial activity wanted to photograph the different types of people that inhabited those places of transit. Ports, cities, embassies, commercial and military outposts enabled the scientific classes and the bourgeoisie to familiarise themselves with images of the Other. In due course, the reduction in size, the lowering of the price of cameras and the simplification of the technique allowed a wider spectrum of society to gain access to photography. In this context, photography began to generate a stereotypical image of folklore and traditional ways of life. This was largely due to the way it seduced anthropologists into adopting this new technology for their studies, thanks to photography's capacity for evocation and its quick and easy execution.

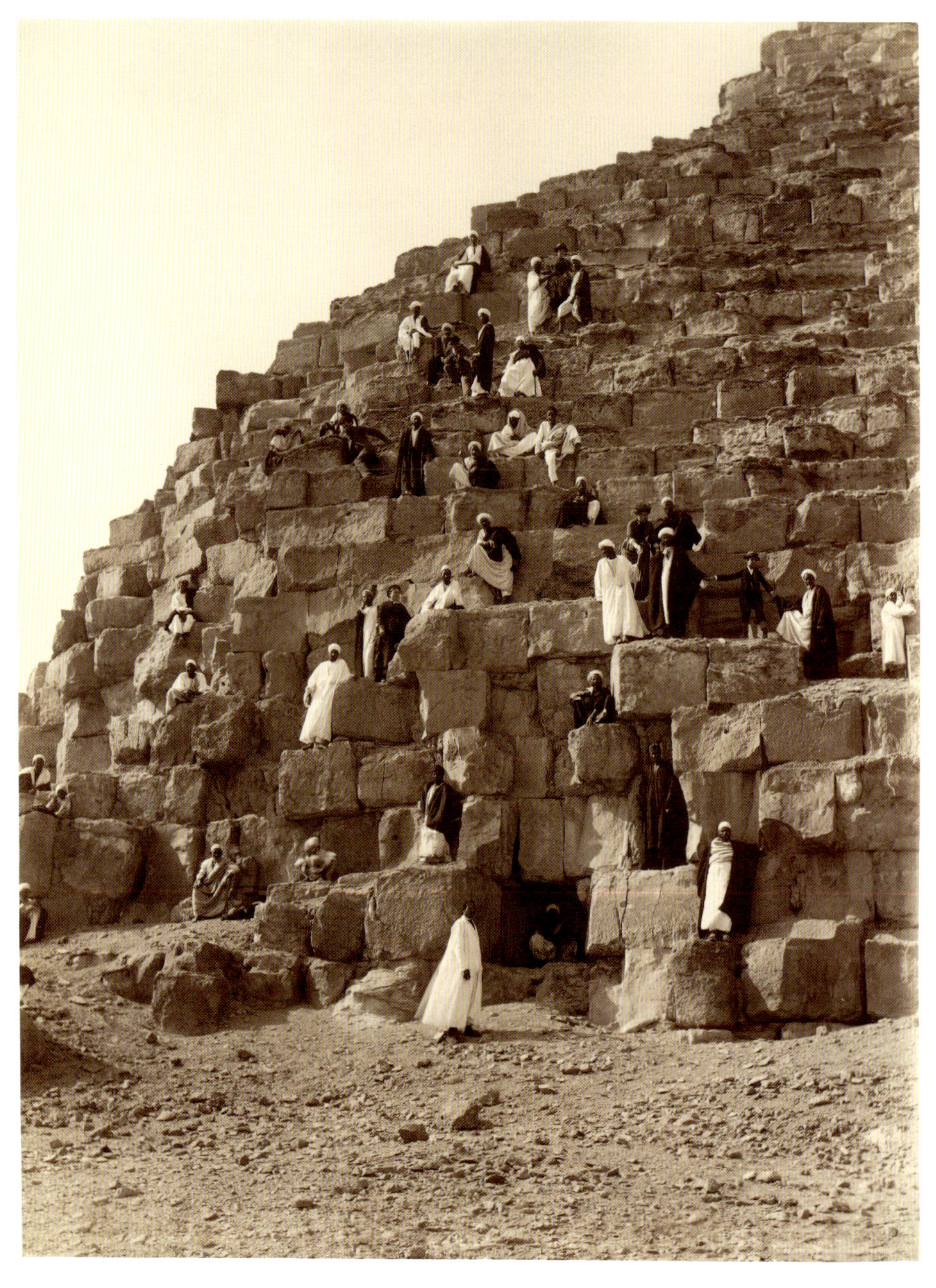

PASCAL SEBAH
Ascent of the Great Pyramid
1870s

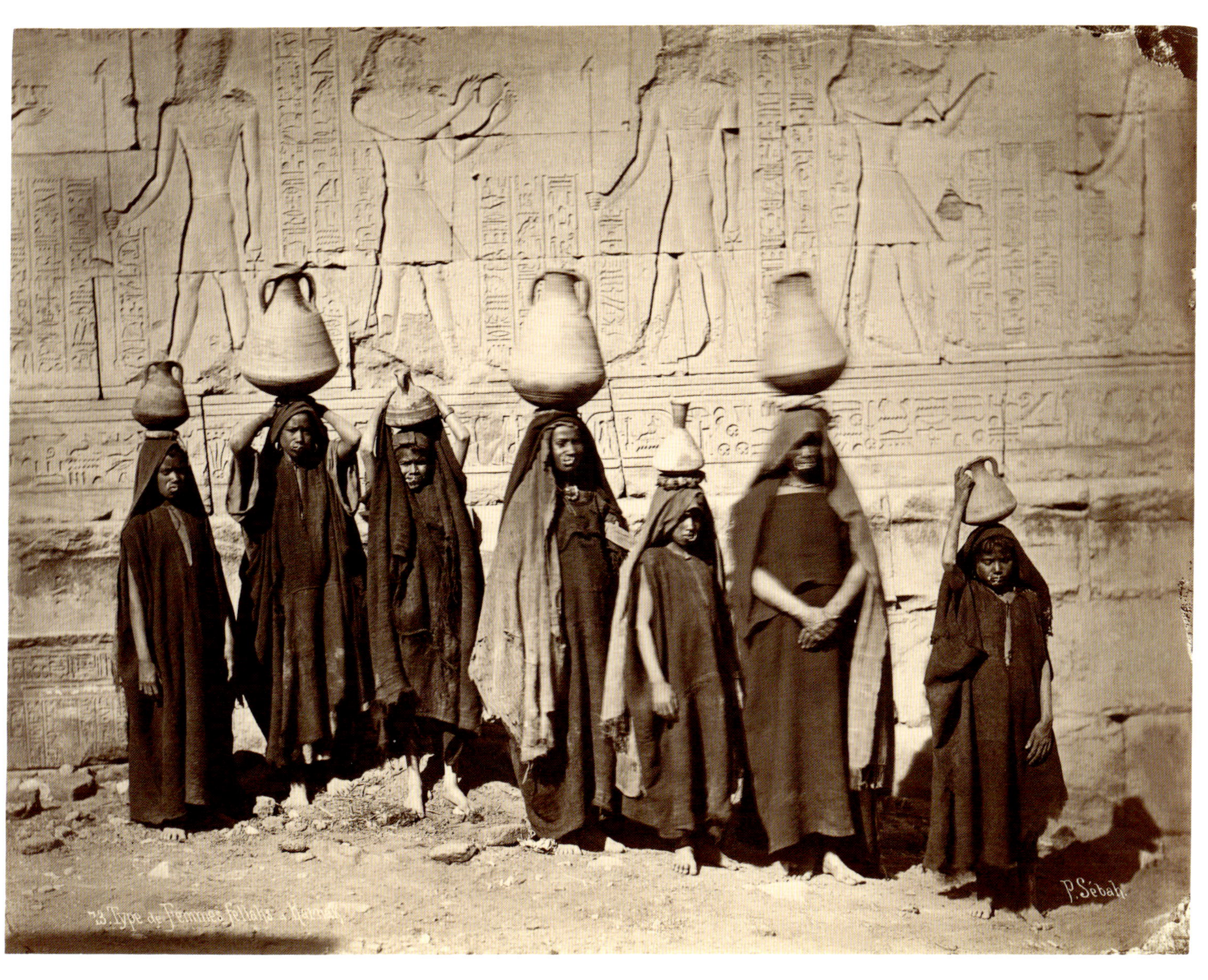

PASCAL SEBAH
Egyptian Village Women
Karnak, 1870s

Photography's allegorical capacity, and the exoticism it subsequently revealed, is one of the most interesting aspects of the way this technique represented the Orient and advanced the study of Orientalism as a result. Photography was not realist; on the contrary, it showed characterisations of ideal types that were thought to have pure forms. Thus the most frequent allegories were the noble savage, the rebellious odalisque, Arab laxity and so on. While these were nineteenth-century mechanisms whose main aim was to sell and commercialise images, they did nevertheless contribute to a visual characterisation of the stereotypes of the Orient in much the same way as literature had done before.

This allegorical sense, open and limitless, generated an interesting but complex reading. Perhaps the most significant example is the recreation in photographic studios of what was seen as Oriental types. A real space is substituted by one recreated in the photographer's premises. Models and photographers agree on a series of techniques in order to create a particular set of postures, gestures and looks. It is not the first time that this happens. Iconographic stereotypes of the Orient can be traced as far back as the fifteenth century when travellers such as Coecke, Nicolai and Ferriol commissioned travelling books with prints depicting Oriental types and customs. It is in studios set up for the occasion that painters and photographers, the first foreigners to set eyes on those hitherto unseen women, cover them with a veil, where they could just as easily have unveiled them. Nonetheless, they reveal something that had previously remained hidden: the way studios can become cameras of dreams to explore a particular culture.

This is the point Albert Londe was making in his book, *La photographie moderne*, 1896. Photographers had to place the inhabitants of a particular destination in their images to give the photograph the right scale and proportions, but also 'to complement the general effect', which should under no circumstances 'make the ensemble look ugly'. In photographs such as *Egyptian Village Women*, or *Ascent of the Great Pyramid*, the human figures appear decontextualised from their surroundings and, therefore, alien and exotic. Once more, only the eye of the photographer seems to have access to those places.

It is undoubtedly in the representation of human beings that the development of Oriental stereotypes can best be analysed. This is due to the fact that the subjects that formulate them place themselves at the same level as the represented figures: they speak the same language, and this allows them to get close and probably to appropriate themselves of the Other. Stereotypes (stereo means solid) are simplified images, commonly accepted as organisations that exist prior to the acquisition of knowledge. Normally used in a negative way, they are also the form that has allowed the West to approximate the East. Perhaps their main interest lies in the fact that they have become engraved in the collective unconscious through repetition and frequent use. In this sense, we should also ask ourselves how, through a slippage in time, the 'there and then' can become the 'here and now'.

What initially started as a *curiositas* for all things Oriental, and later developed into a need to approximate what is now known as cultural constructions (a legacy of the interest in philosophical and political motives, customs and manners since the fifteenth century), became accepted at a particular moment without any questioning. The turning point must be centred in the modern and contemporary era, when the need to know the Orient steers clear of the antagonistic images of previous centuries, based on the remoteness of the Other, and adopts a passion for knowledge more typical of the Enlightenment. Ironically, the encyclopaedic methods and objectives favoured in the eighteenth century recreate a detailed and archaeological image of the Orient that is seen as faithful and, as such, has endured until today.

In the second half of the nineteenth century, with the advancement of printing techniques and the proliferation of optical devices, there is a considerable increase in iconographic density that helps to consolidate the stereotypical types and customs of the Orient. Contrary to what had taken place during the previous four or five centuries, when Oriental motifs were circulated through prints or paintings, those same motifs now seem to be more authentic. The precise capture of the reality associated with photography helps to consolidate those representations in the Western imaginary.

In this sense, the problems arise from the differential contributions of photography to the subject of the Orient, as opposed to those from other cultural manifestations. And beyond that, from the way representation is itself modified according to what it generates. In the case of the photographs in this publication, a first glance will show that they are heavily indebted to earlier and contemporary literary sources, especially travellers and travelling books, where most images reproduce what has already been described in previous pages. In this sense, photography and books share a common characteristic, that of re-writing. Harems, views of Jerusalem and Istanbul, markets, carpet sellers, are motifs that expand through six centuries of Oriental representation. And photography, a new technique that still needs to prove itself, must verify them.

It is the same with painting. The types and motifs of Tapiró or Fabrés, the odalisques inaugurated by Ingres and propagated by Matisse (he painted over forty of them in his Parisian studio to keep up with bourgeois demand), and the *vedute* of Istanbul, Cairo or Jerusalem by Roberts or Lewis reiterate the same types and motifs. To the *vedute*, photography offers the possibility of adding a particular perspective or panoramic view that is difficult to reproduce in painting. To insert Oriental landscapes or views, painting elongates and widens the field of vision for fear that the architecture, which is a constant source of fascination, will not fit the composition. But the invention of panorama solves the problem. The first known panoramic view presents one of the more frequently repeated images in the Western imaginary of the Orient found in painting, literature and photography: Istanbul. At the same time, figuration in the landscape or in nature disappears from these photographs. The fascination is now with human types, since everything is at the service of anthropology.

As we said earlier, the composition and gestures of those types were organised in the studio: a re-codification that destabilises the images, precisely at a time when their meaning should have been subjected to objective demands, as in the case of anthropology and ethnology. An example of this is *Two Women*, where they pose in a studio interior, in front of a backdrop, in the manner of theatrical figures that conform to all of the viewer's stereotypes. The same can be said of the insertion of human figures in images of Egypt. They provide an exact idea of the represented objects, while conforming to an aesthetic composition that distances them from their everyday lives, and the photographed destination from its reality.

In this context, photography acquires yet another function: to serve as a model for any discipline that cannot travel, such as painting, for example. In short, photographers like Schoefft, Bonfils, Leroux, Béchard, etc. – all Western travellers, and highly educated for the most part – offer a view of 'those things that want to be remembered'. In other words, a space that can shift and move from one era to another, and where the study of the camera of dreams that was the Orient for the West can advance.

Gardens of Sand: Commercial Photography in the Middle East, 1859–1905

Clark Worswick

In 1853, a young English merchant named Francis Frith became interested in a new and revolutionary photographic process, the details of which had been published two years earlier in *The Chemist*. Invented by Frederick Scott Archer, a negative was made upon a prepared glass plate, which could in turn produce a positive print. Termed more fulsomely the 'wet plate collodion process', during the latter-half of the nineteenth century Archer's process would come first to revolutionise photography: then, in the next decades, it would make photography almost ubiquitous as the newest 'art science'.

In 1854, at the age of 32, Frith cornered the British market for Greek raisins. After making a fortune from his raisin monopoly, he retired to a life of leisure as a rich gentleman photographer. A founding member of the Liverpool Photographic Society, one of the earliest of its kind in Europe, Frith was both energetic and, as would soon become apparent, frighteningly active and strangely peripatetic. Like many contemporary Englishmen who marched towards the edges of the world, Frith determined to measure that world in a new way.

In September 1856, Frith sailed for Egypt on a yacht propelled by superheated steam. When the emergent photographer reached Egypt – overcome perhaps by a classical education – he was a man possessed by a consuming vision. It was Frith's intent to become the foremost photographer (and stereographer) to document the buildings, ruins and topography of the Middle East. In preparation for this unlikely campaign, he had equipped himself with an 8 x 10 inches camera, a truly splendid monster of a 16 x 20 inches camera, and, finally, a stereoscopic camera that created a 3-D like image. It was Frith's idea, as he picked his way carefully across the sandy wastes of antiquity, to be the first photographer to invent what was to become a catalogue of 'commercial photographic views of the Middle East'. It would be a catalogue of astounding completeness. One had to expect great things from the man who had singlehandedly cornered the Greek raisin market in Britain.

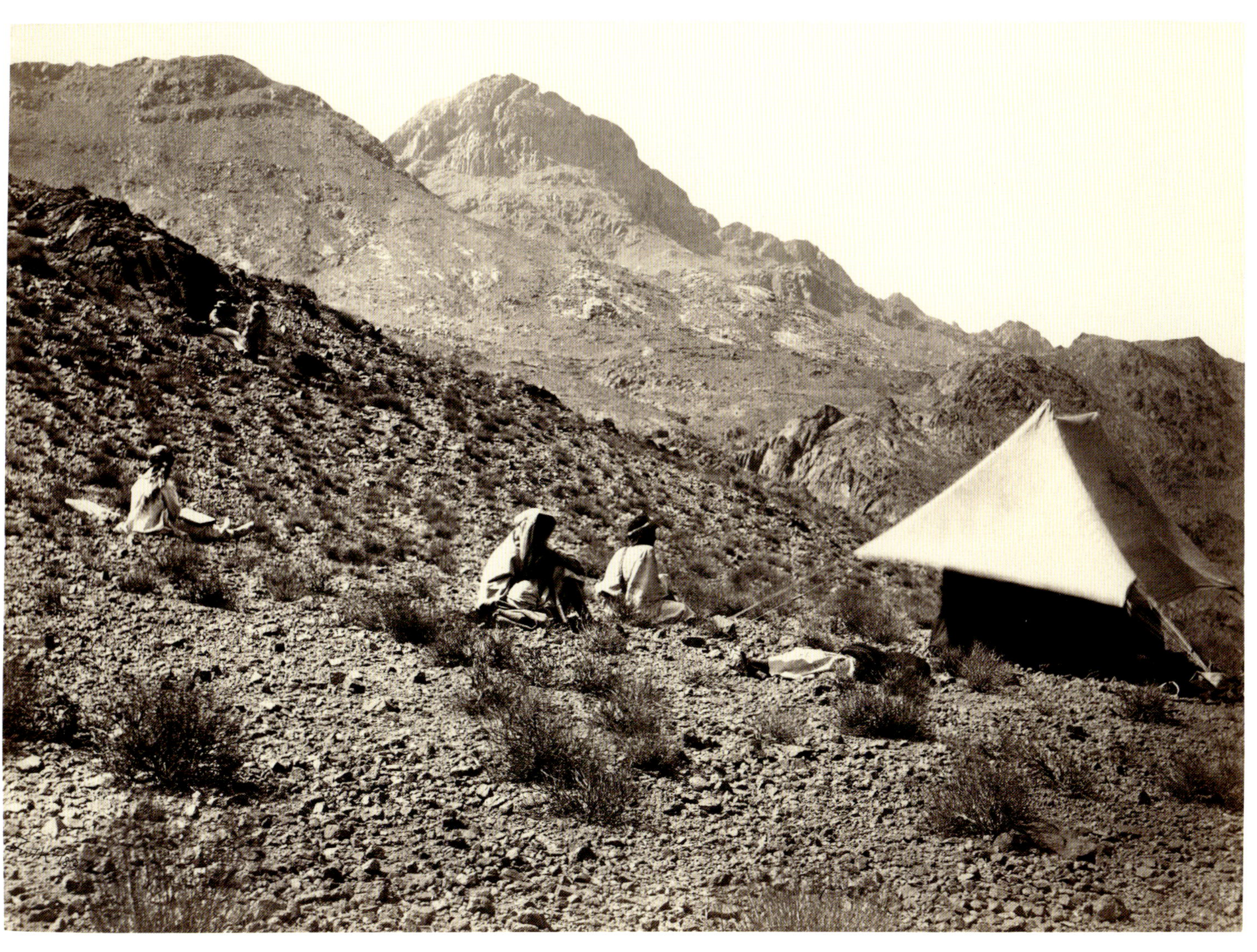

FRANCIS FRITH
The Dark Tent of Francis Frith,
the Summit of Gebel Musa
Sinai, 1857

Frith's dark tent accompanied him on all three of his epic trips to Egypt during the 1850s. He narrated the difficulties of making of a single photograph at this time.

Reaching Alexandria, Frith moved up the Nile to Cairo, and then continued further up river: a nine-hundred-mile journey from the Mediterranean to Abu Simbel, where he made negatives of the startling, half-buried temple complex of Ramses II, which had been completed in 1224 BC.

On his journey, Frith sought the coolness of rock tombs for coating and then developing his plates. But this proved unworkable. The tombs were filled with dust that settled on his plates and caused dark spots to appear on his prints. But there were still other problems for the aspiring photographer. During his photographic operations, Frith describes wild dogs running in slavering packs, insects, sandstorms and attacks by local mobs thirsting for payment of *baksheesh* from the foreigner. In addition there were unruly assistants and the difficulties of avoiding homicidal bandits who wanted to murder his photographic party.

From the perspective of the twenty-first century, it is almost impossible to fathom the difficulties of the then emergent process of photography and the labours of producing even a single picture. For Frith, or anyone else during the mid-nineteenth century who took up the new medium, there were the tortured problems of chemistry and technique: this before the worker ever reached the field. At the beginning of his interest in photography – before a single plate was exposed – the novice had to undergo extensive training, sometimes necessitating months of trial and always-frustrating error. Photographic operations were remorselessly exact, requiring significant scientific knowledge of solutions, development and fixing baths. In addition, they necessitated literally hundreds of pounds of expensive equipment. The awkwardness of these operations was compounded by the difficulties of coating a fresh glass plate with silver-saturated collodion, a process conducted in a dark tent close to where the camera was set up. Once having exposed the plate, the photographer had then to return to the tent to process the picture. All of this had to be done before the wet plate dried out.

Finally, after the now-developed negative had been dried, the plate was coated with a syrupy solution of fresh lacquer, and had then to be carried into the field in its own special unbreakable pot. This latter operation was necessary to preserve the precious exposure from subsequent damage; the scratching and knocks caused by travelling in difficult, out-of-the-way places, often, such as in the Sinai mountains, reached only by camel tracks. In the desert, particularly, one had to be lucky because a photographer needed large supplies of fresh water providentially at hand in order to affect his 'art science'. In Egypt, during Frith's photographic operations in 1856, and while he was hundreds of miles from a ready supply of chemicals, it is still difficult to imagine how hard it must have been coating a 16 x 20 inches photographic plate. In the stifling heat of the darkened tent, with one hand Frith held the huge plate, while with the other he poured liquid collodion impregnated with silver across the glass surface in order to create a smooth film of completely even consistency.

Whatever Frith thought at the beginning of his commercial venture to Egypt, a different man emerged from the deserts surrounding the Second Cataract of the Nile, a thousand blistering miles into the belly of the African continent. No photographer had ever attempted to do what Frith did, combining multiple cameras of new and differing formats with a then relatively new photographic process.

Frith's first trip to Egypt lasted from September 1856 to July 1857. His first series of photographs was published in 1857 by Negretti & Zambra of London, but also in France and America in an edition of one hundred stereos, while his larger-format prints were published by Thomas Agnew & Sons of London. The commercial results of this first expedition were spectacular. To his photography Frith had brought an 'eye' that was unique, fresh and unexpectedly detailed. *The*

Times delivered a glowing review of his work: '[the photographs] carry us far beyond anything that is in the power of the most accomplished artist to transfer to his canvas.' Impressively, Frith's reputation was established: not only as an artist, but also as a businessman who had proved there was both an intense interest and almost a thirst amongst the public for Middle Eastern 'views'.

In October 1857, Frith made his second trip, with the aim of conducting a much larger survey of the Middle East. From Cairo he set out to Sinai, Palestine and Syria, where he took pictures of Jerusalem, Bethlehem, Damascus, Baalbek and the surrounding deserts: the biblical centres of the European classical imagination. Frith travelled in an eccentric wickerwork carriage, which he'd brought with him from England to serve as both darkroom and sleeping quarters. As Frith described his vehicle, '[it was] overspread with a cover of white sailcloth to protect it from the sun [and it] was a most conspicuous and mysterious-looking vehicle and it excited amongst the… populace a vast amount of ingenious speculation… it was full of moon faced beauties, my wives all! – and great was the respect and consideration which this view of the case provided for me'.[1]

Near the end of the following year, after an absence of some months from the Middle East, in 1858 Frith set out from England on his third and last trip to Egypt. Only two words come to mind to describe these journeys: grand opera. His last journey was to prove the most gruelling of all his photographic expeditions. Indeed, of all the photographic expeditions undertaken during the nineteenth century, only one other comes close to Frith's in risk and the difficulties undertaken. This was a journey of the mid-1860s of another British commercial photographer named Samuel Bourne, who made a 'solitary' ten-month sojourn in the Himalayas accompanied by sixty mountain porters to carry his equipment.

Describing Frith's third and last trip to Egypt in 1859, the photographic historian Helmut Gernsheim wrote:

> The demand for views of the Near East [now] seemed insatiable, despite the arduous journey and extreme discomforts. On this trip he went further up the Nile than any photographer had been before, travelling beyond the Fifth Cataract, about 1,500 miles from the Nile Delta. A hundred years ago few travellers ventured beyond the Second Cataract, which could be reached by boat. The continuation of the journey to the most remote ancient remains, some 500 miles further south, had to be made on dromedaries. Accompanied by his dragoman [a local guide and expedition organizer], a cook, two guides and a boy, Frith covered the distance in eighteen days, taking as little baggage as possible, apart from the photographic outfit.[3]

Upon his return to England from his last trip, Frith was able to capitalise on both his work and his travels in a way that few commercial photographers of the nineteenth-century Middle East would ever be able to do again. Instead of letting others publish his work, the photographer now set up his own firm of Francis Frith & Co. (of Reigate). His three journeys resulted in no less than seven books published from Frith's Middle Eastern work. From the 1860s to the 1890s, Frances Frith & Co. issued additional prints and portfolios of photographic views of Italy, Spain, Portugal, Austria, Switzerland and Germany. By the end of the nineteenth century it had been forgotten that, in the late 1850s, Frith's commercial intuition had posited that, with proper and careful attention, a wet plate collodion negative could be printed many times over. It was based solely upon this intuition that Frith's firm became the earliest purveyor of commercial views of the Middle East in a manner that no other nineteenth-century photographic firm was able to follow.

Other commercial photographers would shortly appear upon this scene and it was these photographers who would fill out the gaps of imagination that Frith had not touched upon. Strangely, in the late 1860s and early 1870s, one of these photographers was to be an employee of Frith. In the following decades, commercial photography in the Middle East became a work of astonishing imagination, and these pictures of people, trades and types, the activities of the cities, routes of pilgrimage and scenes of daily life would echo the creative imagination that Frith had first carried to the new 'art science' of photography.

Doing the Work: Commercial Photography in the Middle East

In the period between 1859 and 1905 there arose in the Mediterranean littoral an audacious and unique conjunction of talented professional photographers who took up the photographic documentation of the Middle East. The construction of a vision of this place – wedged between the archaeological past, and a twentieth-century industrial future – was a joint effort of diverse ethnicities and tangled religious beliefs. The raw genius devoted to this work resulted from a startling configuration of talent the likes of which was never seen in any other place, or at any other time, in the medium of photography. For forty-five years it was 'a work in progress' created by Armenians, Egyptians, English, Turks, French men and women, Greeks, Germans, Italians, Persians, Arabs and the curious Antoine Beato, a naturalised resident of Corfu, who became an expatriated British subject and resided for the better part of his life in Luxor, the ancient capital of Egypt. During this time commercial photographers made a series of now forgotten journeys that criss-crossed both the period and the human topography of the Middle East.

In the space of a comparatively short time, these photographic artists also measured their artistic accomplishment against millennial landscapes, while they documented cultures that had never been recorded before in this way. For the first time, between 1859 and 1905 a cadre of commercially motivated artists evolved a totally new narration in counterpoint to the classical typologies of the Middle East. Studios were set up in Istanbul, Smyrna, Luxor, Cairo, Tunis, Beirut, Damascus and Mecca. A few of these studios existed for a brief moments but some survived for decades, and the photographs they compiled, in aggregate, were simply staggering bodies of work.

Equally important, the production of this work coincided with both the decline of century-old dynasties in North Africa and Turkey, but it was also a period when Europe and the West 'rediscovered' the forgotten millennial cultures and the people of the Middle East. Significantly, the work of the commercial photographer during the nineteenth century was carried out with large plate glass negatives, which reveal an acutance and technique possibly never recaptured in later commercial photographic technologies of both the twentieth and twenty-first centuries.

To isolate a single example of the diversity of these careers, and 'the work' undertaken, one could cite the example of Sulayman al-Hakim, a resident in the Asruniya district of Damascus. At the present moment al-Hakim remains the only known Arab nineteenth-century photographer of the Middle East. Outside of the al-Hage collection (now rumoured to be in the Qatar collections), today most of al-Hakim's photographs are unknown and are almost impossible to find. It remains one of the conundrums of the twenty-first century that, now forgotten, photographers like al-Hakim, who documented Damascus including the destruction of the Great Mosque by fire in 1893, created some of the core 'humanistic documents' of the nineteenth century. Such is the rarity of al-Hakim's work that, during the period 1961–88, only six lots of the photographer's work appeared in the most important compendium of worldwide photography sales.[4]

For most of his commercial working life, al-Hakim resided in the longest continuously inhabited city in world. Even by the late nineteenth century, the eighth-century city of the Umayyad sultans remained virtually unchanged. We know

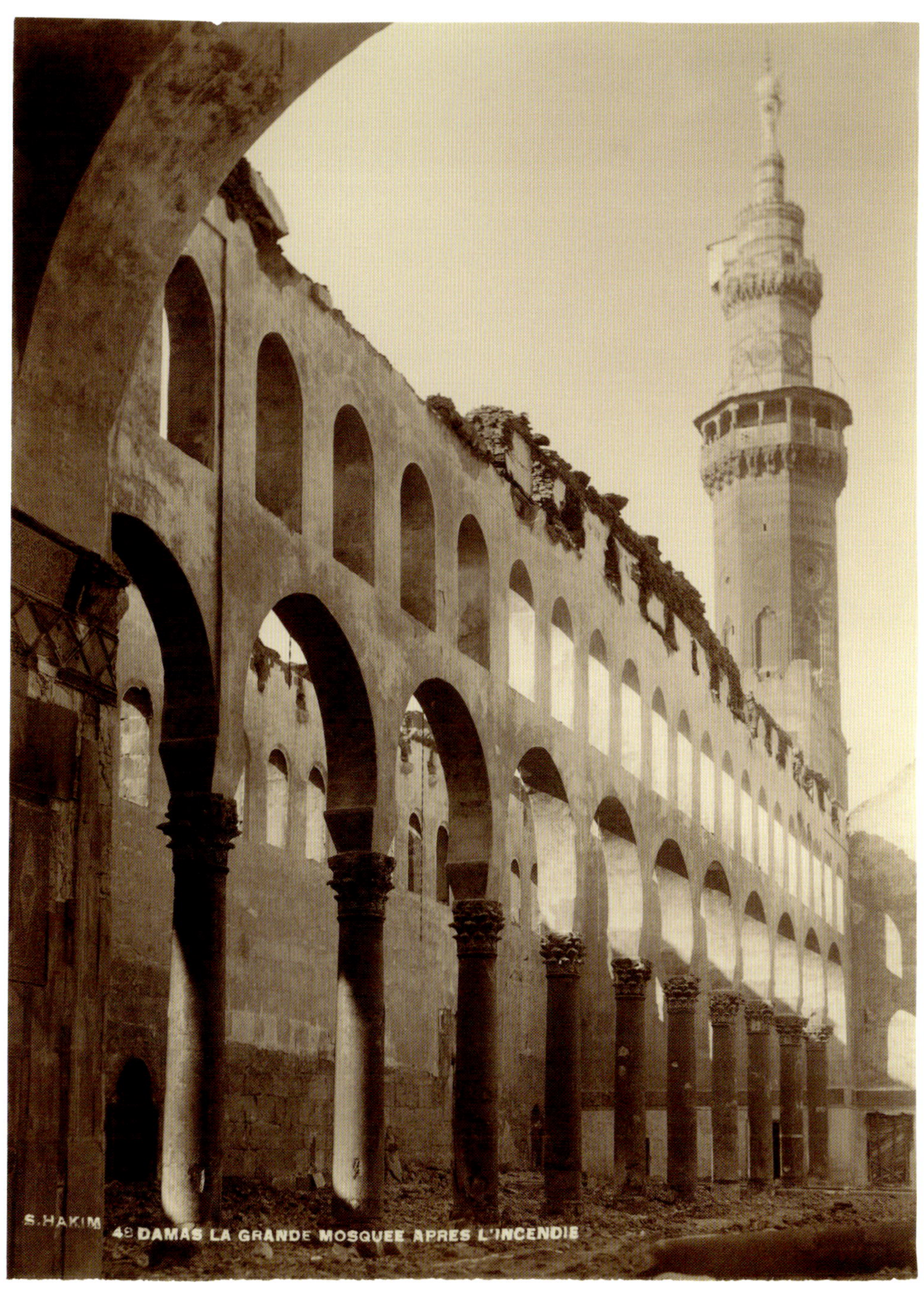

SULAYMAN AL-HAKIM
Ruins after the 1893 Fire, Umayyad Mosque
Damascus, 1893

In 1893, a catastrophic fire destroyed much of the mosque, including Byzantine mosaics dating from the building's construction in the eighth century and which had survived for 1,178 years. Also destroyed was the largest golden mosaic in the world.

that al-Hakim printed the work of other contemporary photographers, and he over-printed his name on their work, yet today his own work is so scarce – such as his mosque pictures – that in the photography world virtually no one remembers him. So obscure today is al-Hakim's memory that Ken Jacobson, in his monumental book of nineteenth-century photographer's biographies, can cite only five sentences in regard to the current knowledge about the photographer and his life's work.[5]

Today, when considering the careers and pictures of many photographers of the Middle East during the nineteenth century, their work remains a virtual secret. Even after decades of research and the pursuit of pictures, I often have the feeling that I am dealing simply with shadows. To illustrate this point turn only to three careers out of scores of photographers active in the nineteenth-century Middle East. First, there is the career and work of F. Quarelli of Beirut. A photographer of the 1880s, Quarelli made a series of distinguished yet rarely seen photographs of 'native types' of Lebanon. His surviving photographs, as known to us today, number perhaps twenty. Next, there is Otto Schoefft, of Cairo and Alexandria, whose early work in the 1860s is virtually impossible to find, and who listed himself on the back of his photographs as '*O. Schoefft, Photographe de la cour d'Egypte*'. It was Schoefft, recognised now by only a few surviving pictures, who crafted an almost literary and heroic vision of his Egyptian and Bedouin subjects. Finally, there is the great mystery of Sayyid Abd al-Ghaffar Tabeeb Makkah (Doctor of Mecca), believed to be of Indian or Malay birth, whose work documenting the holy city in the mid-1880s is almost never seen and whose bibliography remains opaque despite two generations of scholarly research. An additional point of interest to these now nearly invisible careers is that none of the photographers cited above, nor their works, appear in the collected worldwide photographic auction records of the period 1961–88.

The single most difficult textual problem besetting any study of nineteenth-century photography of the Middle East is simply the paucity of distinguished, rare and mostly inaccessible pictures available for publication. This fact – combined with the scarcity of bibliographical texts detailing the lives of nineteenth-century photographers – has until recently made the creation of a book on Middle Eastern commercial photography a project fraught with difficulties. With the appearance some years ago, however, of Nissan Perez's book *Focus East, Early Photography in the Near East (1839–1885)*, and more recently Ken Jacobson's *Odalisques & Arabesques: Orientalist Photography 1839–1925*, much has been revealed about the concerns and fascinations of nineteenth-century Middle Eastern photographers.

One then turns, however, from bibliographical difficulties to the larger problem of finding grand Middle Eastern pictures of the nineteenth century. It is the oddest circumstance, but after decades of thinking about this problem I blame this absence of remarkable pictures upon the then newly introduced nineteenth-century Cook's *Tour of Egypt and the Holy Land*. It was Thomas Cook & Son who, in the 1880s, introduced package tours to the Middle East: 'Every Expenditure Provided For… The Acme of Travel Without Trouble.' In a kind of Gresham's law of commerce, an economic maxim that relates to counterfeit money driving out good money, package tourists suddenly appeared in the Middle East in ungodly hoards, eager to patronise the commercial photographers of the region, who in turn supplied ready-made travel souvenirs in the form of photographic albums. For a few years the result of this new custom was a kind of commercial photographic nirvana. By the mid-1880s, however, it appeared there were too many photographic studios in operation in the Middle East. In a corollary to Gresham's law, supply rose to demand, with a drastic falling off of photographic vision and quality.

Photographic 'art' changed into flat and often uninspired confections of 'native types' along with tired banquets of ancient monuments. It is in this work, which is undistinguished and banal, that a conundrum of nineteenth-century Middle Eastern commercial photography arises today. The task of the collector or the museum curator is fixed like a lodestar upon unearthing the great pictures. One trolls through the archives. One opens decades of photographic auction catalogues in order to discover great pictures of the nineteenth century made in the Middle East that have avoided the twin wrecks of mediocrity and deteriorated condition.

The final irony of Middle Eastern photography and its scarcity appears at this point. As much as ninety-eight percent of the work purchased in the shops of Middle Eastern nineteenth-century photographers was carefully pasted down onto album pages that have proved to be highly acidic. The triage of the distinguished nineteenth-century Middle Eastern photograph has been horrendous. Almost universally the nineteenth-century photographic albums supplied by the photographers of Cairo or Istanbul – who created these pictures – have caused them to fade away into acidified oblivion. The work of the collector proceeds: he must undertake the work of discovering the comparatively few important pictures that have survived this artistic holocaust. After decades of searching one comes to the conclusion that only one picture in two hundred has survived this immense wreck. If the work of the Middle Eastern photographer during the nineteenth century entailed the creation of remarkable pictures… today the work of the twenty-first century is finding them.

1859–1905: The Commercial Studios

In Cairo or Beirut, of the scores of photographers who undertook the commercial wager of establishing a studio in the Middle East during the nineteenth century, most lasted less than a few short seasons. The setting up of a commercial photographic studio in the Middle East was always beset by risk. In Cairo, studios appeared, like that of W. Hammerschmidt (1860–65) and Royer & Aufiere (1860s), only to disappear. Local 'native' support for these establishments proved ephemeral. For those few artists that survived, commercial photography in the nineteenth-century Middle East had other hazards.

During the winter seasons from the late 1850s to the late 1870s, too few European tourists appeared in the Middle East to generate enough custom for a commercial photographic studio to survive. A photographer sometimes waited weeks for a single customer. It was reported by Henri Rombau, an early assistant in the Bonfils firm of Beirut, that the studio once went for fifteen days without a single client. For the photographer intent on making his pictures, there were other problems of uncooperative assistants and transport, and problems with the donkeys and camels that carried the apparatus and chemicals. There were additional uncharted business risks, both artistic and financial, that were nothing less than daunting, such as recalcitrant tribes, sunstroke, bad water and difficult, if not impossible, conditions of travel across deserts that have recorded the hottest temperatures on earth.

Against the vastness of the scale of human time in the Middle East, the nineteenth-century commercial photographer's work was barely fifty years in duration.

With the success of the pocket Kodak camera in the1890s, literally everyone, everywhere, took up 'instant photography'. Without so much as a glance backwards at the accomplishments of the nineteenth-century commercial photographer of the Middle East, the medium passed into extinction. With the studios went a whole oeuvre of large-plate, intensely formalist studio photography. Gone, too, was work that was invariably closely detailed and observed. The recorded memories of these

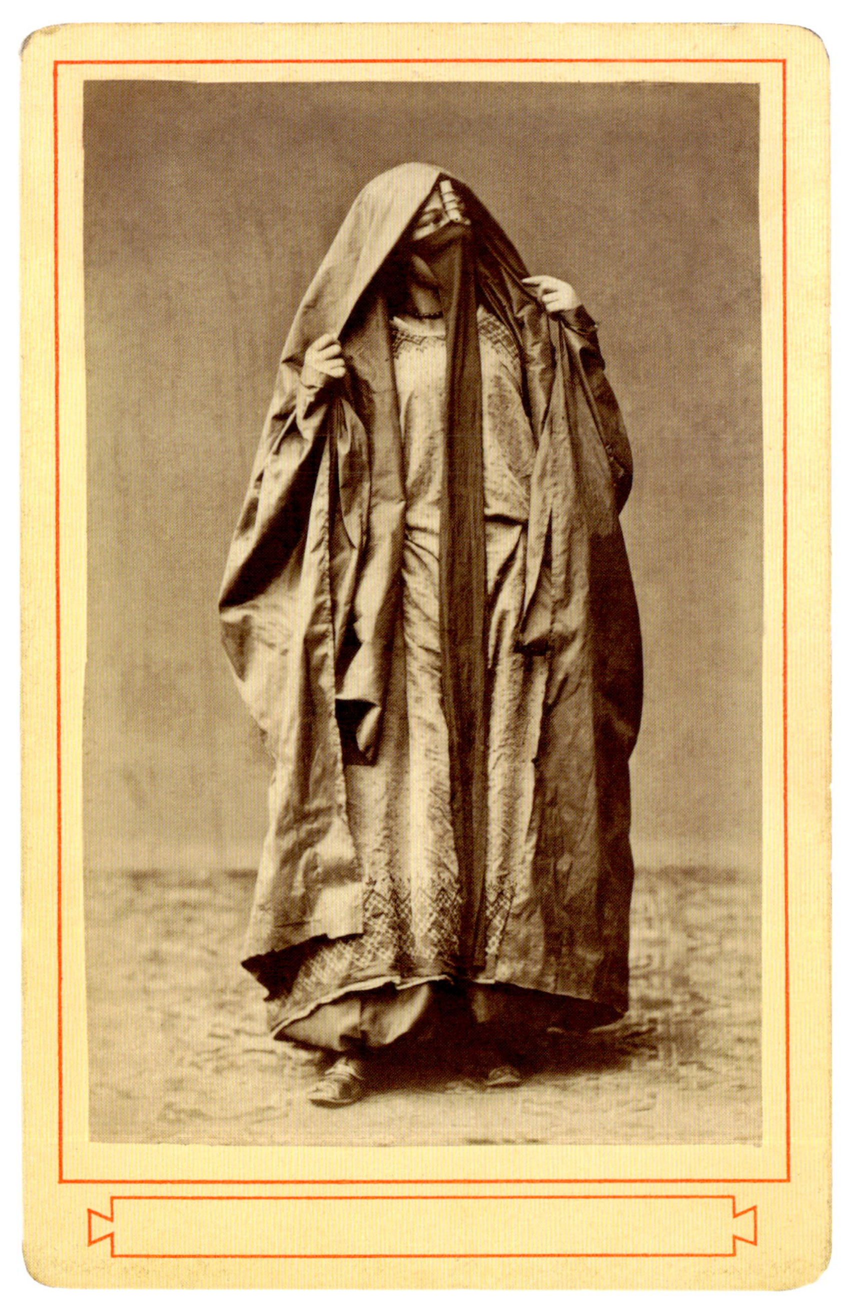

OTTO SCHOEFFT
Woman Wearing a Face Mask
mid-1860s

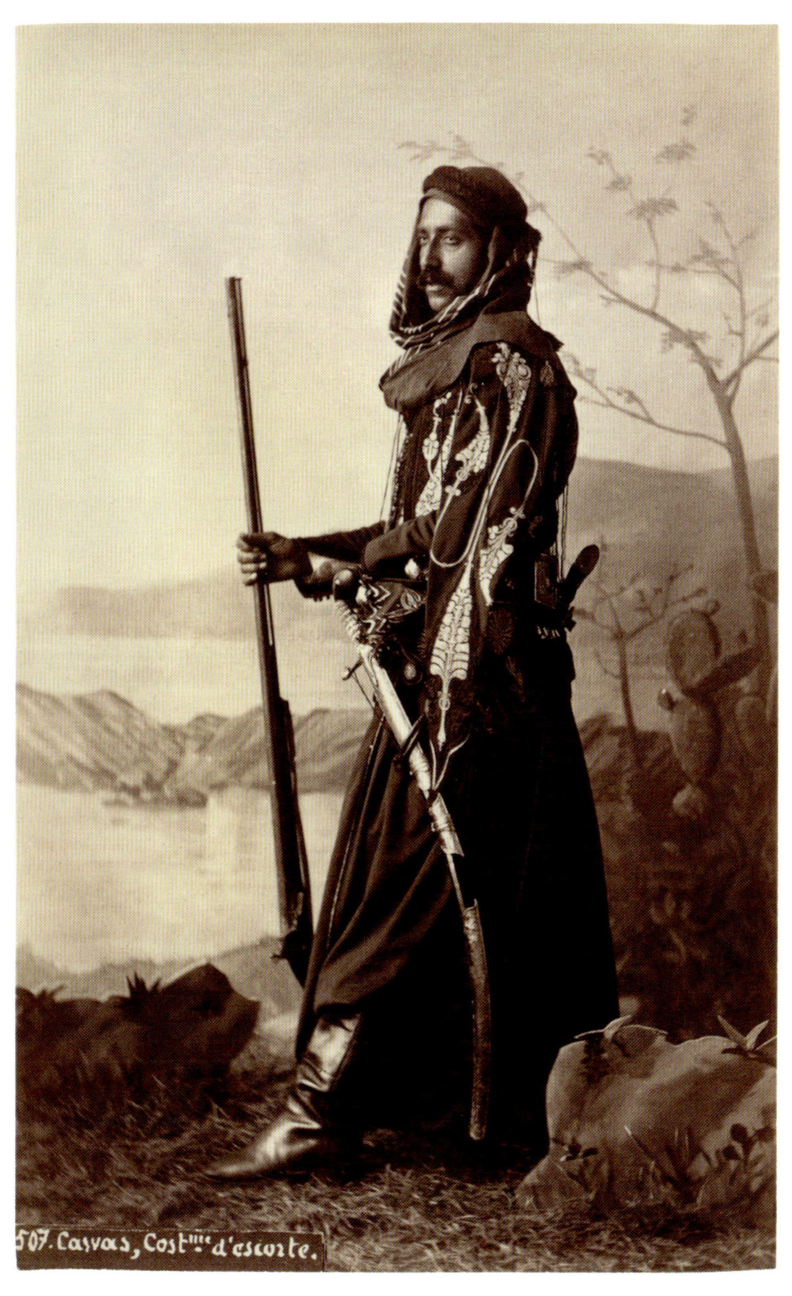

F. QUARELLI
Middle East Captain of the Armed Escort
1870s

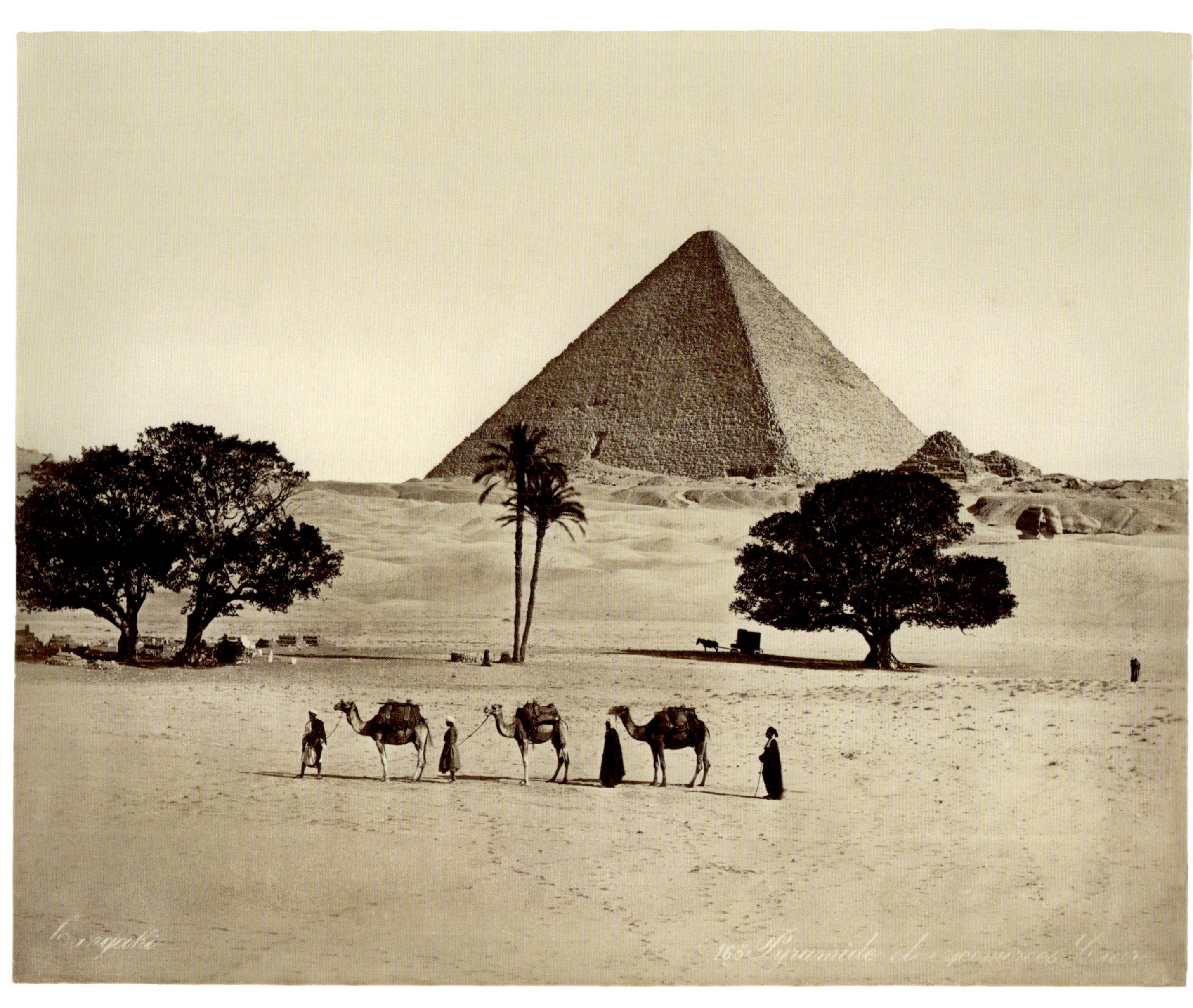

GEORGE AND CONSTANTINE ZANGAKI
Pyramid, Camels and Photographer's Van
1880s

photographers, their accomplishments, the records of their remarkable journeys and even in some cases their names were faced with extinction.

Like many of the extinctions wrought by time in the Middle East, the great commercial photographic firms of the nineteenth century expired in unremarked silence. A few years after the turn of the century, their negatives were sold off in the souks by the hundredweight for scrap glass. In turn, skilled darkroom workers, who had previously produced photographic masterpieces, now only found work producing abbreviated versions of extraordinary pictures in the new format of the picture postcard. Thousands, then millions upon millions of postcards were produced that shrank the Middle East down to 80 x 120 cm (3½ x 5 inches). From the end of this narrative, we return to the beginnings.

It is May 1859. Above the Third Cataract of the Nile, Francis Frith is on his third and last trip. His aim was to penetrate the upper Nile and to embark on the longest photographic expedition ever undertaken in Egypt, throwing down a marker for the future and making a 1,500-mile, Victorian epic-journey, purely photographic in nature. It would be difficult to duplicate (and it never was). In his own words Frith describes the making of a single photograph. The narrative itself is epic.

> The difficulties which I had to overcome in working with collodion, in those hot and dry climates, were also very serious. [At the Second Cataract, one thousand miles from the mouth of the Nile], with the thermometer at 120–130° in my tent, the collodion actually boiled when pouring upon the glass plate. I almost despaired of success. By degrees, however, I overcame this and other difficulties; but suffered a good deal throughout the journey from the severe labour rendered necessary by the rapidity with which every stage of the process must be accomplished in climates such as these; and, from excessive perspiration, consequent on the suffocating heat of a small tent, from which every ray of light, and consequently every breath of air, was necessarily excluded.

[1] *Egypt & Palestine Photographed and Described by Francis Frith, 1858–1859*, vol. II.

[2] See: *Photographic Journeys in the Himalayas, Samuel Bourne 1863–1866*, superbly edited by Hugh Rayner, Bath: Pagoda Tree Press, 2009.

[3] Helmut & Alison Gernsheim, *The History of Photography 1685–1914*, New York: McGraw-Hill, 1969, p. 286.

[4] Gary Edwards, *The International Guide to Nineteenth-Century Photographers and Their Work*, Boston: G.K. Hall, 1988, p. 237.

[5] Ken Jacobson, *Odalisques & Arabesques: Orientalist Photography 1839–1925*, London: Bernard Quaritch, 2008, p. 204.

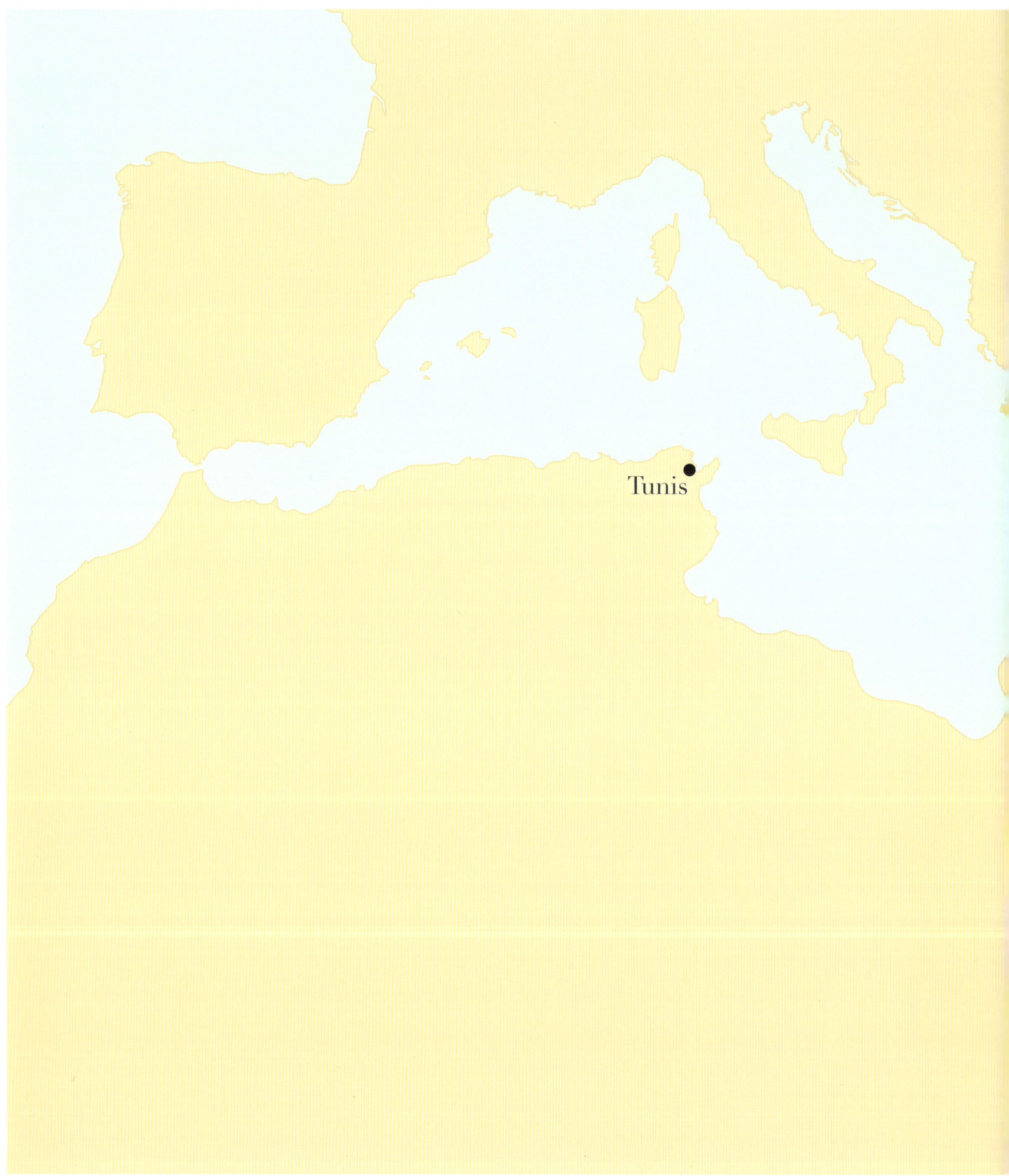
Tunis

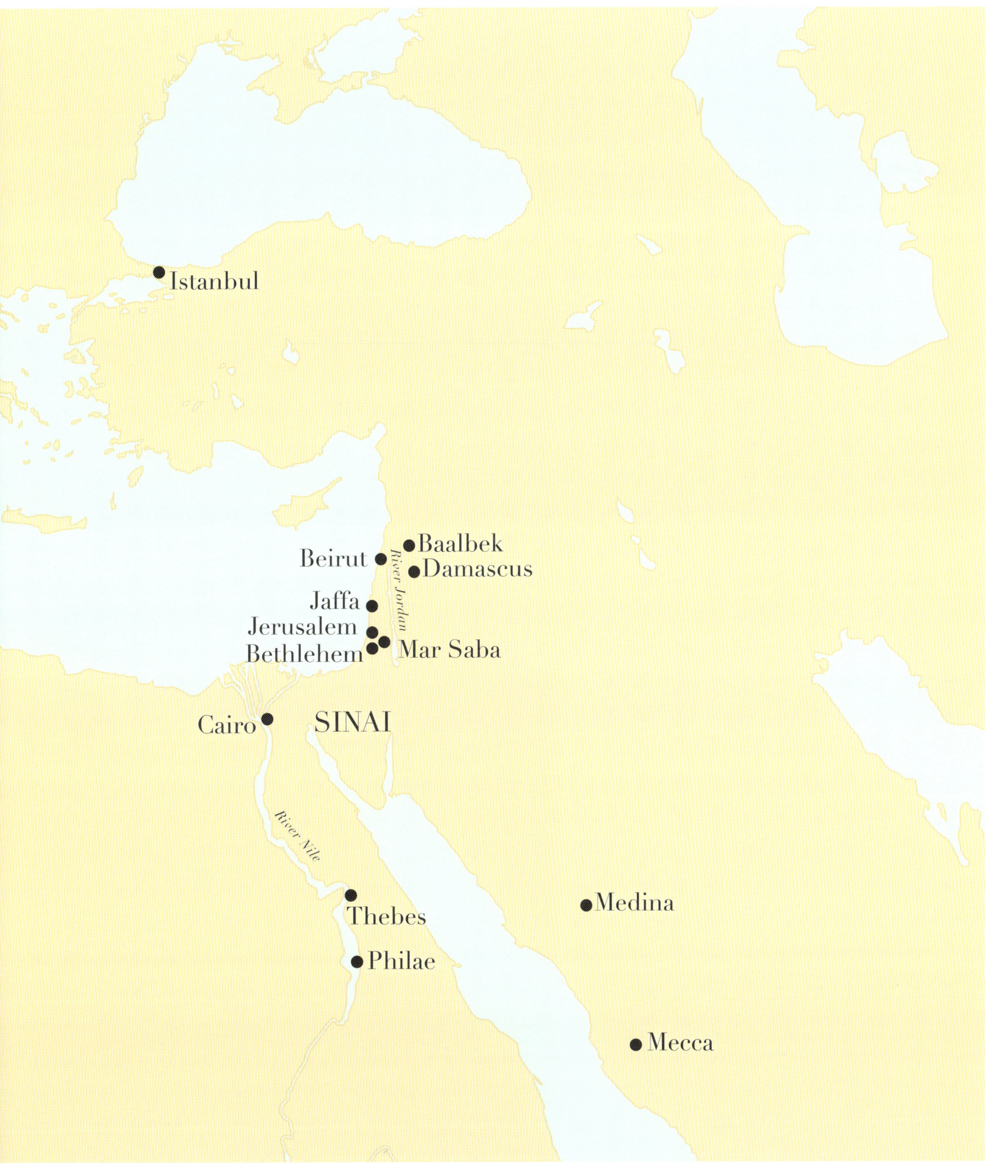
Istanbul
Baalbek
Beirut
River Jordan
Damascus
Jaffa
Jerusalem
Bethlehem
Mar Saba
Cairo
SINAI
River Nile
Thebes
Philae
Medina
Mecca

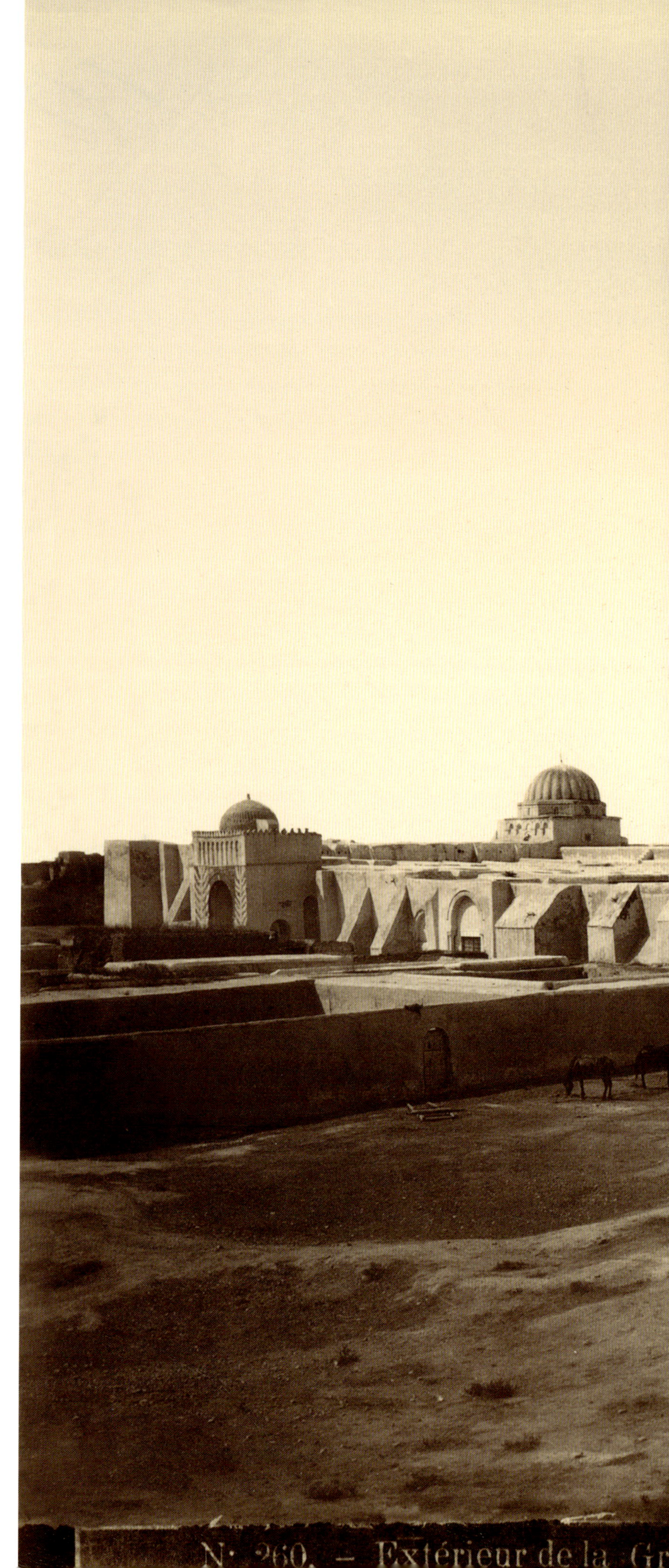

GARRIGUES
Great Mosque of Kairouan
Tunis, 1880s

The Mosque of Uqba, also known as the Great Mosque of Kairouan, is the fourth oldest in Islam, and was built by the Arab general Uqba ibn Nafi from AD 670 at the founding of the city. The mosque is spread over a surface area of 9,000 square metres and is considered the oldest place of worship in the western Islamic world, as well as a model for all later mosques in the Maghreb. It was from Kairouan that the invasions of Spain (AD 711) and Italy (AD 827) were mounted by the Arabs.

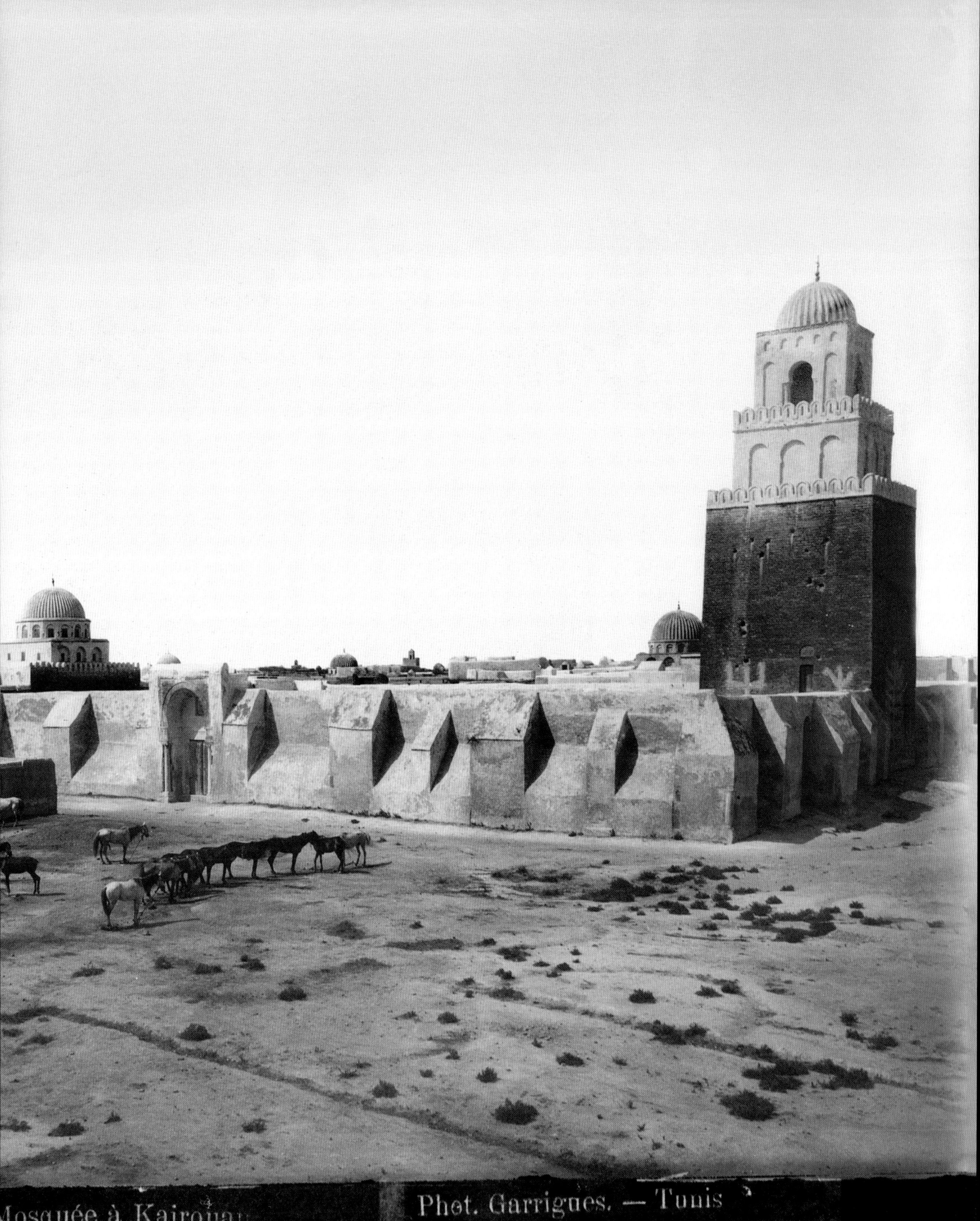
Mosquée à Kairouan.
Phot. Garrigues. — Tunis

The women dress, like the men, handsomely. Indoors they wear, I am told, a Sudayriyah, or bodice of calico and other stuffs, like the Choli *of India, which supports the bosom without the evils of European stays. Over this is a Saub, or white shirt, of the white stuff called* Halaili *or* Burunjuk, *with enormous sleeves, and flowing down to the feet; the* Sarwal *or pantaloons are not wide, like the Egyptians', but rather tight, approaching to the Indian cut, without its exaggeration. Abroad, they throw over the head a silk or a cotton* Milayah, *generally chequered white and blue. The* Burka, *all over El Hejaz, is white, a decided improvement in point of cleanliness upon that of Egypt.'*

Richard F. Burton, *Pilgrimage to El Medinah and Meccah*, 1855

ALEXANDRE LEROUX
Women with Veils
Algeria, 1880s

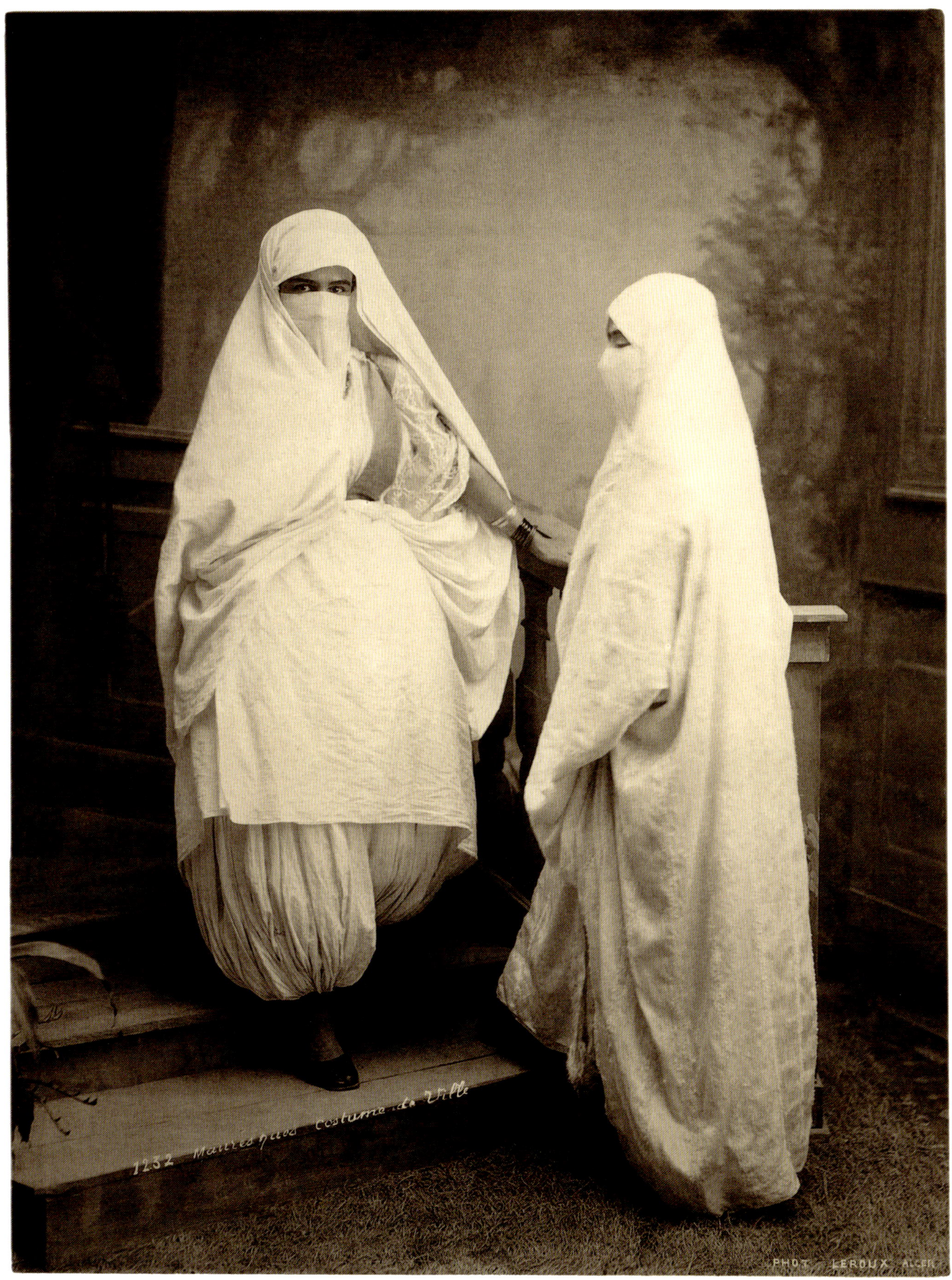
1232 Mauresques costume de Ville
PHOT. LEROUX ALGER

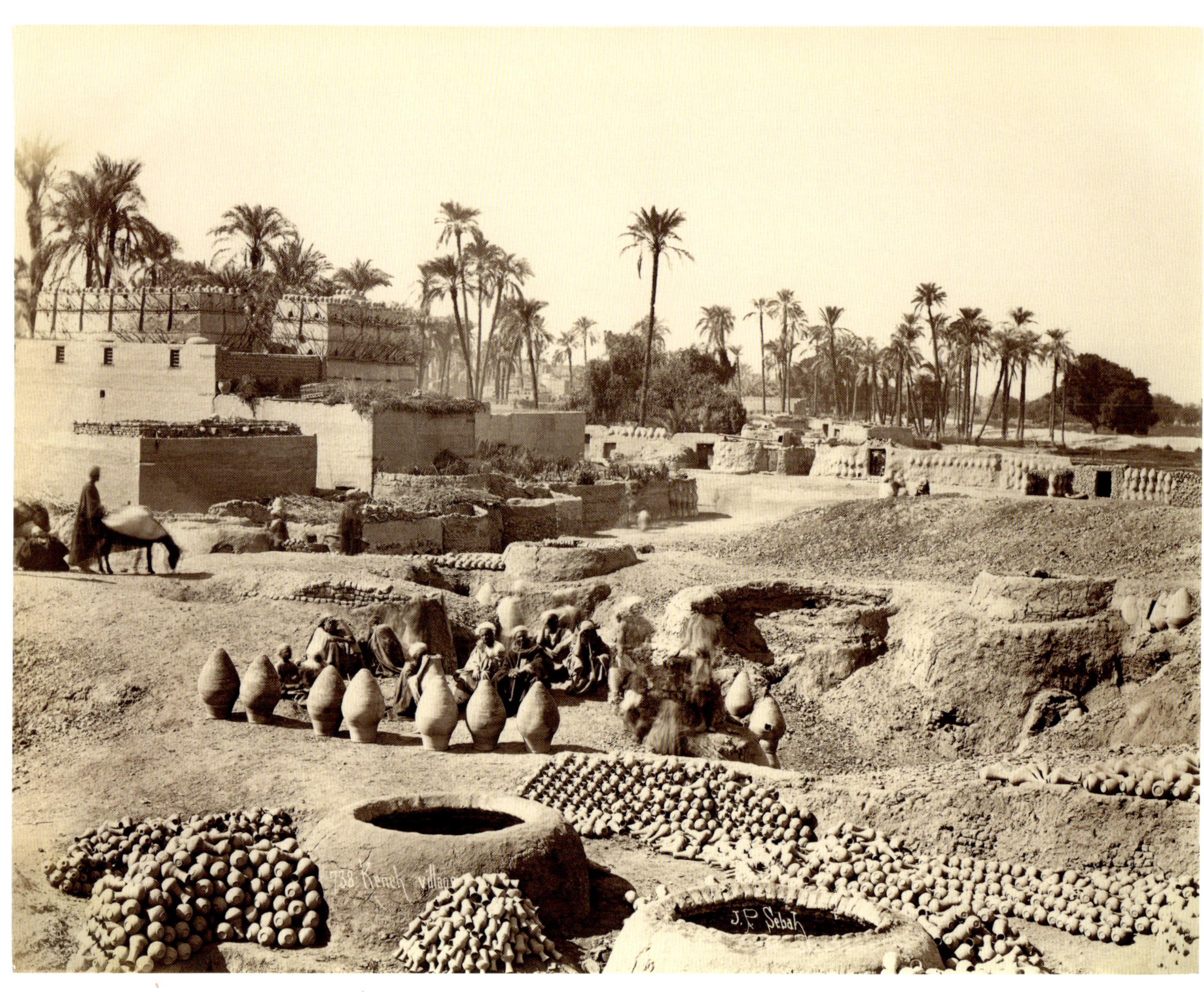

PASCAL SEBAH
Qena Village
1870s

The village, 650 kilometers up the Nile from Cairo and close to the ruins at Dendera, has for more than three millennia specialised in making a drinking vessel called a *gullah*, which is exported to the Arabian Peninsula.

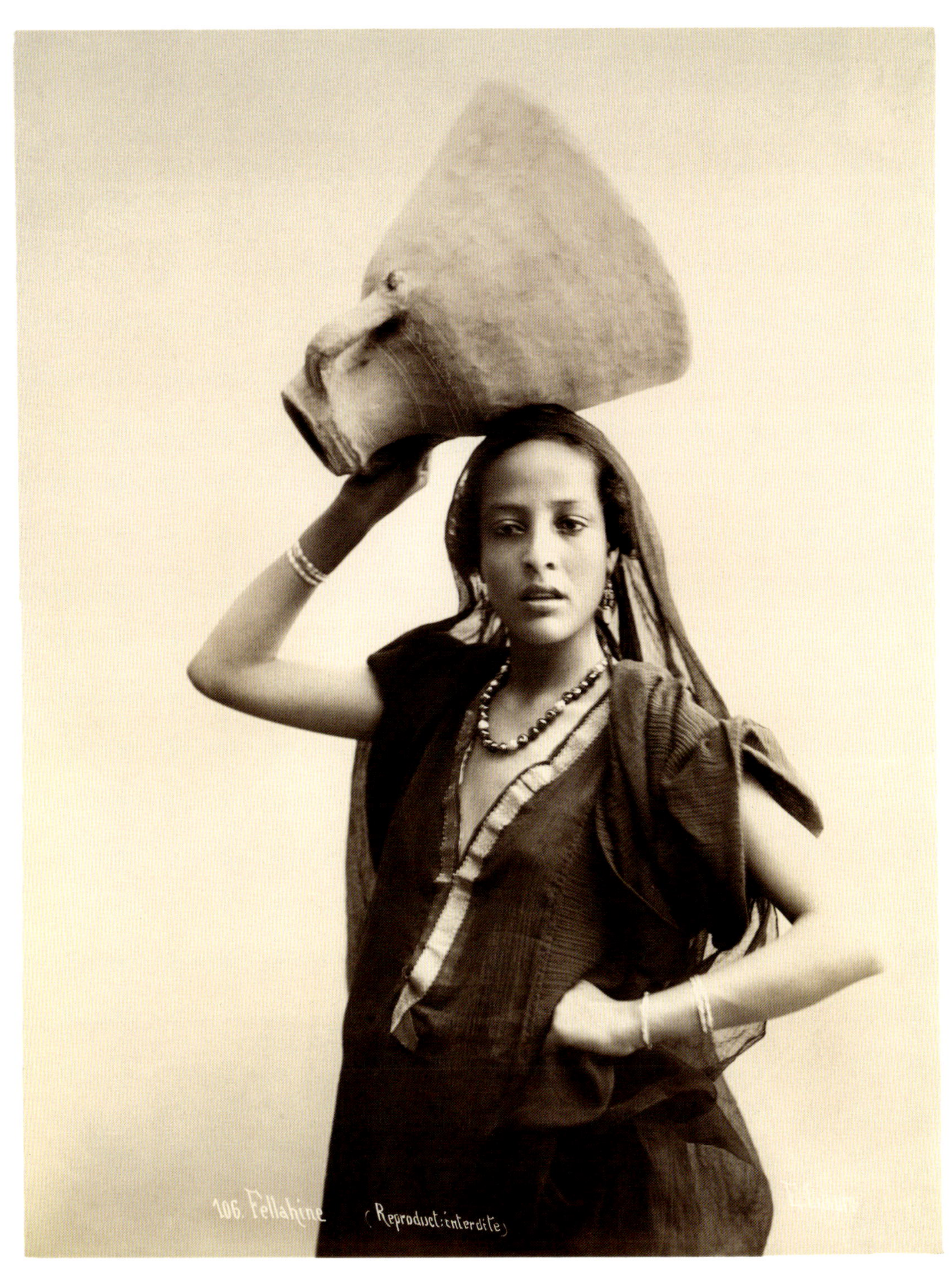

E. LAURO
Woman with Water Pot
Egypt, 1890s

Greeks and Romans, on their pilgrimage to Egypt, never failed to sail up the Nile, beyond Thebes and on to the island of Philae. There they received their last initiation, in the form and poetic guise of a sacred drama, according to which the sons of Hermes agreed to reveal the greatest secret of their religion to laymen or foreigners of their choice... They turned the story of Isis and Osiris into a tale entitled One Thousand and One Nights, *and renamed the island of Philae as* Anis-el-Vogoud, *meaning* Life's Delights. *This is a wonderful place notable for its solitude, its exquisite charm and its ability to provoke the deepest, most unforgettable emotions through its mysterious wilderness, sadness and tenderness.*

Edouard Shure, *Shrines of the Orient*, 1898

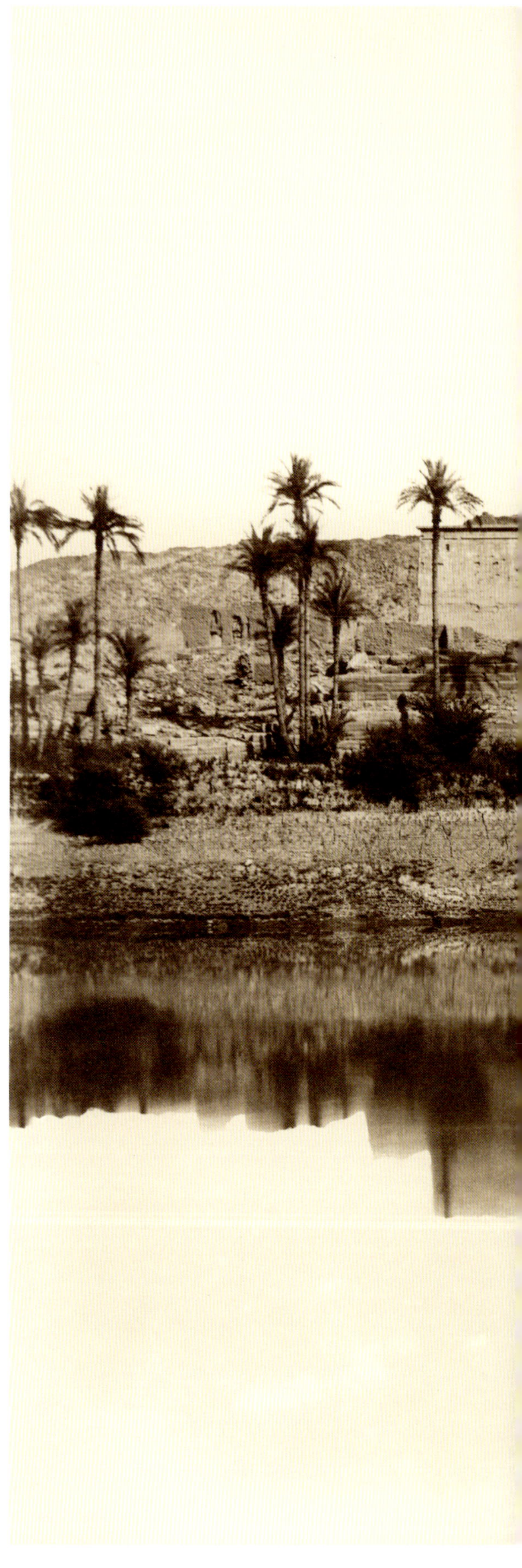

ANONYMOUS
Temple of Isis at Philae Island
1870s

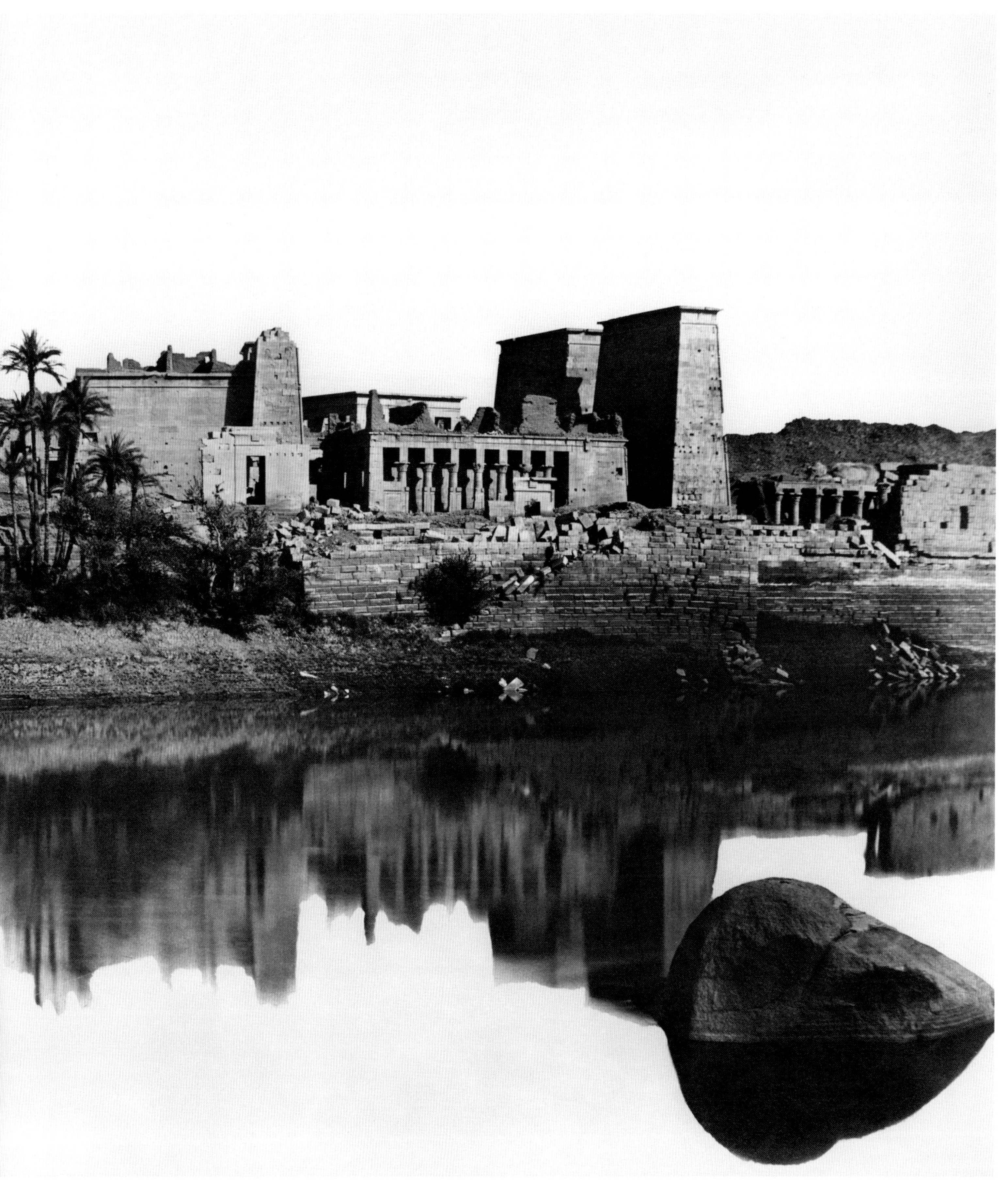

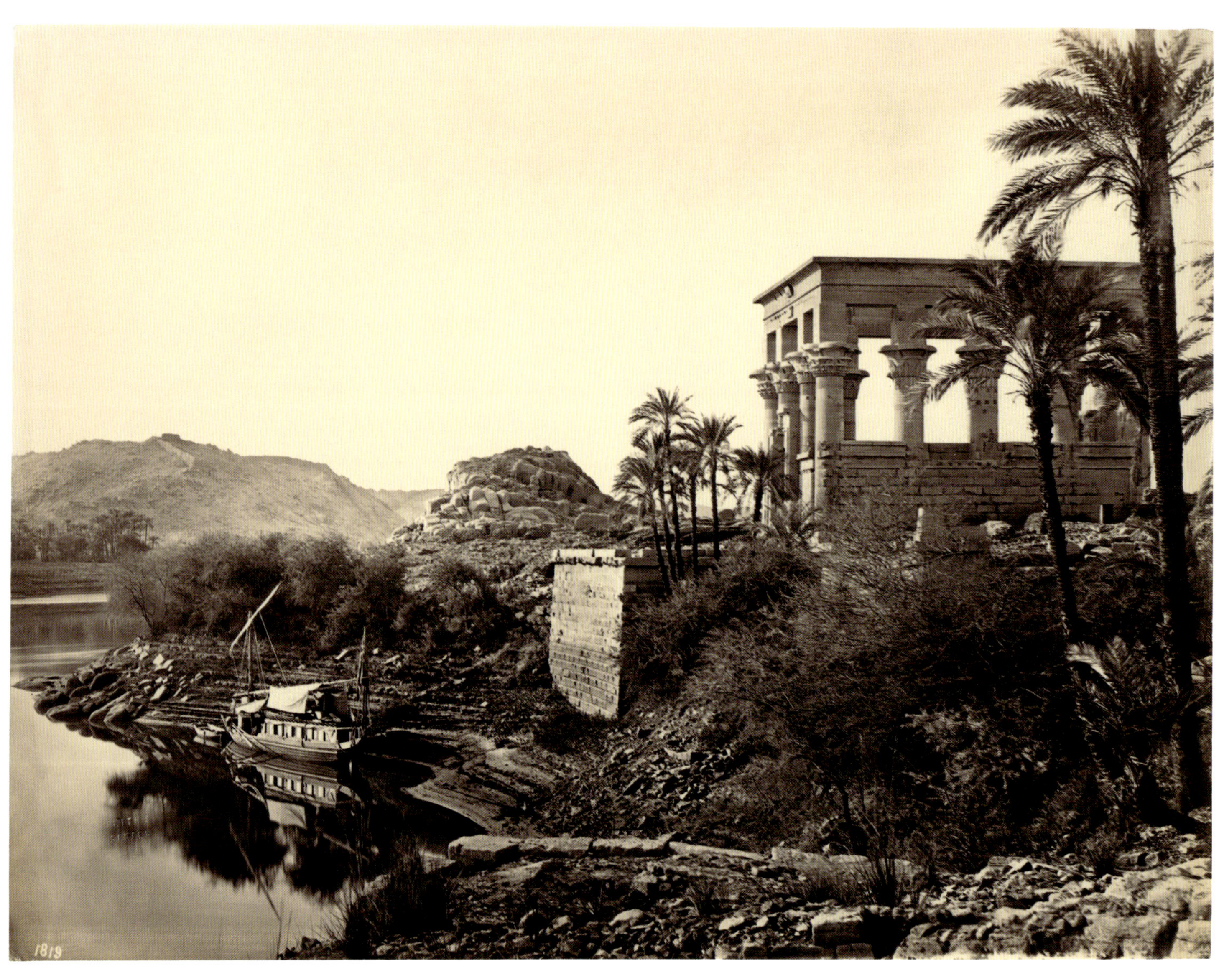

FRANK MASON GOOD
The Nile with Ruins at Philae with the Photographer's Dahabieh
1868–69

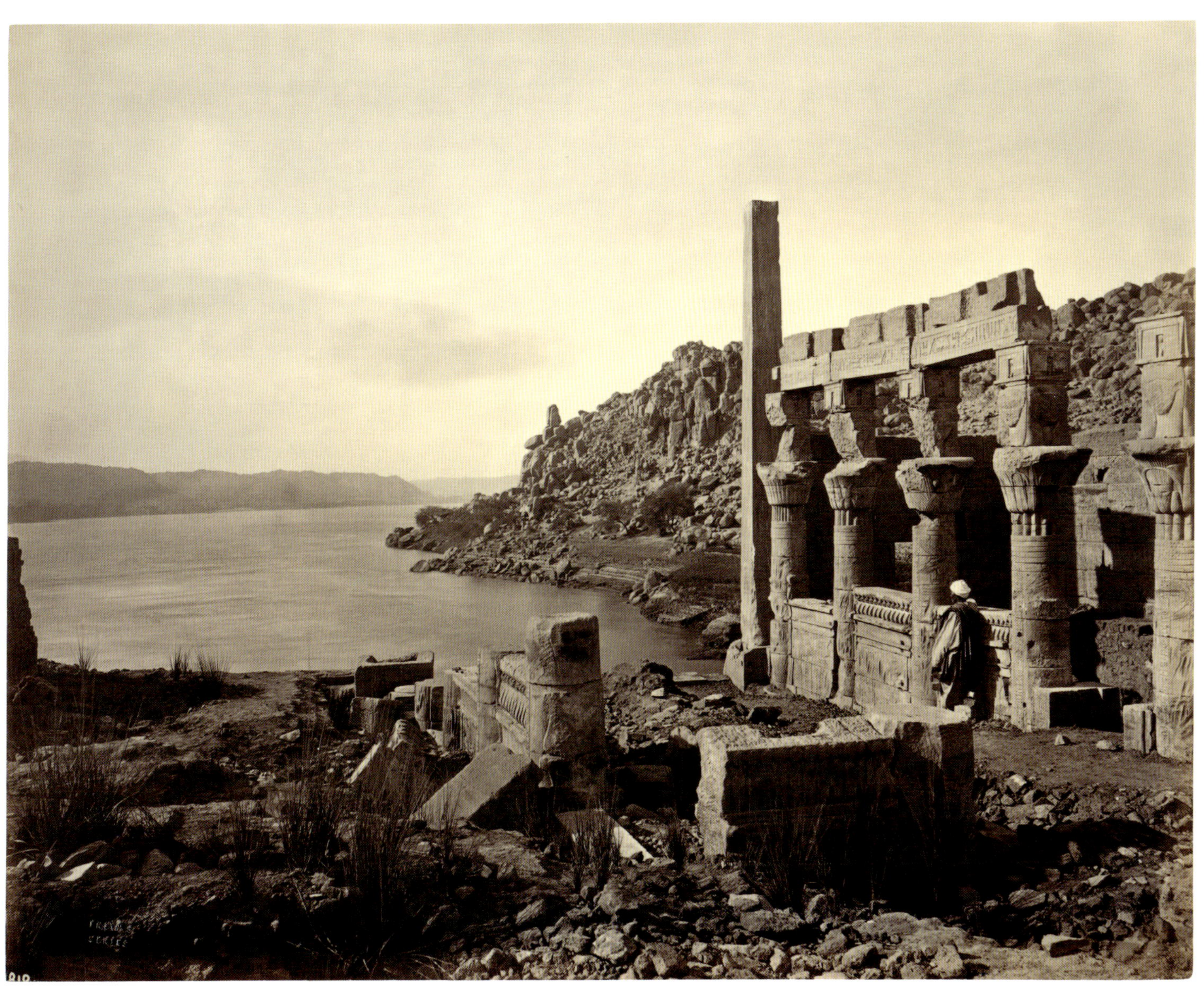

FRANK MASON GOOD
The Nile from Philae
1868–69

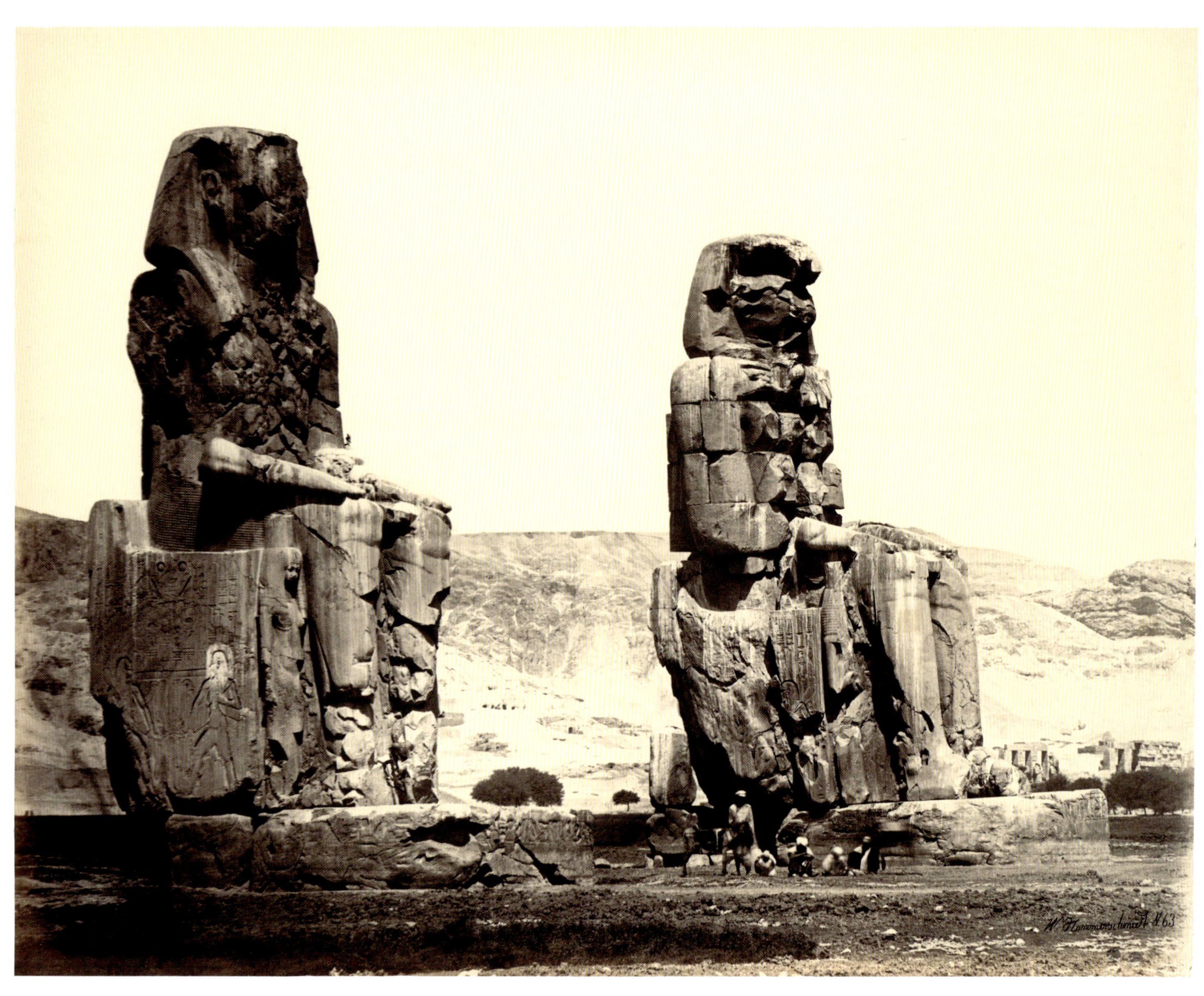

WILHELM HAMMERSCHMIDT
Colossi of Memnon
Thebes, 1860

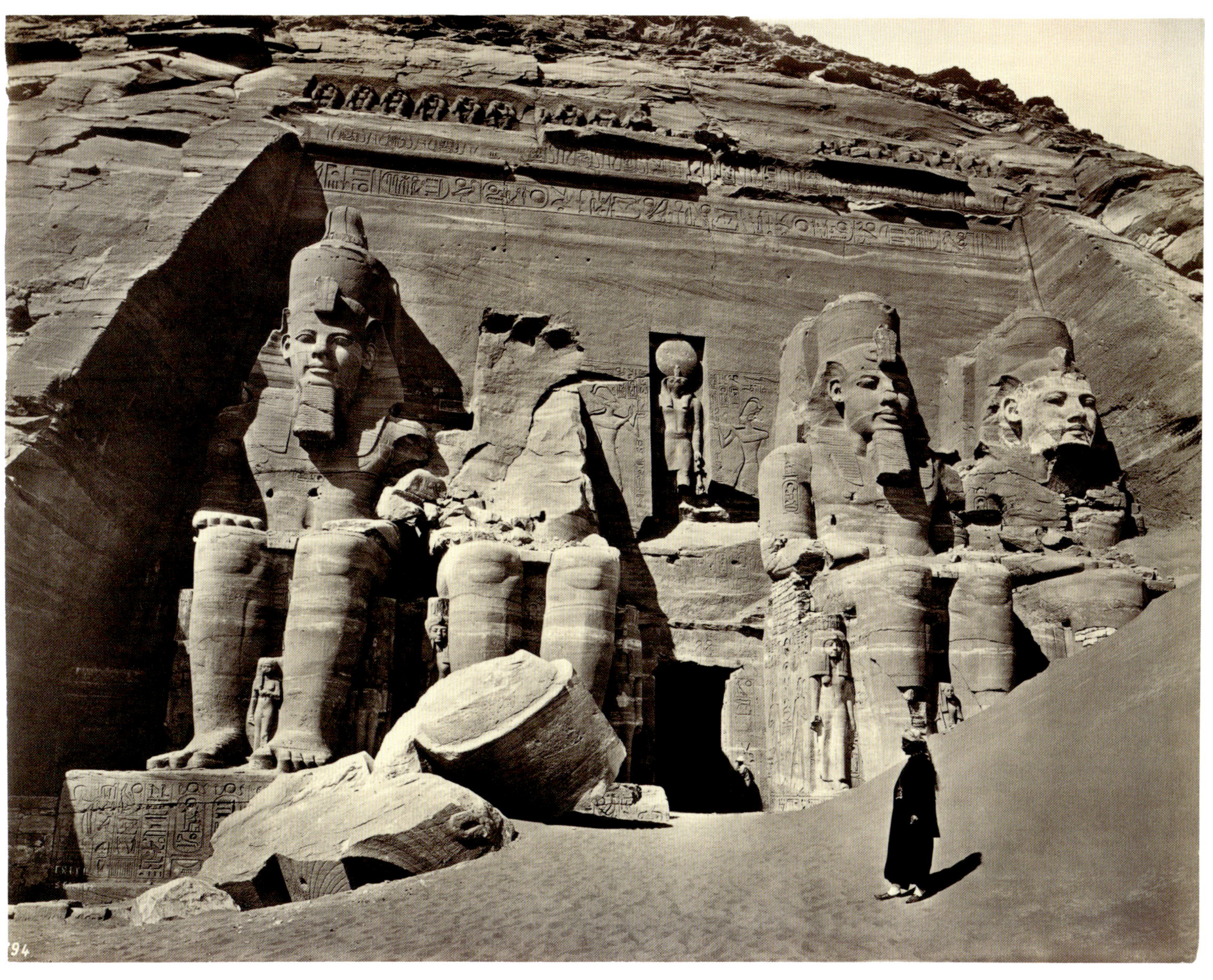

FRANK MASON GOOD

Abu Simbel, Man with the Black Robe

1868–69

Built for Ramesses II (1295–25 BC), the larger of the two temples penetrates 56 meters into the rock and the four colossal statues stand 20 meters high. During the eons since it was built, sand often obscured the temple. In the 1960s, with the construction of the Aswan High Dam, the temples were cut out of the rocks bordering the Nile and, in a massive undertaking to save this archaeological treasure, moved to a new location.

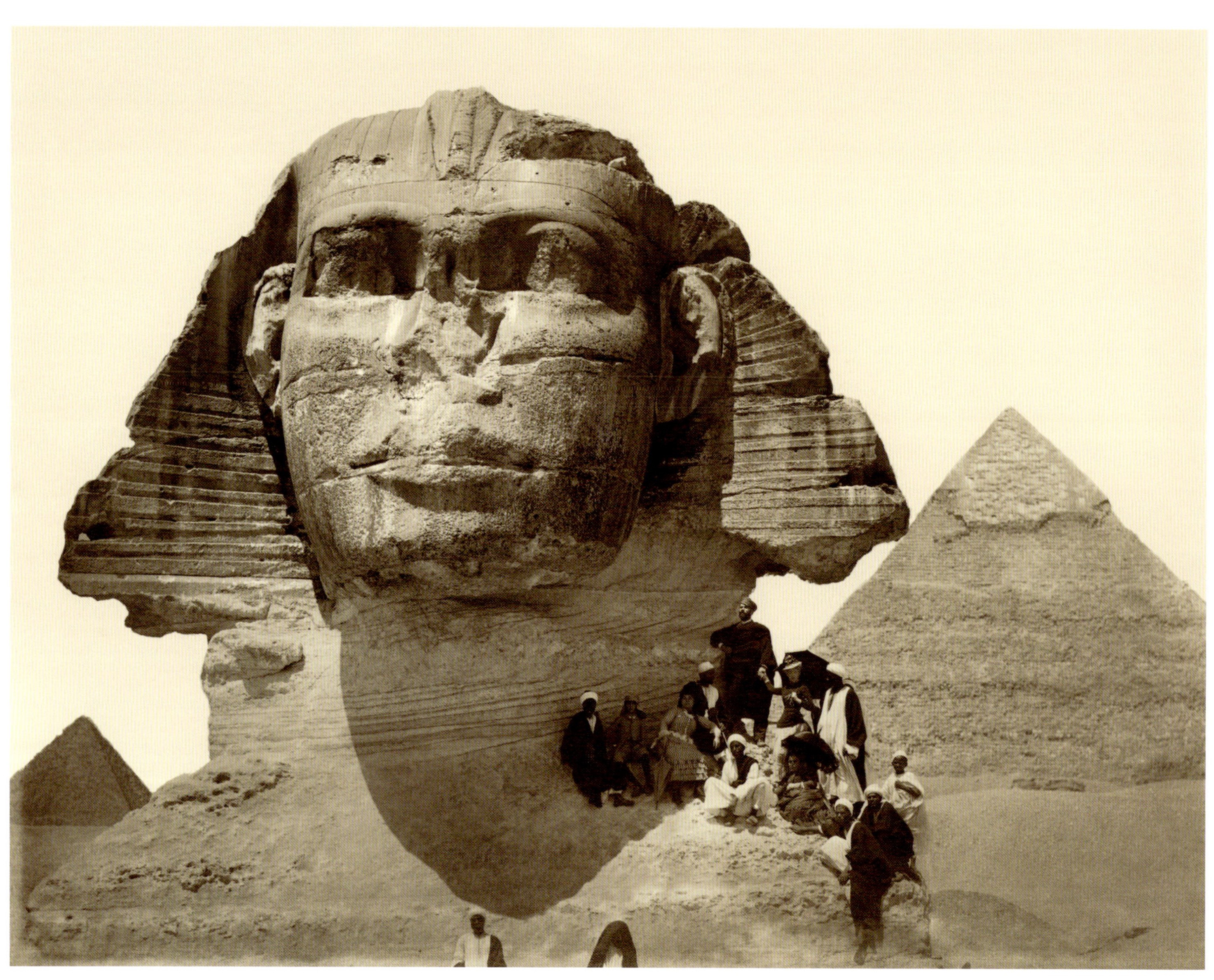

ABDULLAH FRÈRES
Sphinx
1886

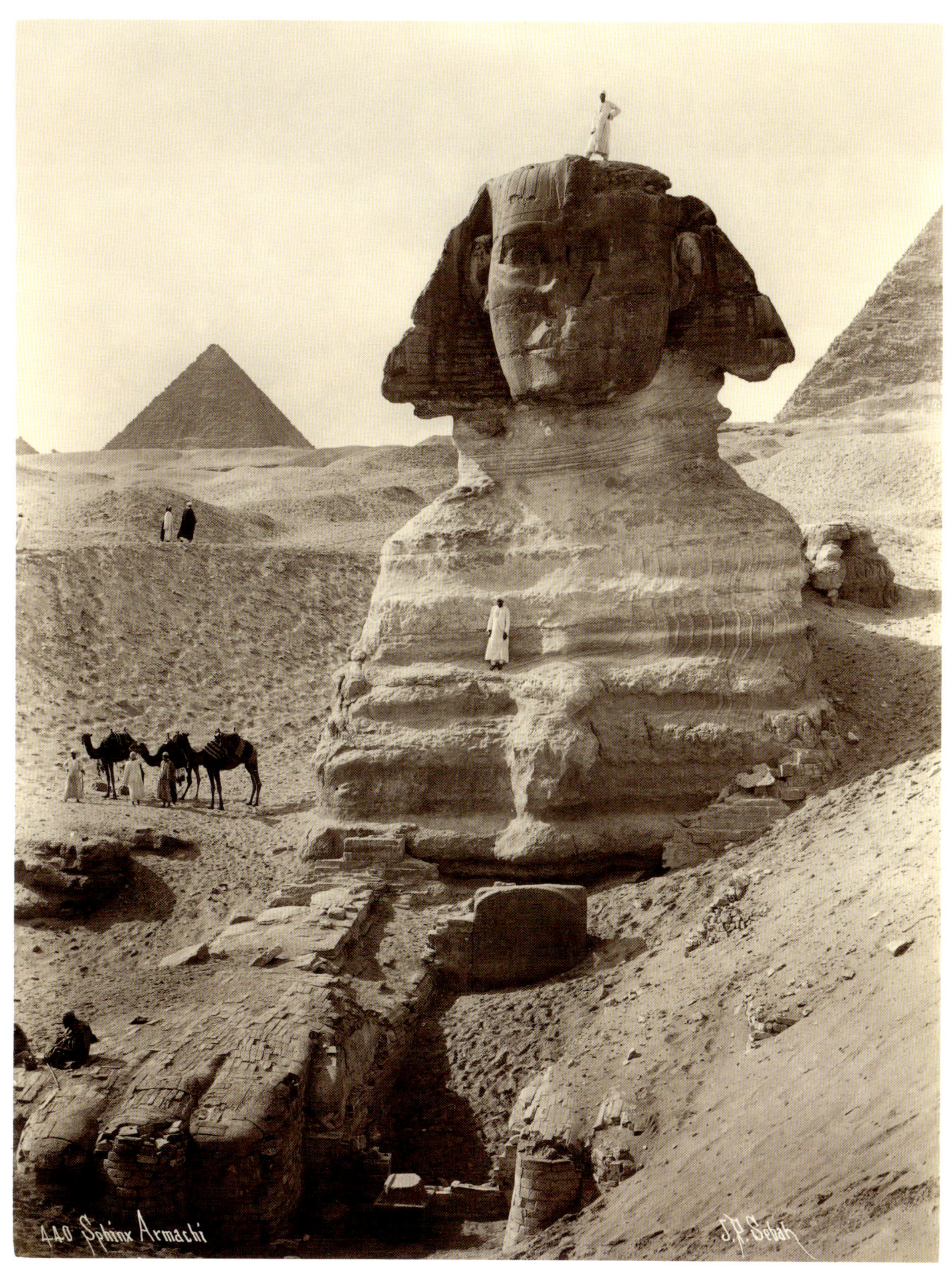

JOHANNES SEBAH
The Sphinx after Excavation
1890s

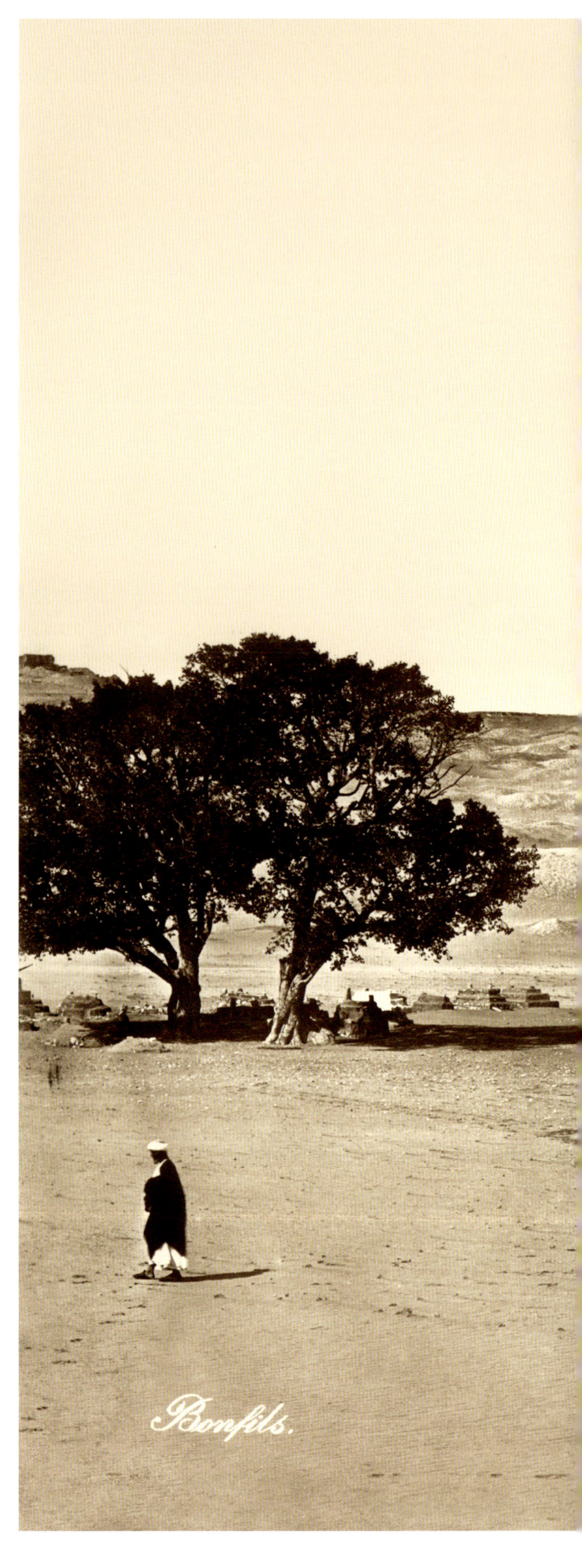

FÉLIX BONFILS
Great Pyramid of Cheops
Cairo, 1860s

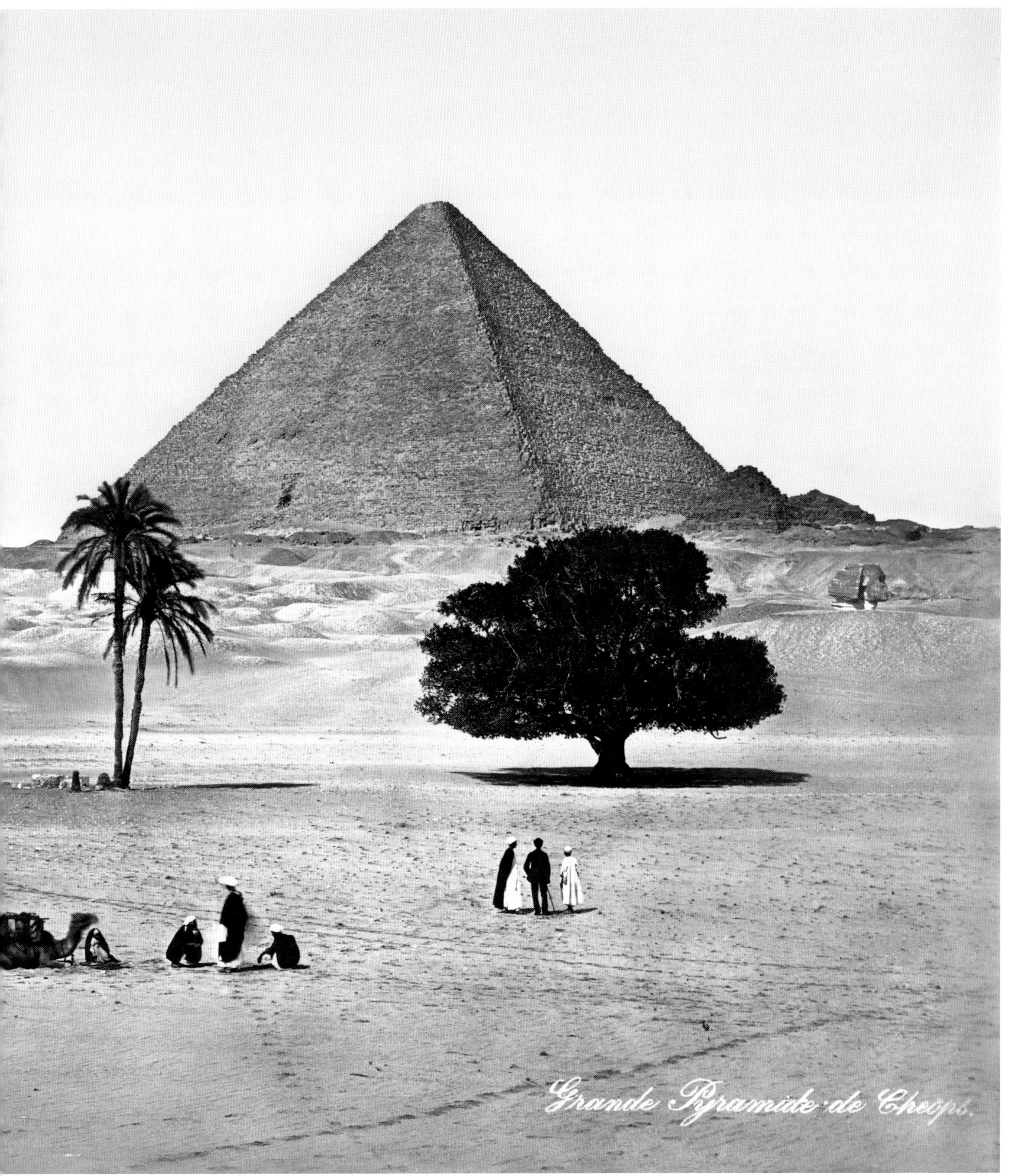
Grande Pyramide de Cheops.

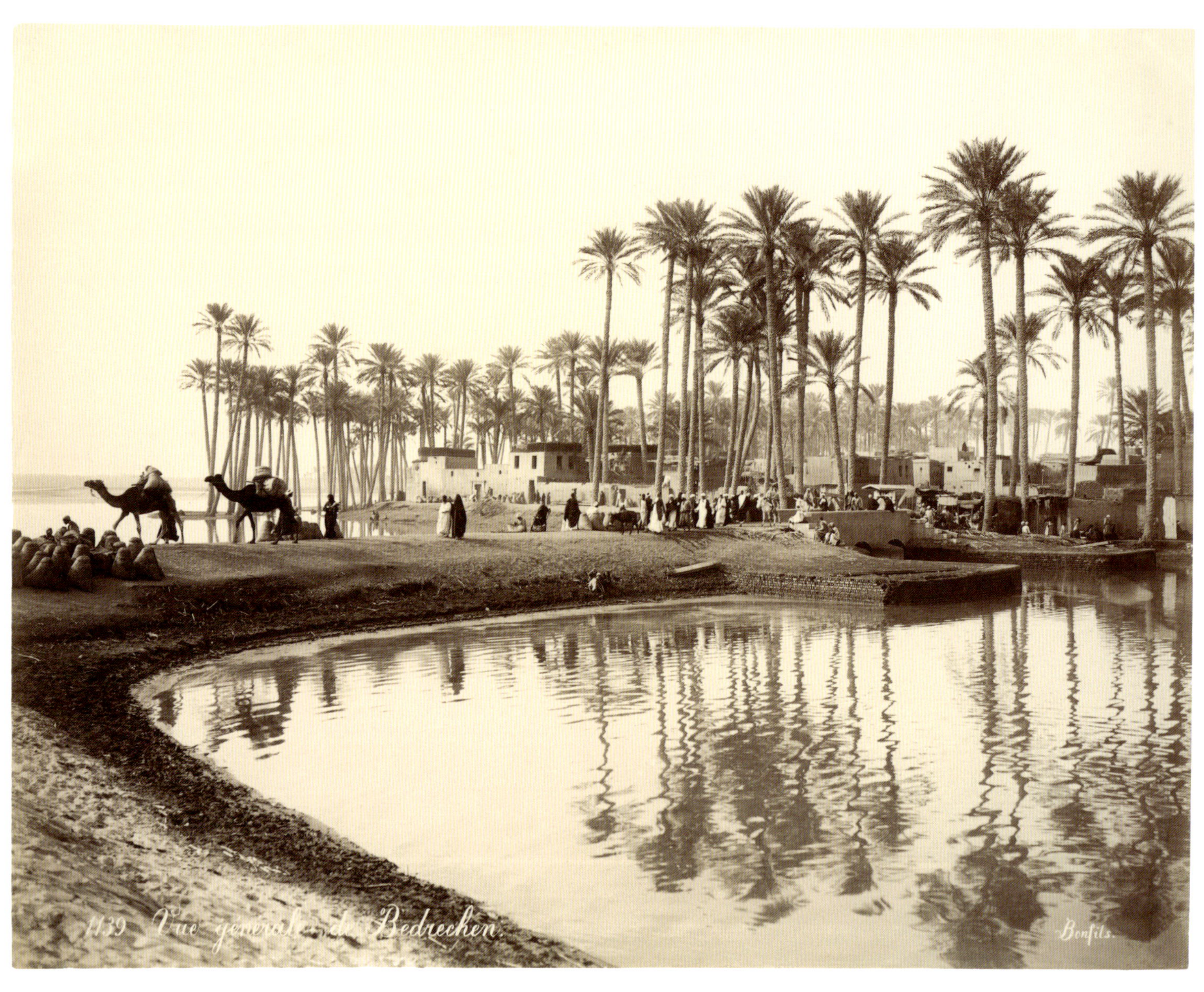

FÉLIX BONFILS
Oasis and Nomads
1870s

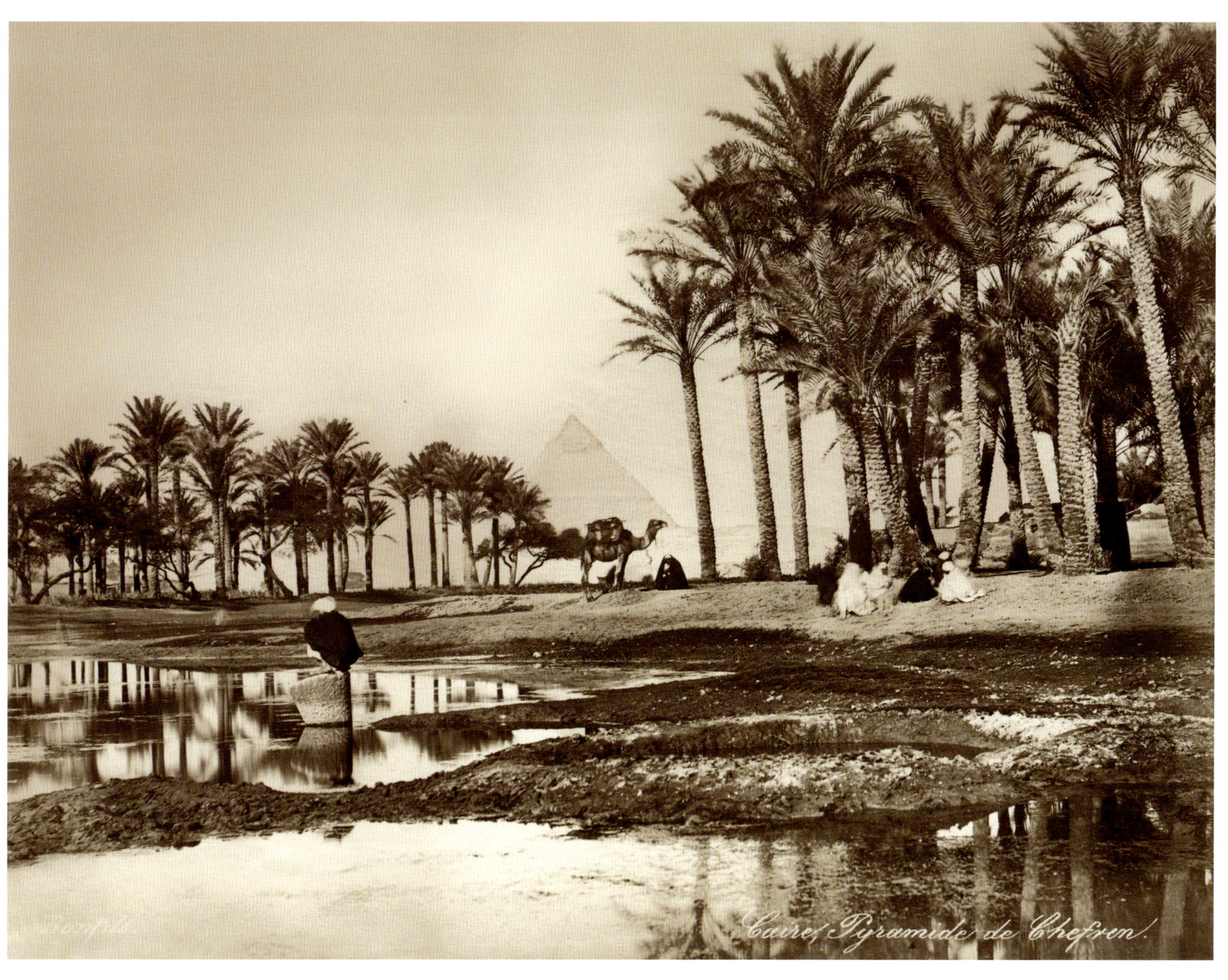

FÉLIX BONFILS
Pyramid of Khafre
1880s

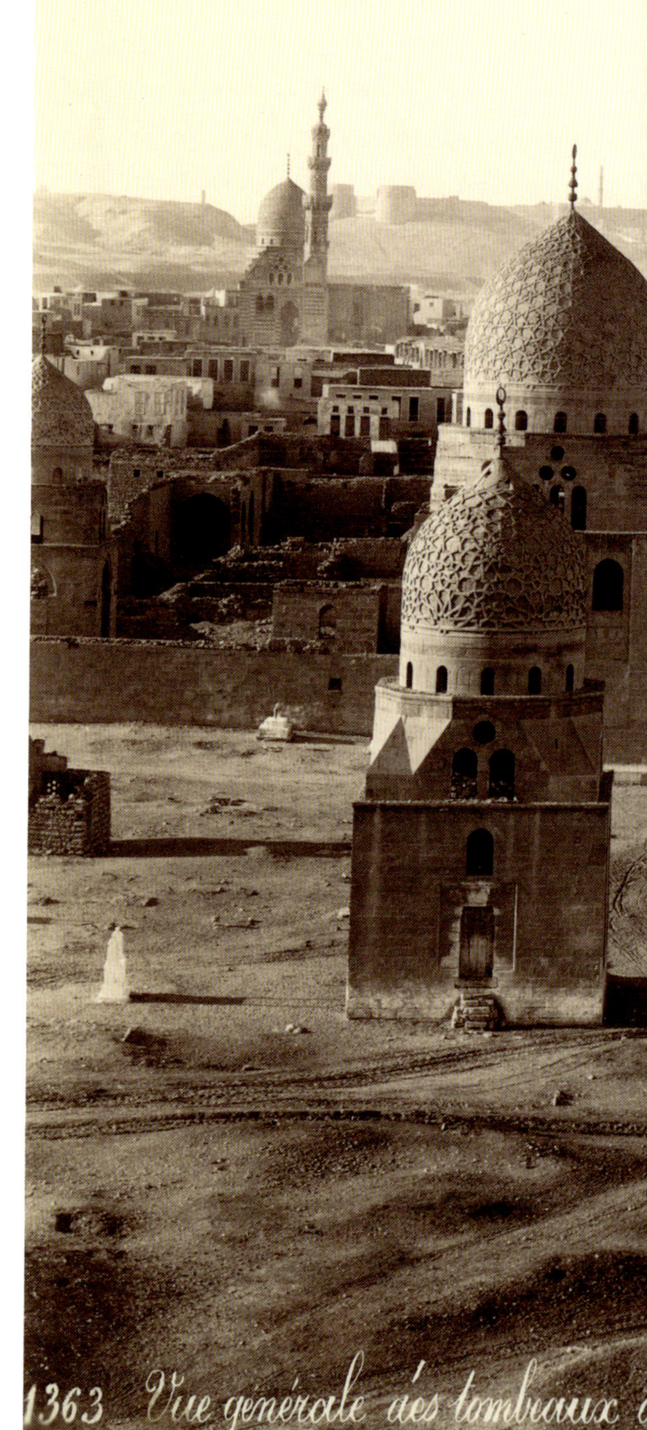

FÉLIX BONFILS
The Northern Cemetery Tombs of the Mamluk Caliphs
Cairo, 1870s

The dome in the foreground is the tomb of Gani Bak; the large dome behind it is the mausoleum of Sultan al-Ashraf Barsbay; beyond to the left is the mausoleum of Qaytbay; the small ribbed dome in the middle distance is the tomb of Khadiga Umm al-Ashraf; the squat dome on the right is the oratory of al-Rifai.

The 'Mamluk phenomenon', as the scholar David Ayalon has called it, was of great political importance and long-lived; in the Middle East it lasted from the ninth to the nineteenth centuries. In the Mamluk system, young boys were captured and trained within the Islamic world to become formidable soldiers loyal to an older Mamluk master. Enslaved mainly from areas near the Caucasus (largely Circassia and Georgia), and from Turkic areas north of the Black Sea, these young slaves always had non-Muslim backgrounds. Over time, Mamluks became a powerful military caste in various Muslim societies, including Egypt, the Levant, Iraq and India. Most notably, Mamluk factions seized the sultanate for themselves in Egypt and Syria in a period known as the Mamluk Sultanate (1250–1517). Famously, the Mamluk Sultanate defeated both the Mongols and the Crusaders.

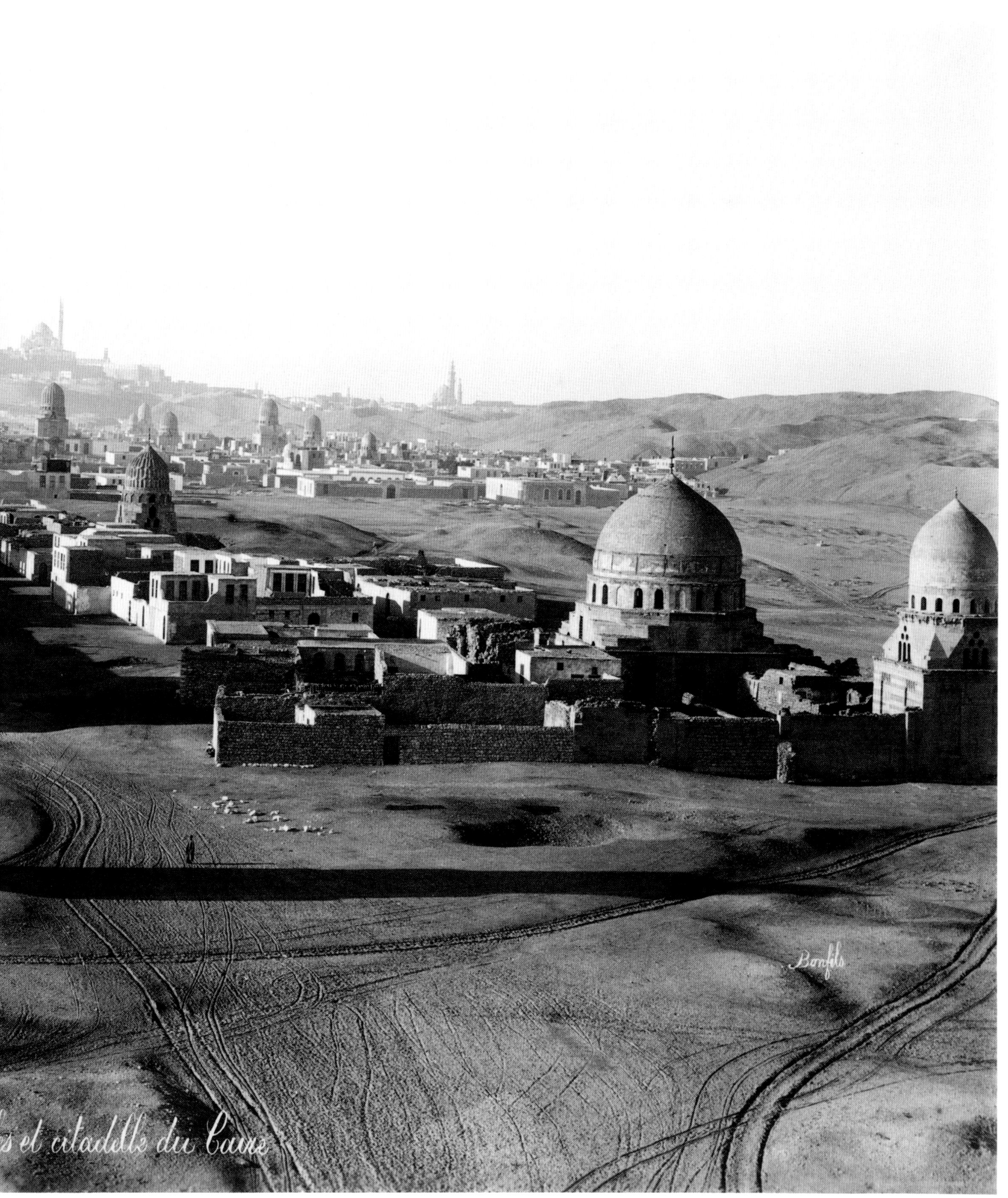
Bonfils
...s et citadelle du Caire

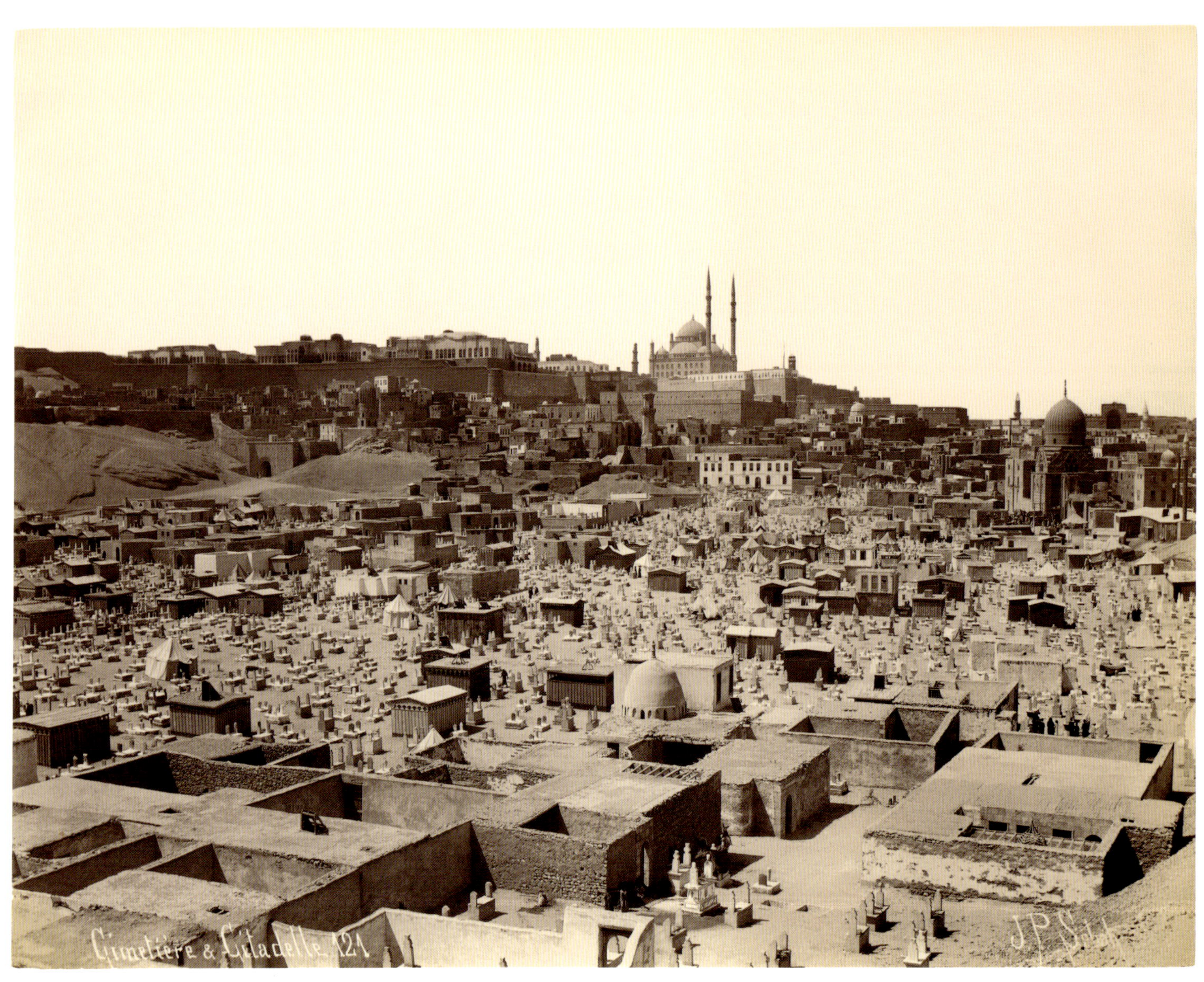

PASCAL SEBAH
Cairo, Citadel and the Northern Cemetery
1870s

The Northern Cemetery (Tombs of the Caliphs). View across the cemetery towards the Citadel and the Mosque of Muhammad Ali.

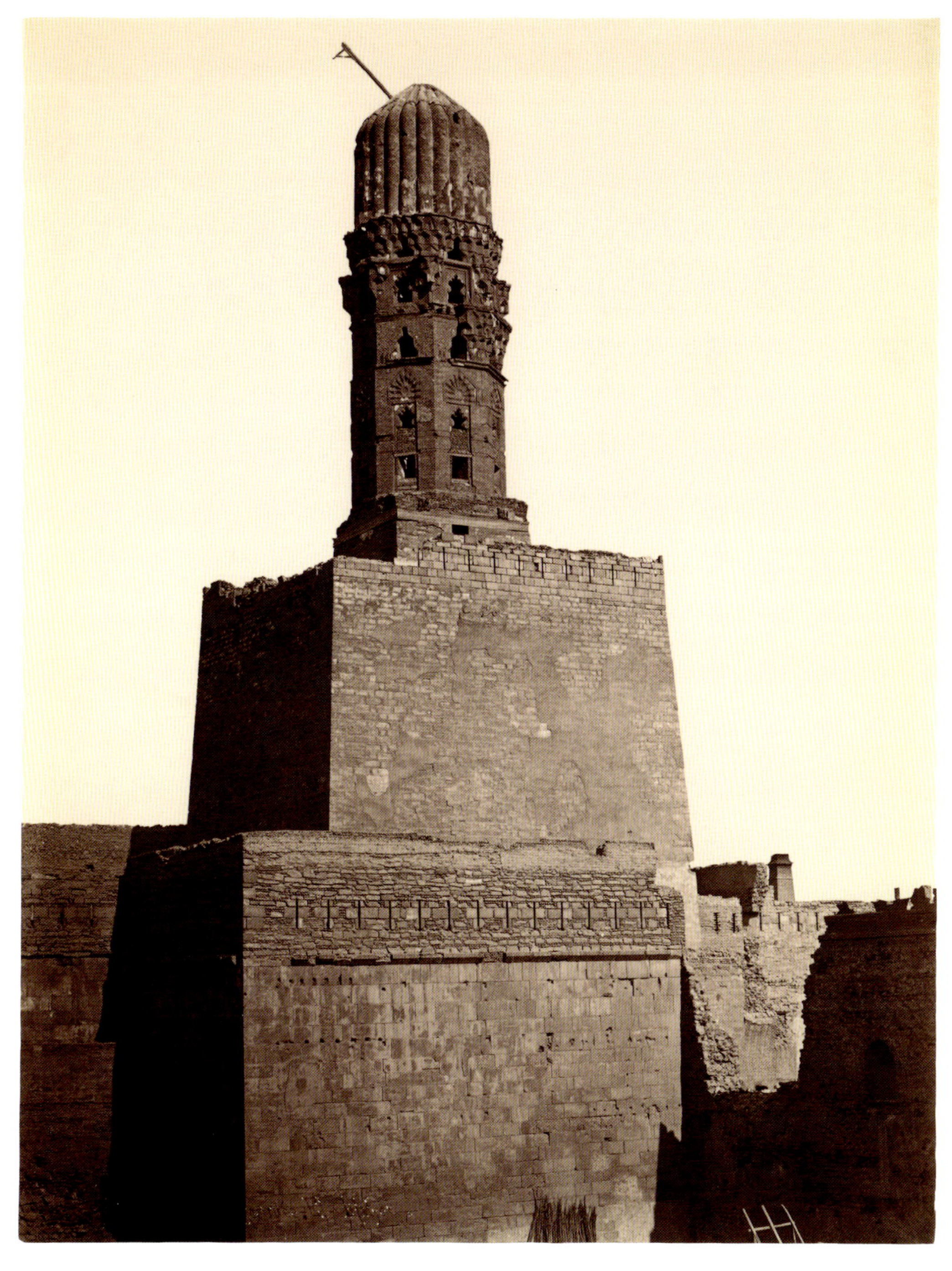

PASCAL SEBAH
Mosque of al-Hakim
Cairo, 1870s

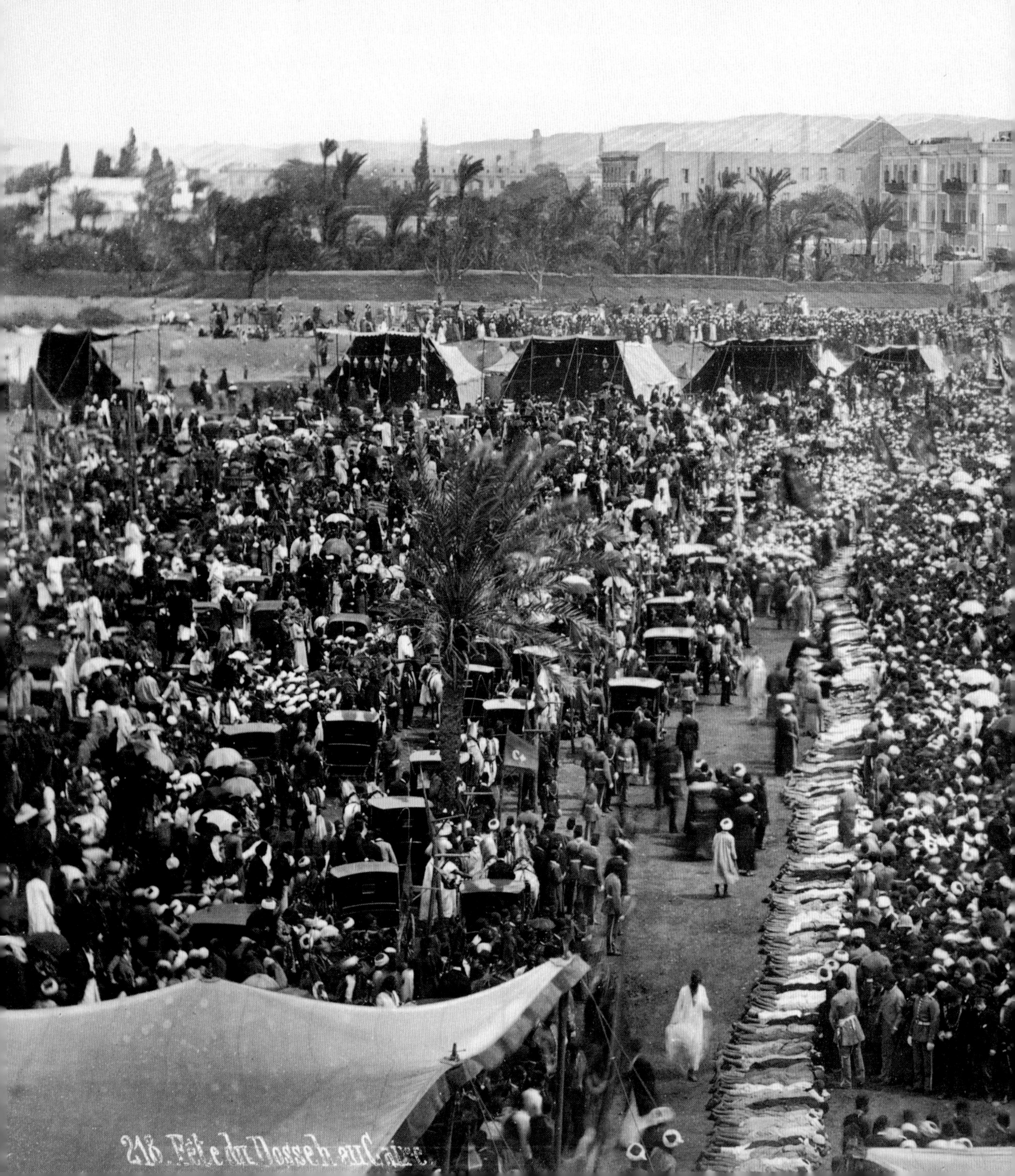
216. Fête du Dosseh au Caire.

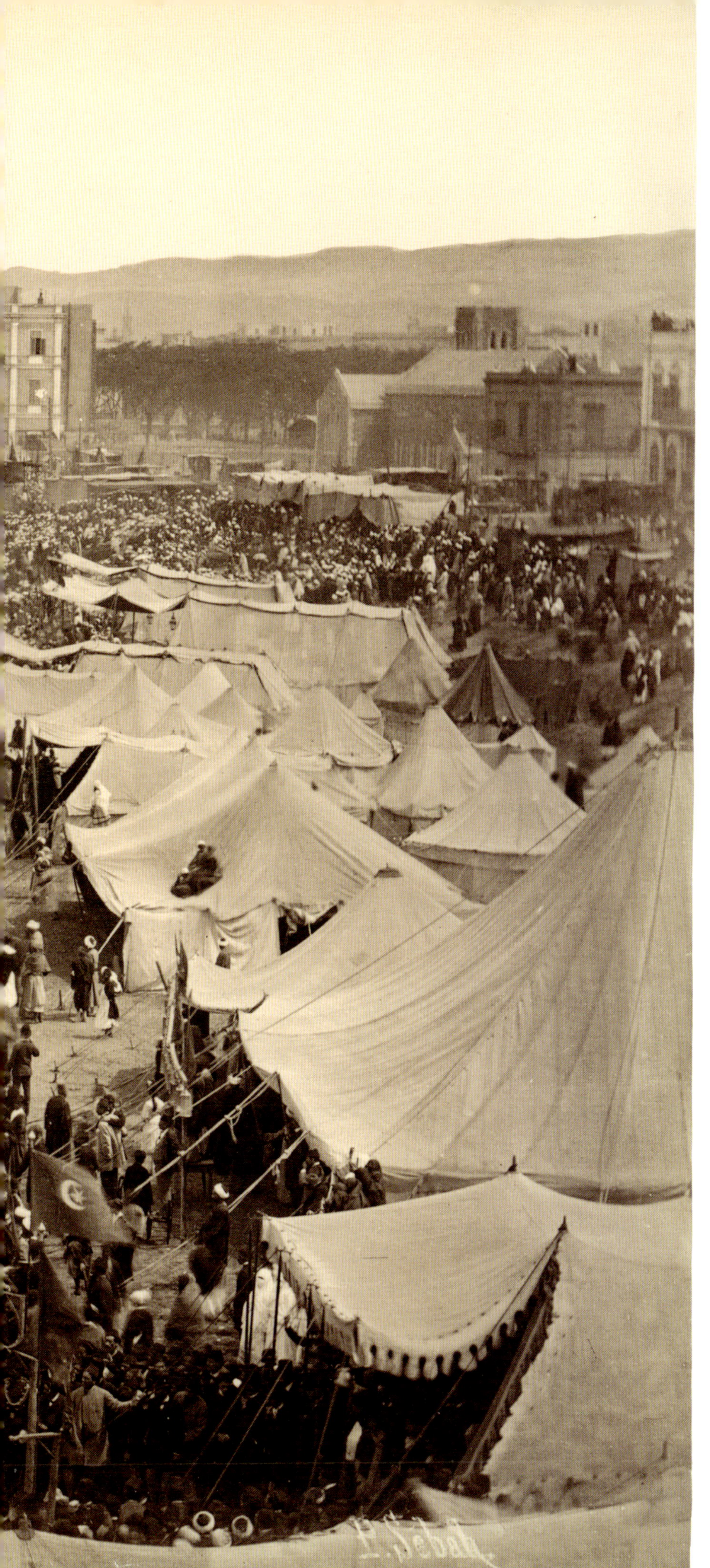

PASCAL SEBAH
The Day of Treading
Cairo, 1870s

'The Day of Treading' in Cairo was an annual religious ritual of the Dervishes. The Dervishes lay face down in a row. Their sheikh then rode on horseback across his followers. Those whose bones broke under the hooves were assumed to have been sinners. After 1881, the sheikh walked across a living carpet of his followers.

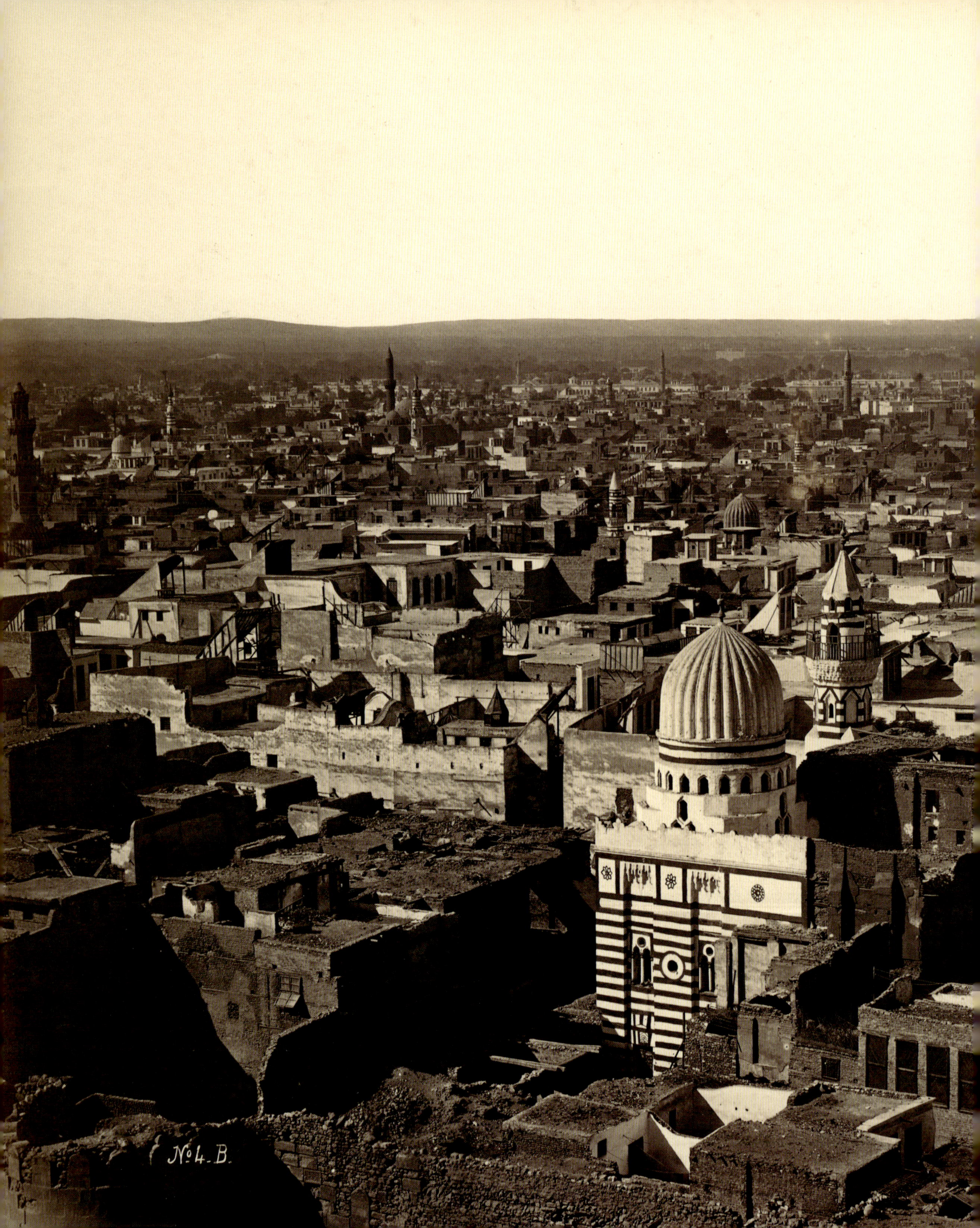
Nº4_B.

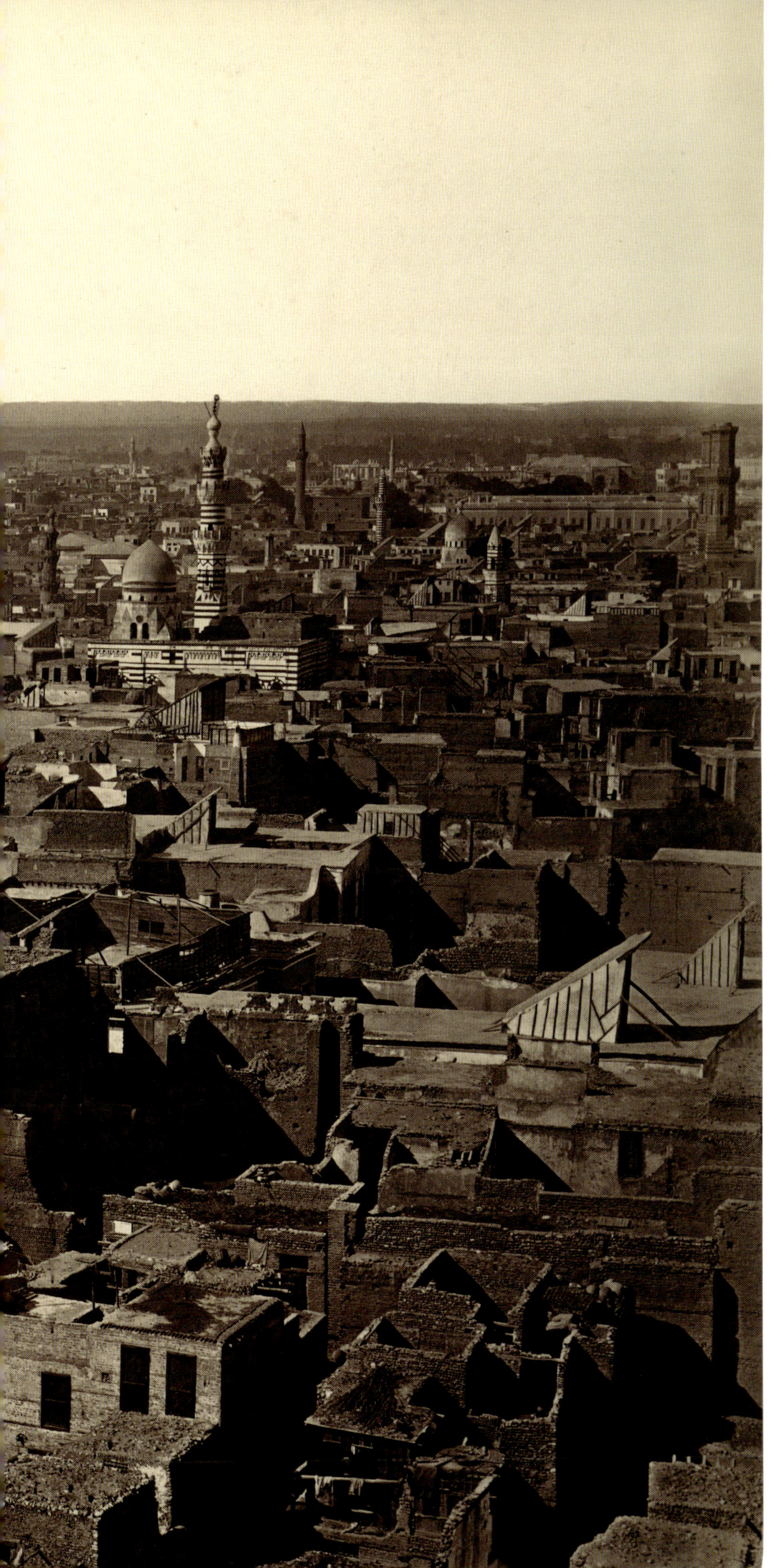

PASCAL SEBAH
View of Cairo and the Mosque of Aslam al-Silahdar in the Foreground
early 1870s

This photograph is a part of a mammoth ten-plate panorama of the city.

PASCAL SEBAH
Tomb of Kait Bey (Qaytbay)
Cairo, 1870s

The tomb of Qaytbay is constructed from layered courses of tura limestone taken from the Great Pyramid. Finished in the reign of the Egyptian Pharaoh Khafre (2520–2494 BC), the stones removed from the Great Pyramid can still be seen as parts of these structures.

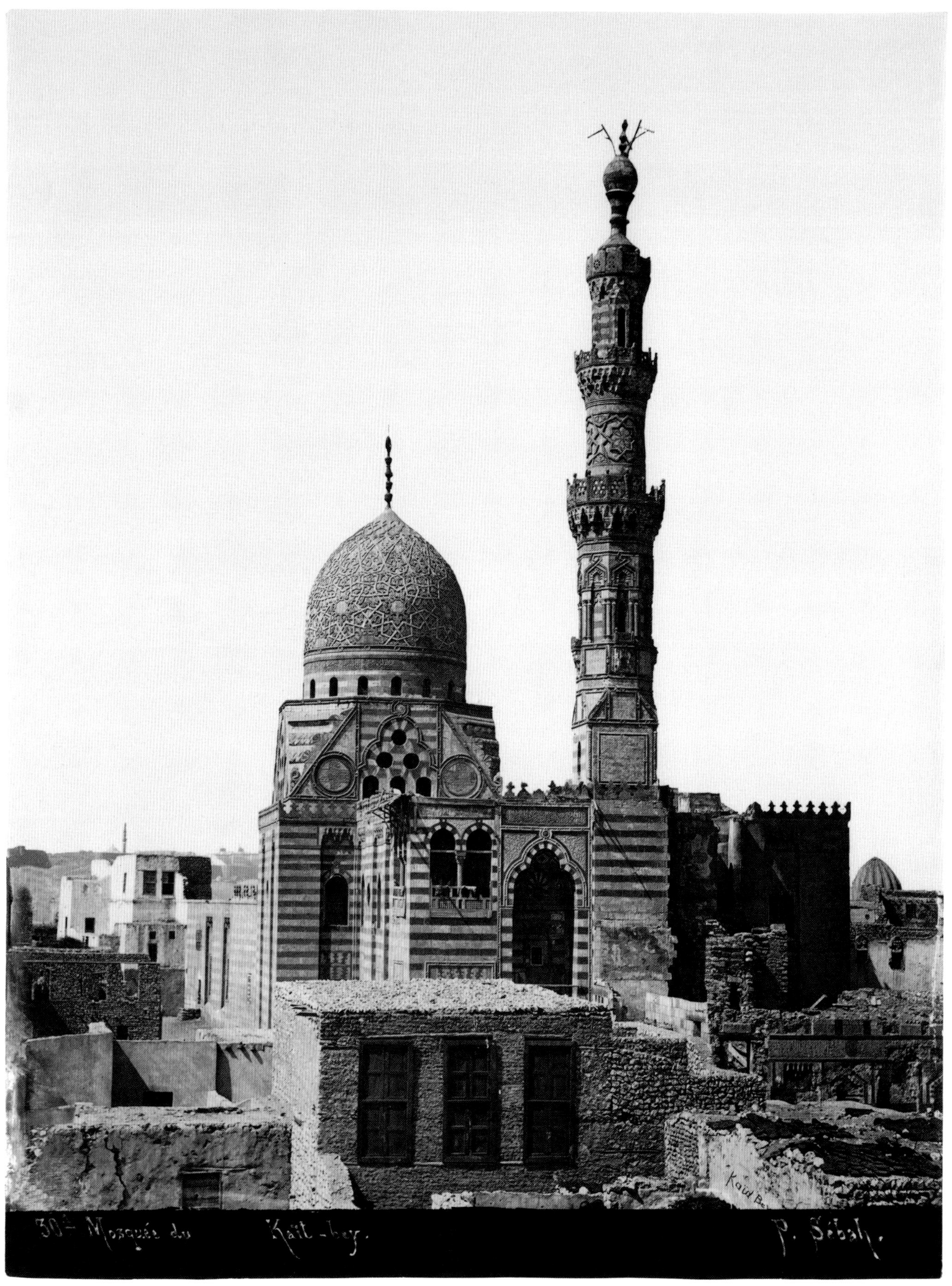
30e Mosquée du Kaït-bey.
P. Sébah.

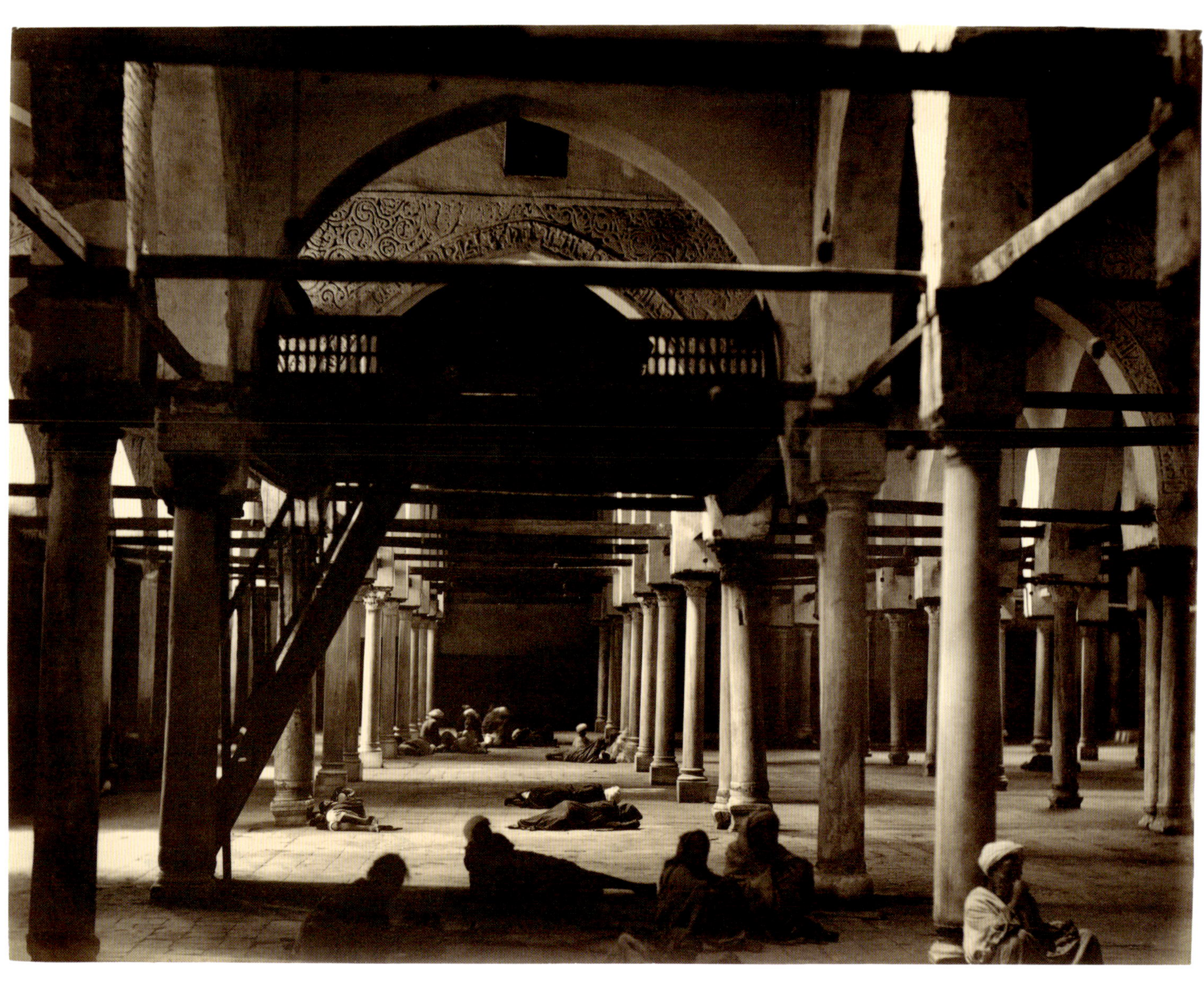

PASCAL SEBAH
Inside the Mosque of al-Azhar
Cairo, 1870s

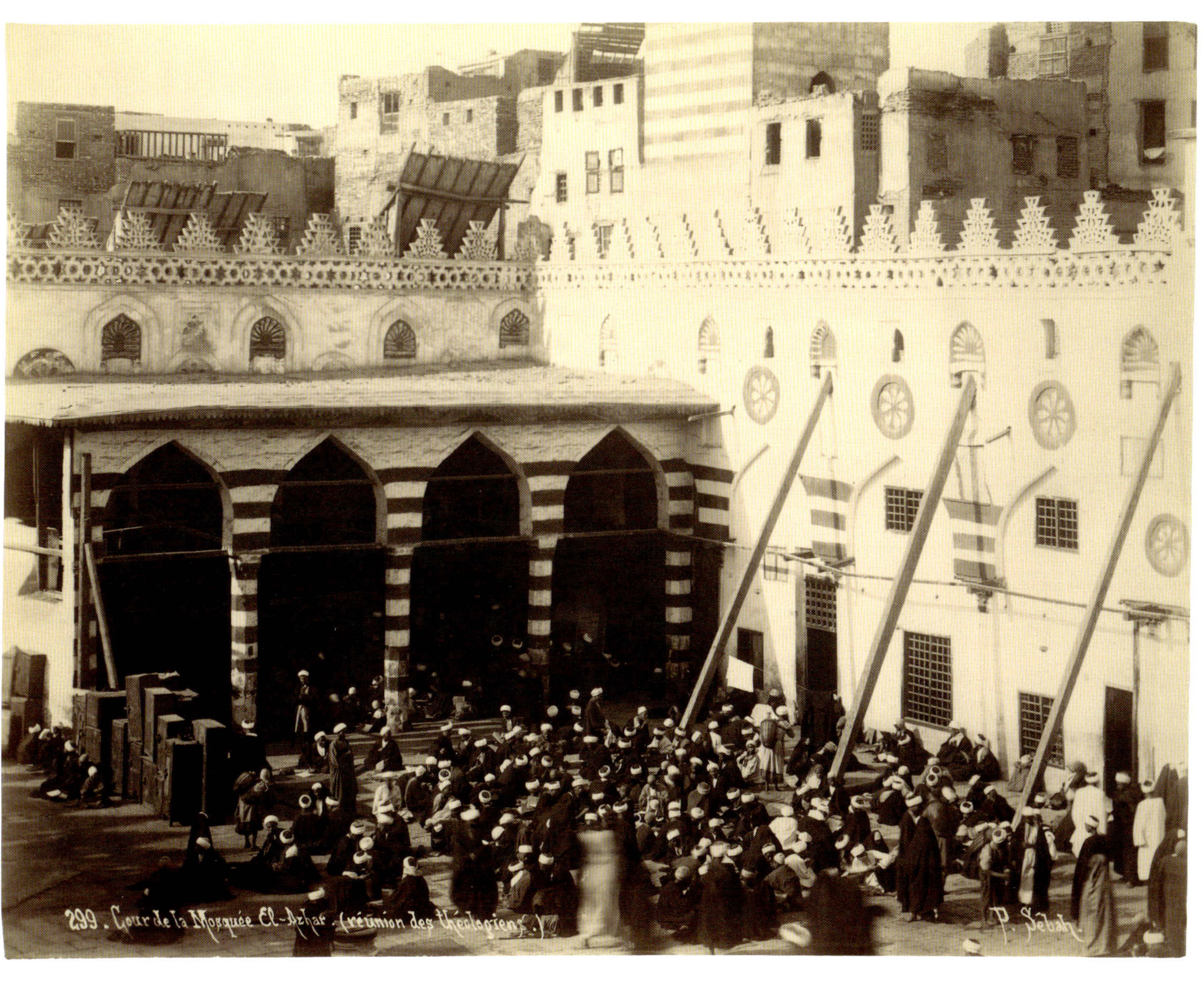

PASCAL SEBAH
Mosque of al-Azhar, Meeting of the Theologians
Cairo, 1870s

The foundations of modern Cairo were established in 969 AD by Gawhar al-Siqilli, a Fatimid general of Greek extraction from Sicily, who conquered Egypt from the base of the Fatimid caliphate situated near Kairouan in Tunisia.
In 989 AD some 17 years after the dedication of the al-Azhar Mosque, 35 scholars were hired, to develop, as an adjunct to the mosque, what became the oldest continuously-run university in the world. For over a thousand years al-Azhar University has been regarded as the foremost institution in the Islamic world for the study of Sunni theology and Sharia law.

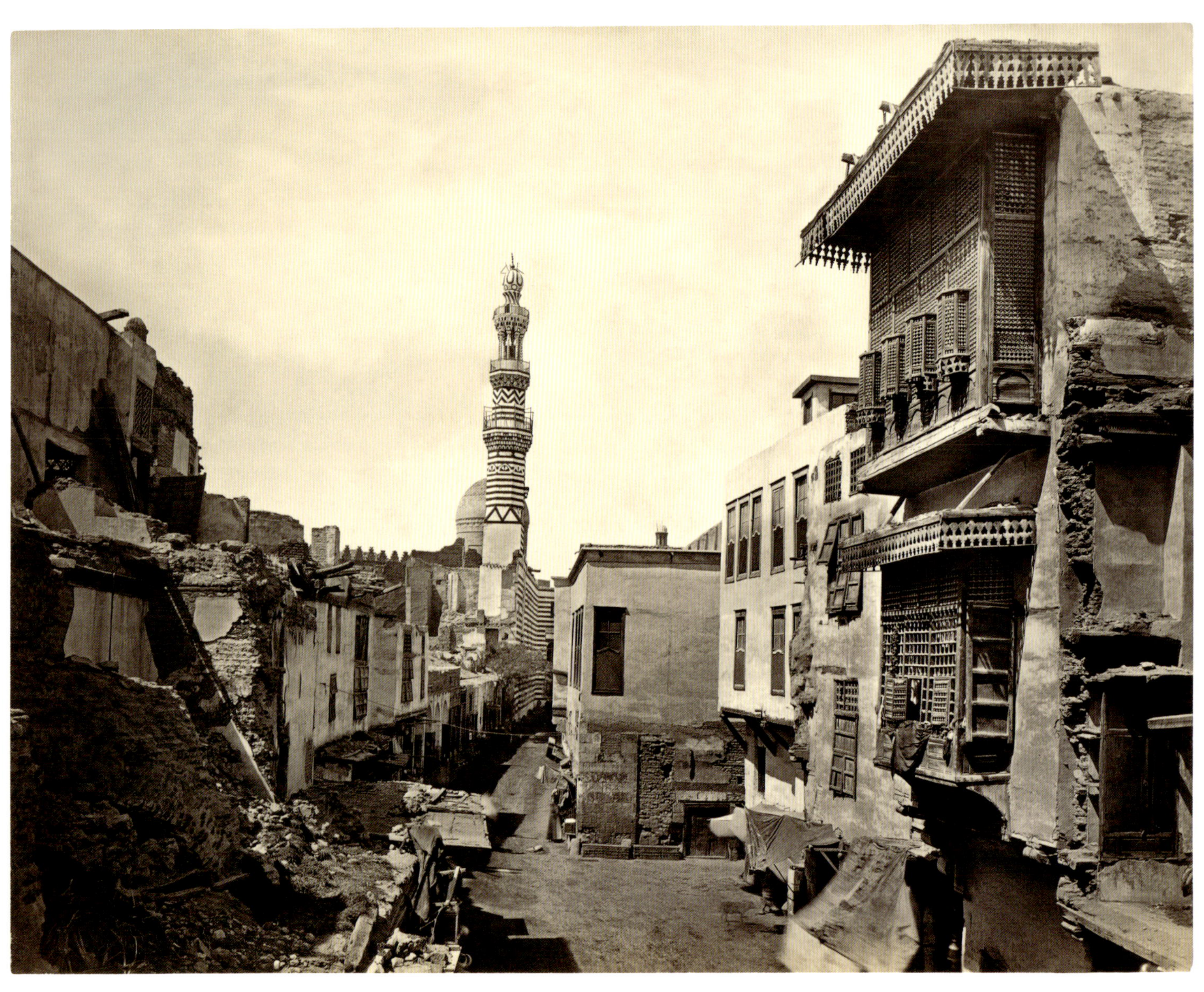

FRANK MASON GOOD
Cairo Street
1868–69

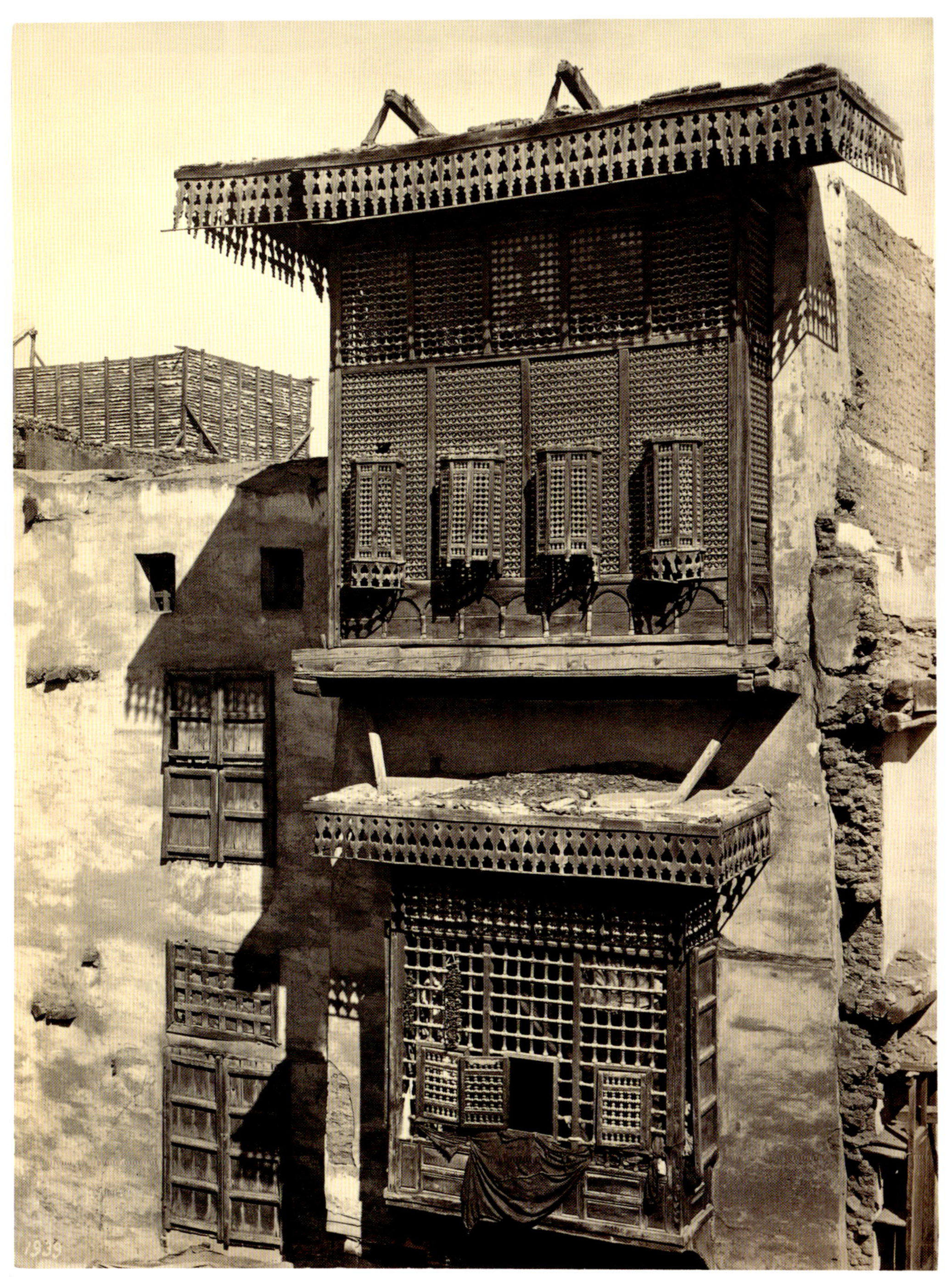

FRANK MASON GOOD
House with Mashrabiyas
Cairo, 1868–69

In both the Turkish and the Arab houses, a screened window overlooking the street is called a *mashrabiya*. It allowed women to see out, while, modesty intact, hiding the female inhabitants of the household from the city beyond.

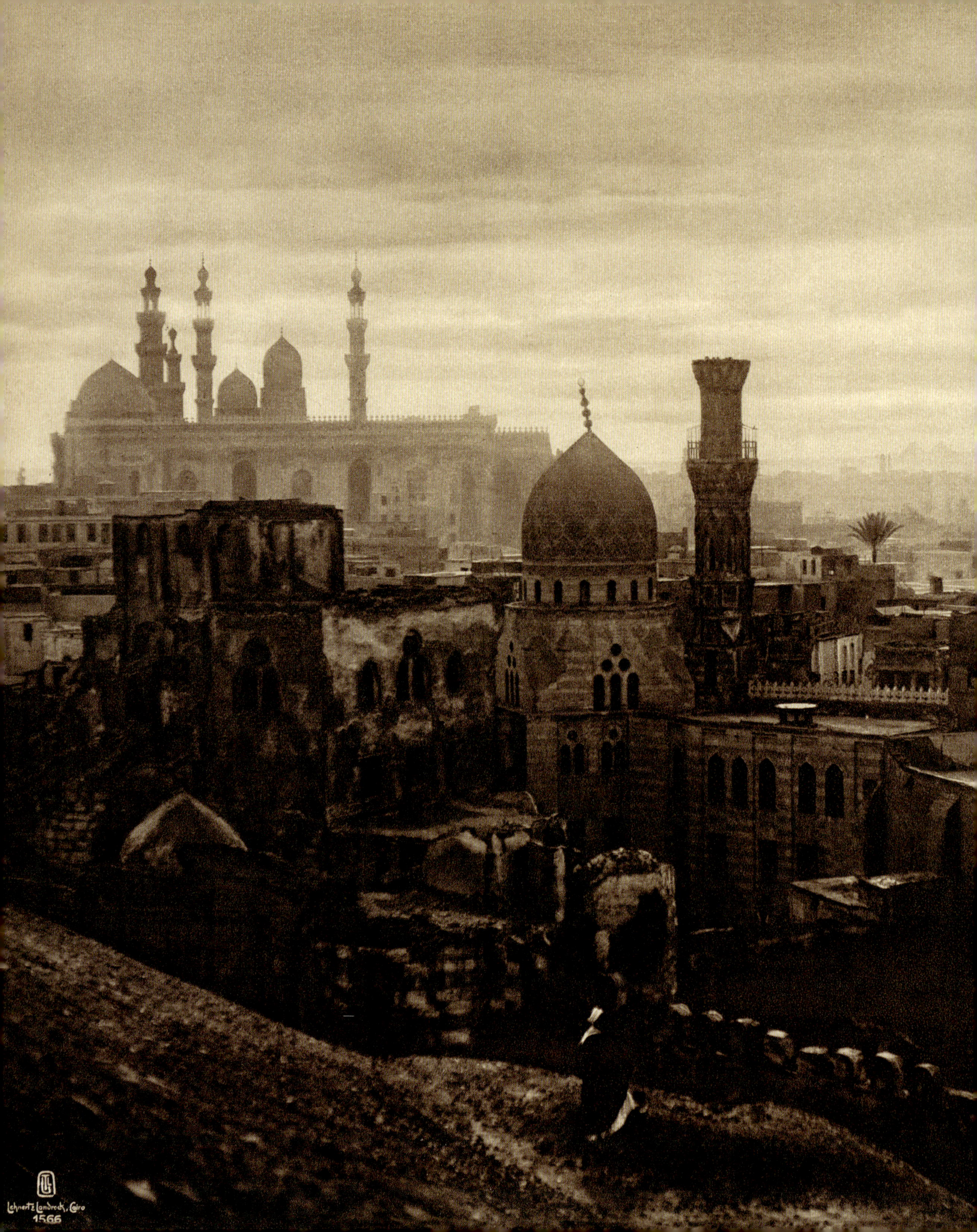
Lehnert & Landrock, Cairo
1566

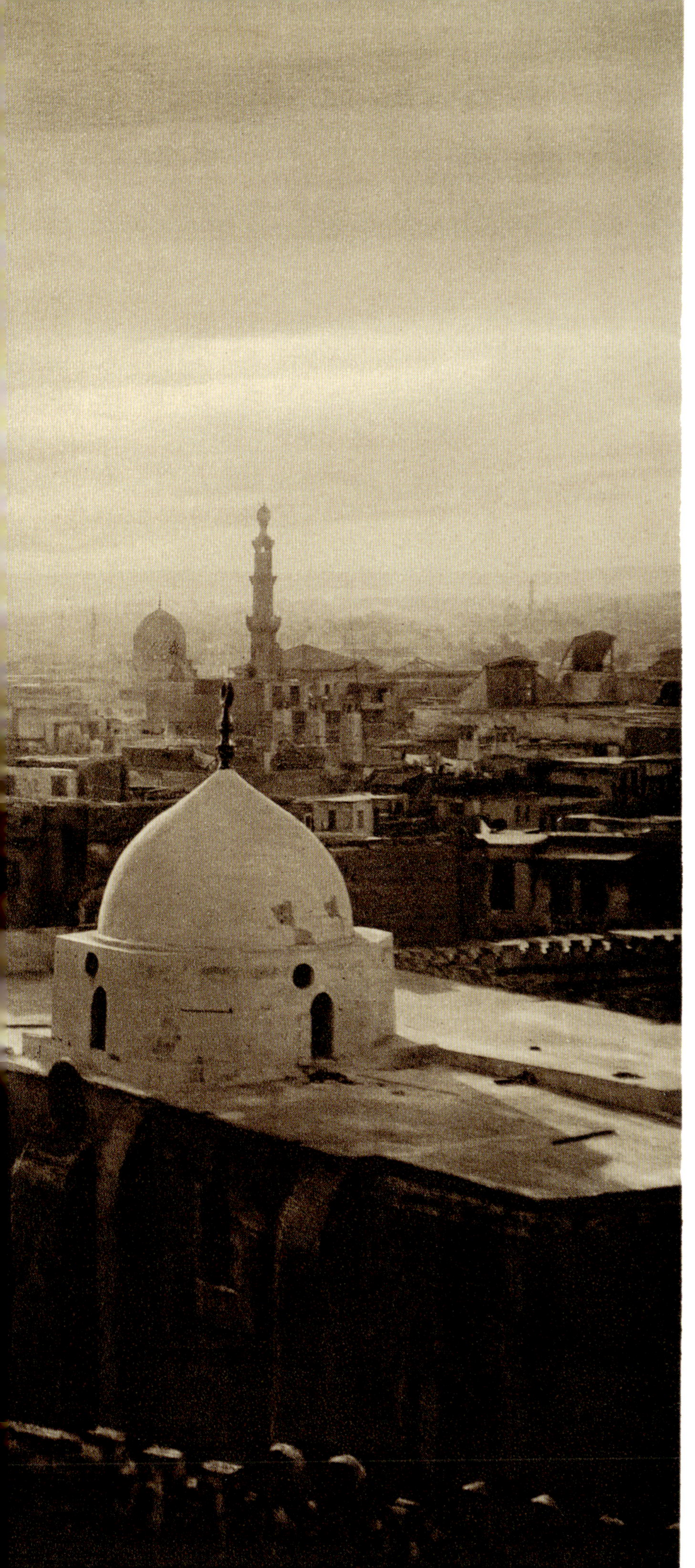

LEHNERT AND LANDROCK
Sunset, Cairo
c. 1905

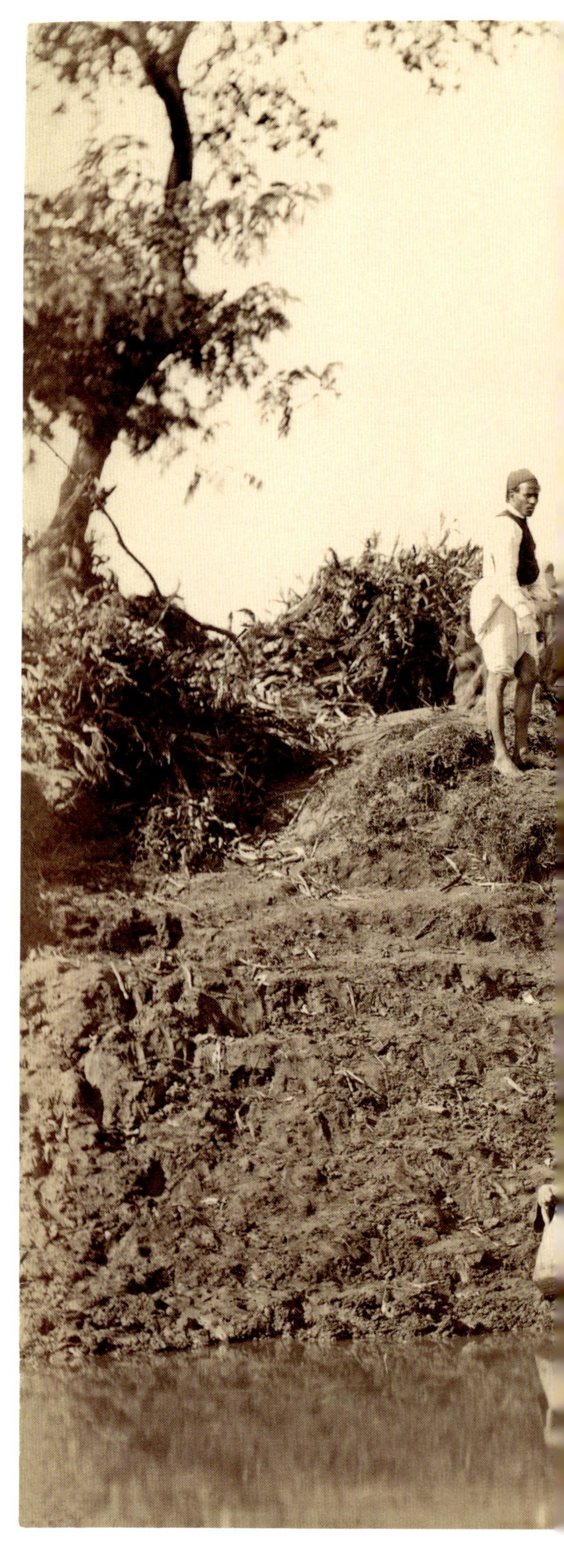

PASCAL SEBAH
Step Irrigation called Shaduf
1880s

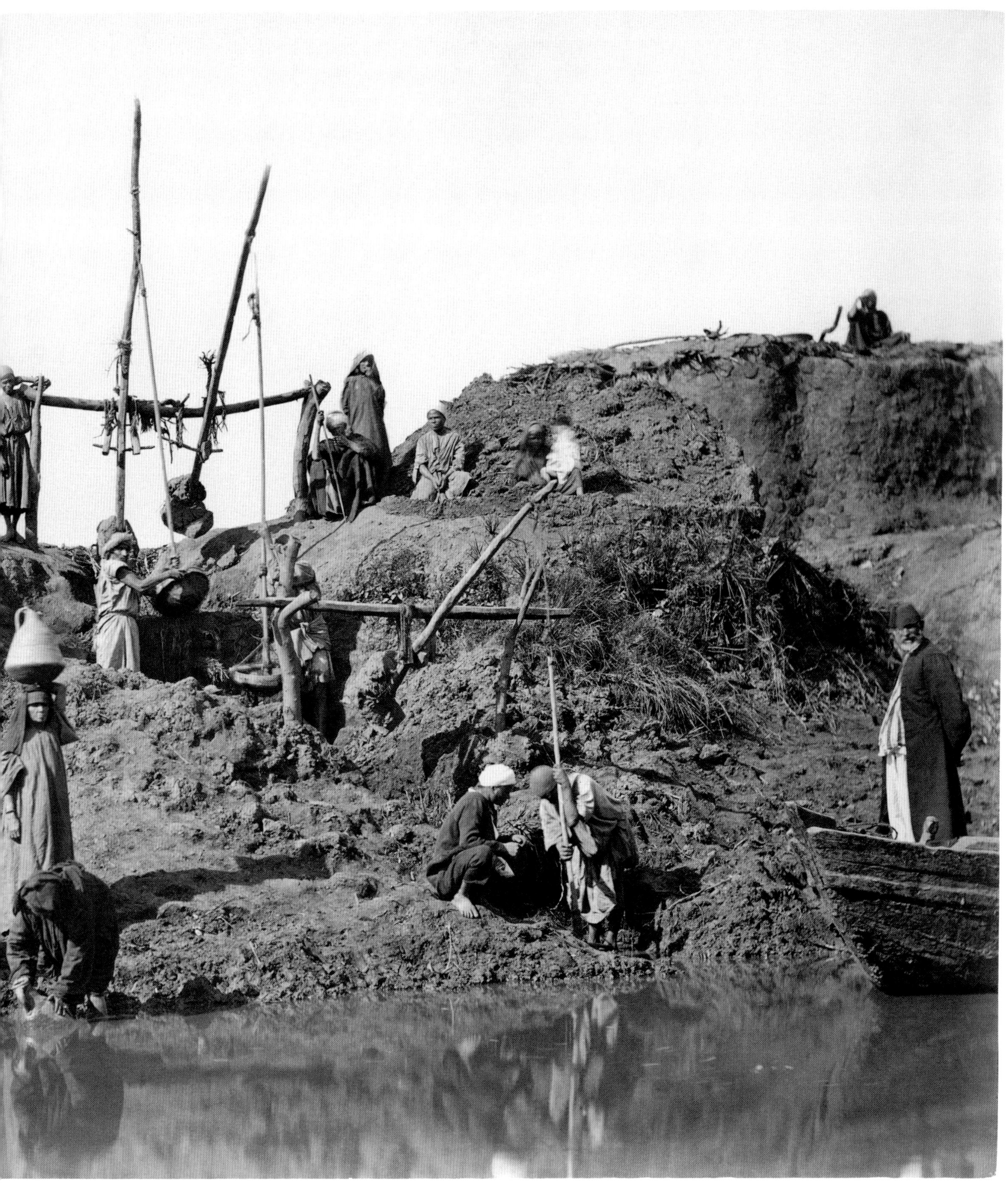

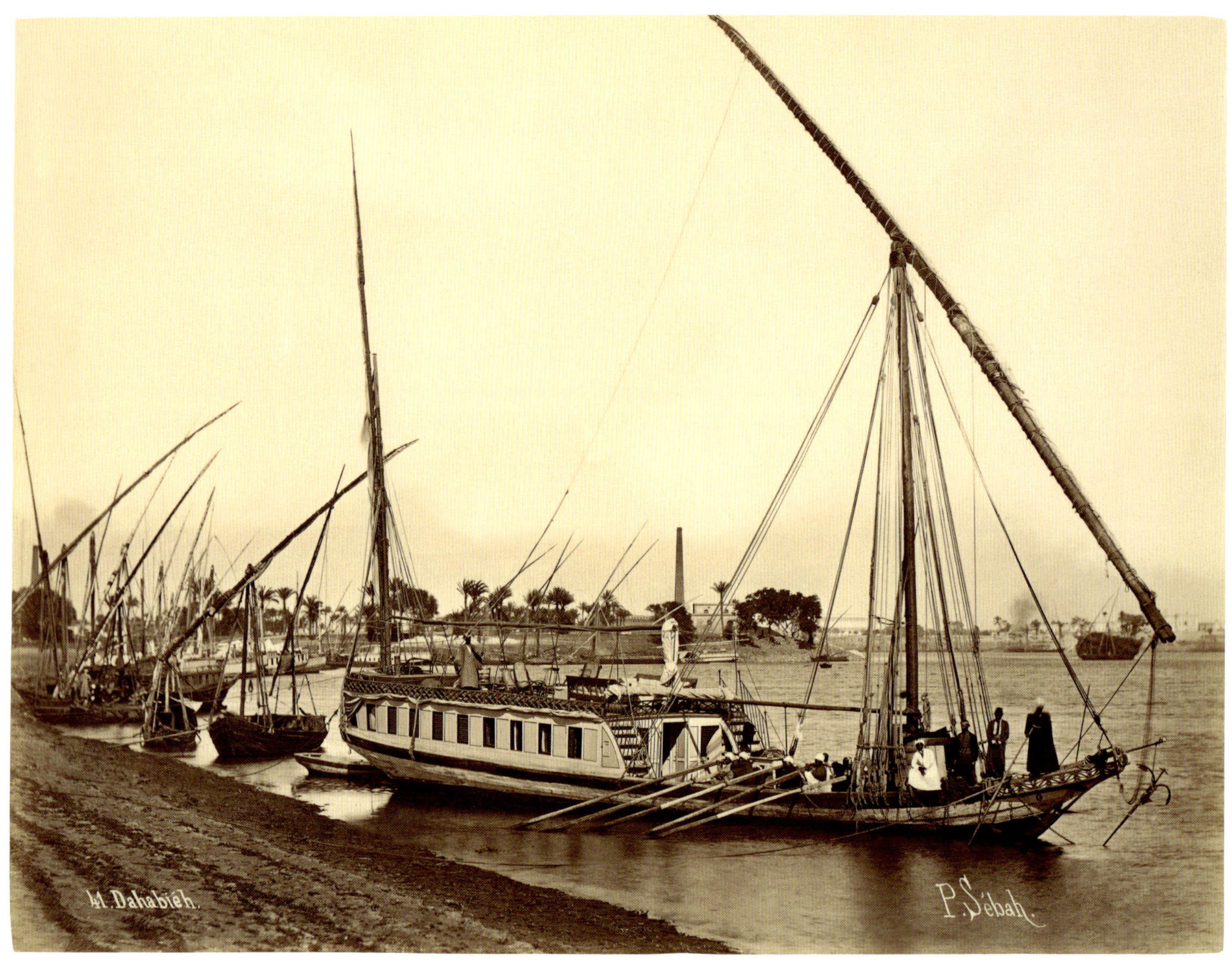

PASCAL SEBAH
Dahabieh *on the Nile*
1870s

Today, it is easy to forget the tremendous hardships endured by nineteenth-century photographers travelling the Nile towards Upper Egypt. Abu Simbel from the Mediterranean is a three-thousand-kilometer round trip. For these voyages, Europeans engaged a *dahabieh*, complete with crew, captain, cook and personal servants for a journey that would often last several months.

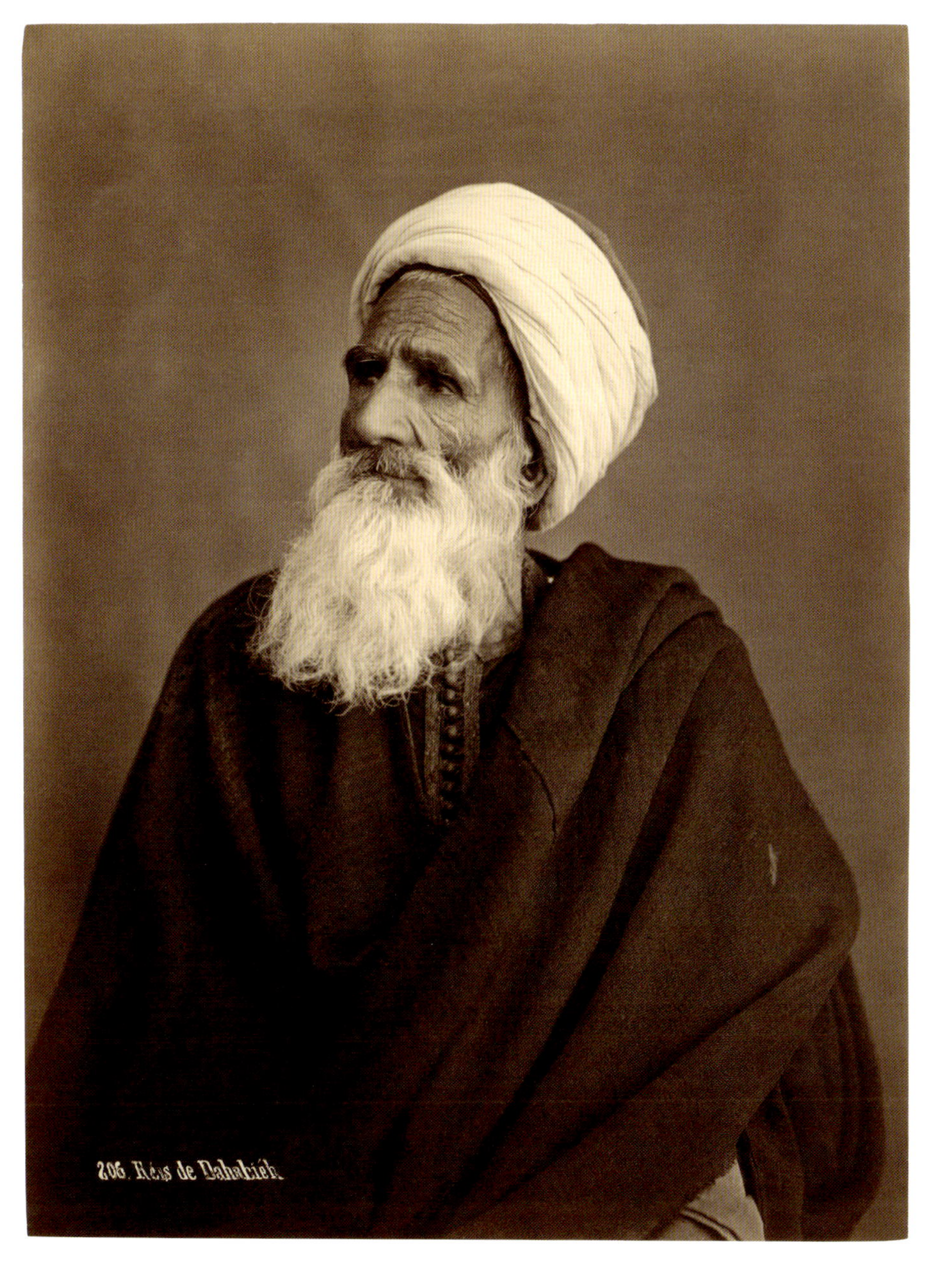

PASCAL SEBAH
Dahabieh *Ship's Captain*
1870s

LEHNERT AND LANDROCK
Nile Sunset
Cairo, 1905

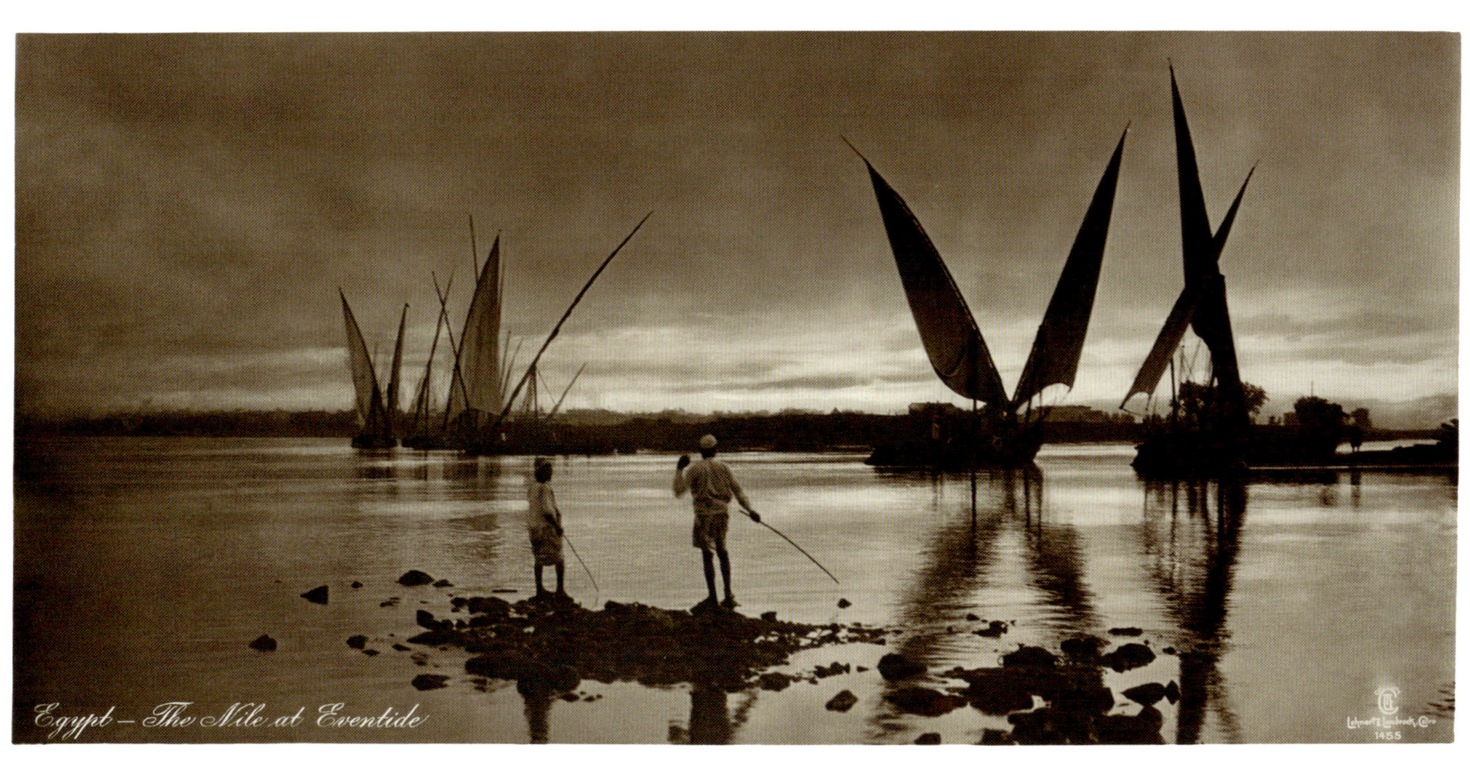
Egypt – The Nile at Eventide
1455

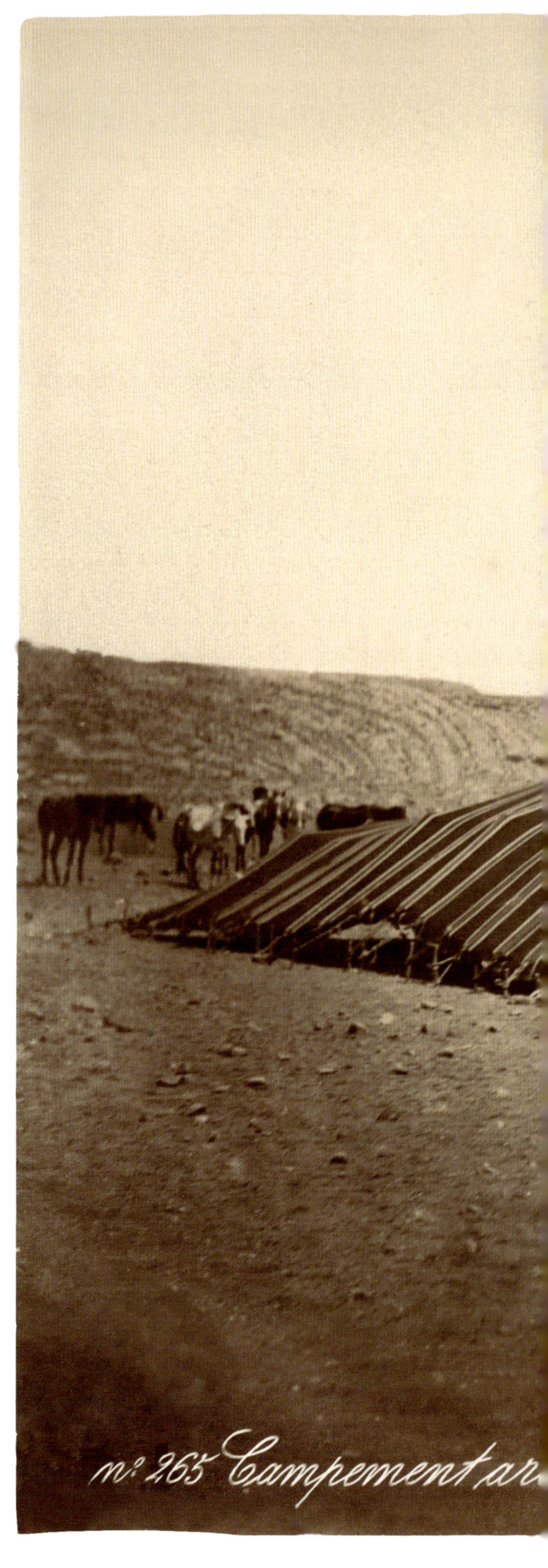

ANONYMOUS
Camp in the Desert
1880s

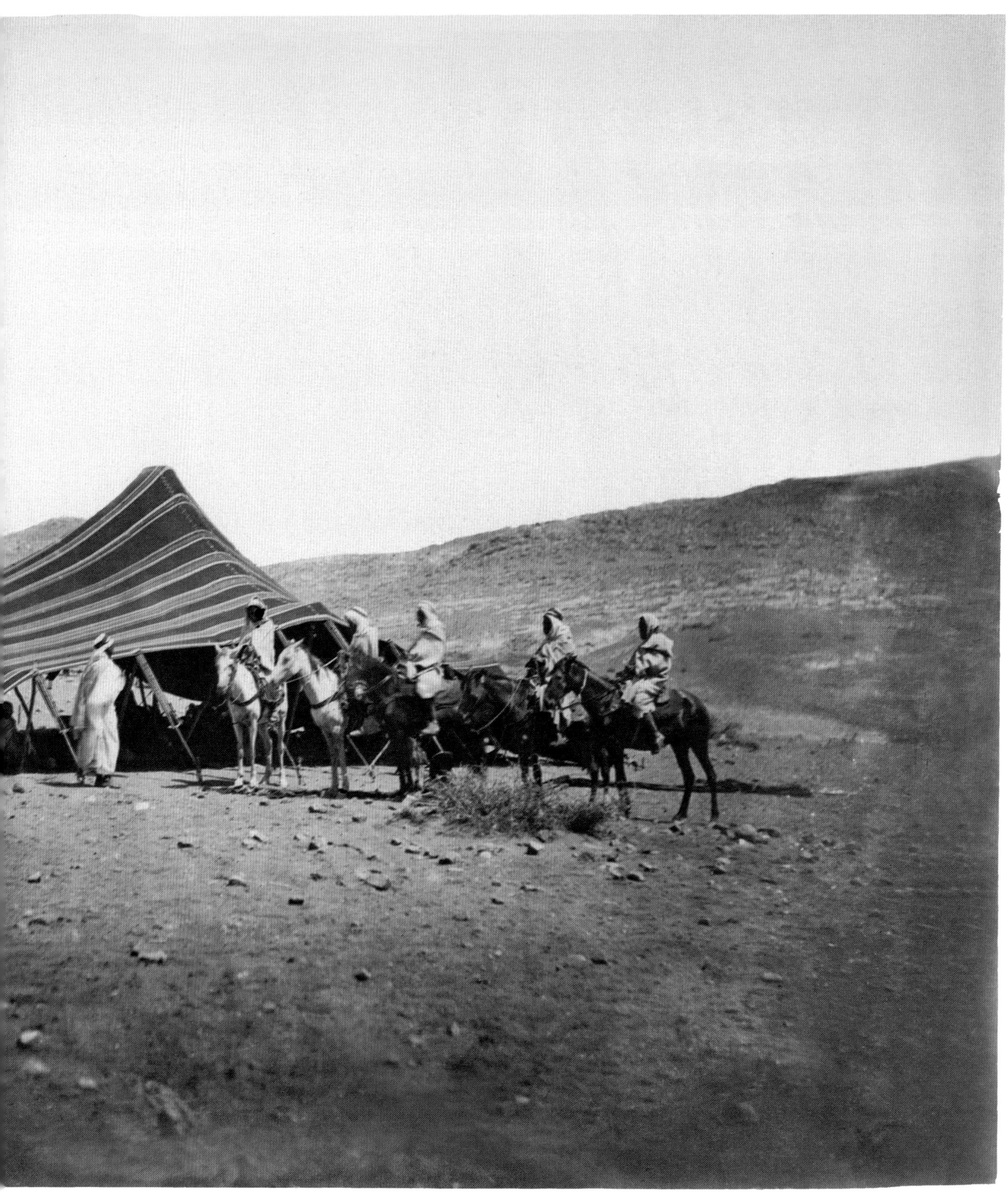

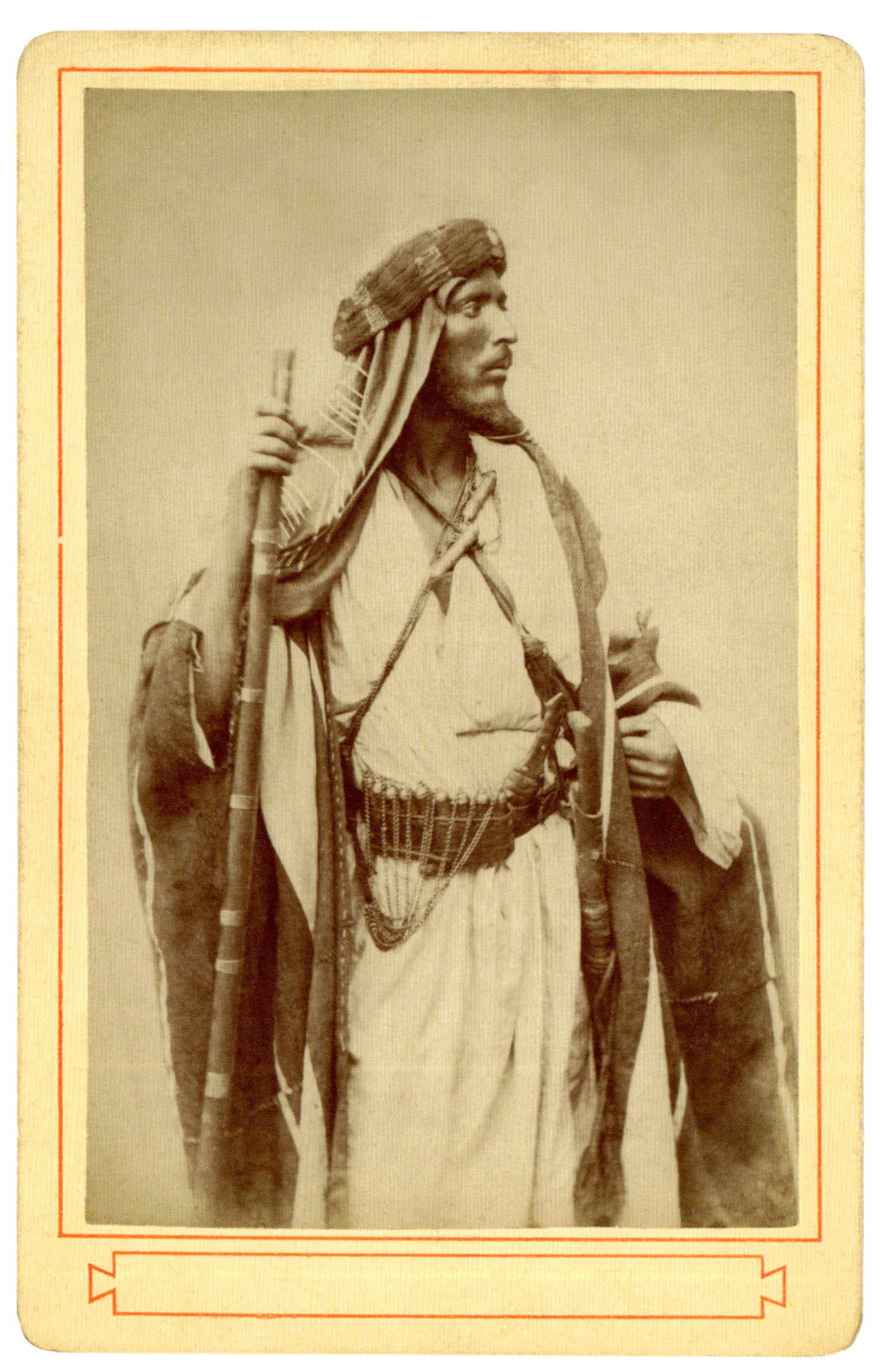

OTTO SCHOEFFT
Chief with Rifle
mid-1860s

Otto Schoefft's photographs made during the mid-1860s form an almost unique vision in Middle Eastern photography, entailing the creation of highly idealised subjects and a 'documentation' detailing a series of 'types'.

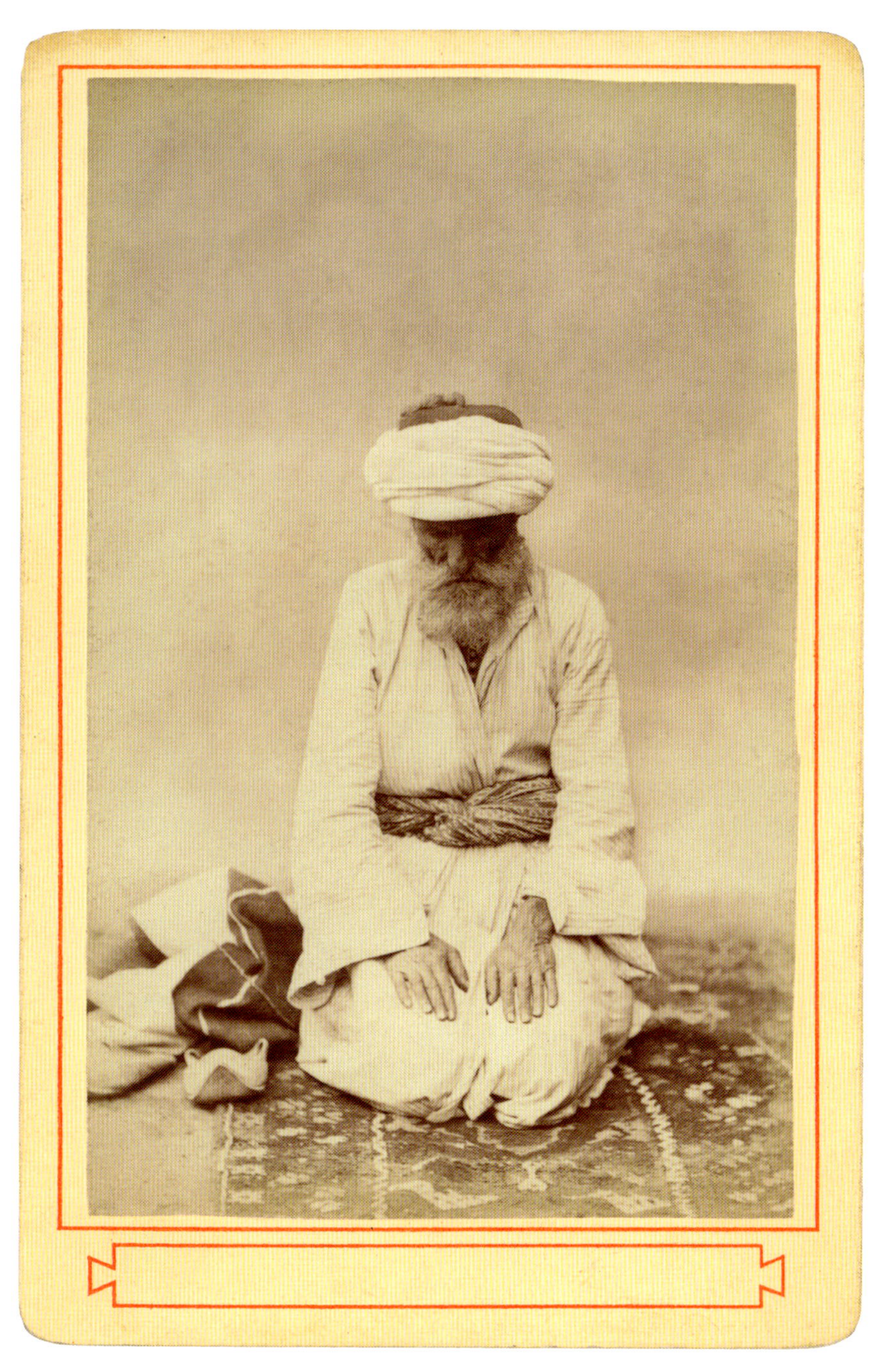

OTTO SCHOEFFT
Man Praying
mid-1860s

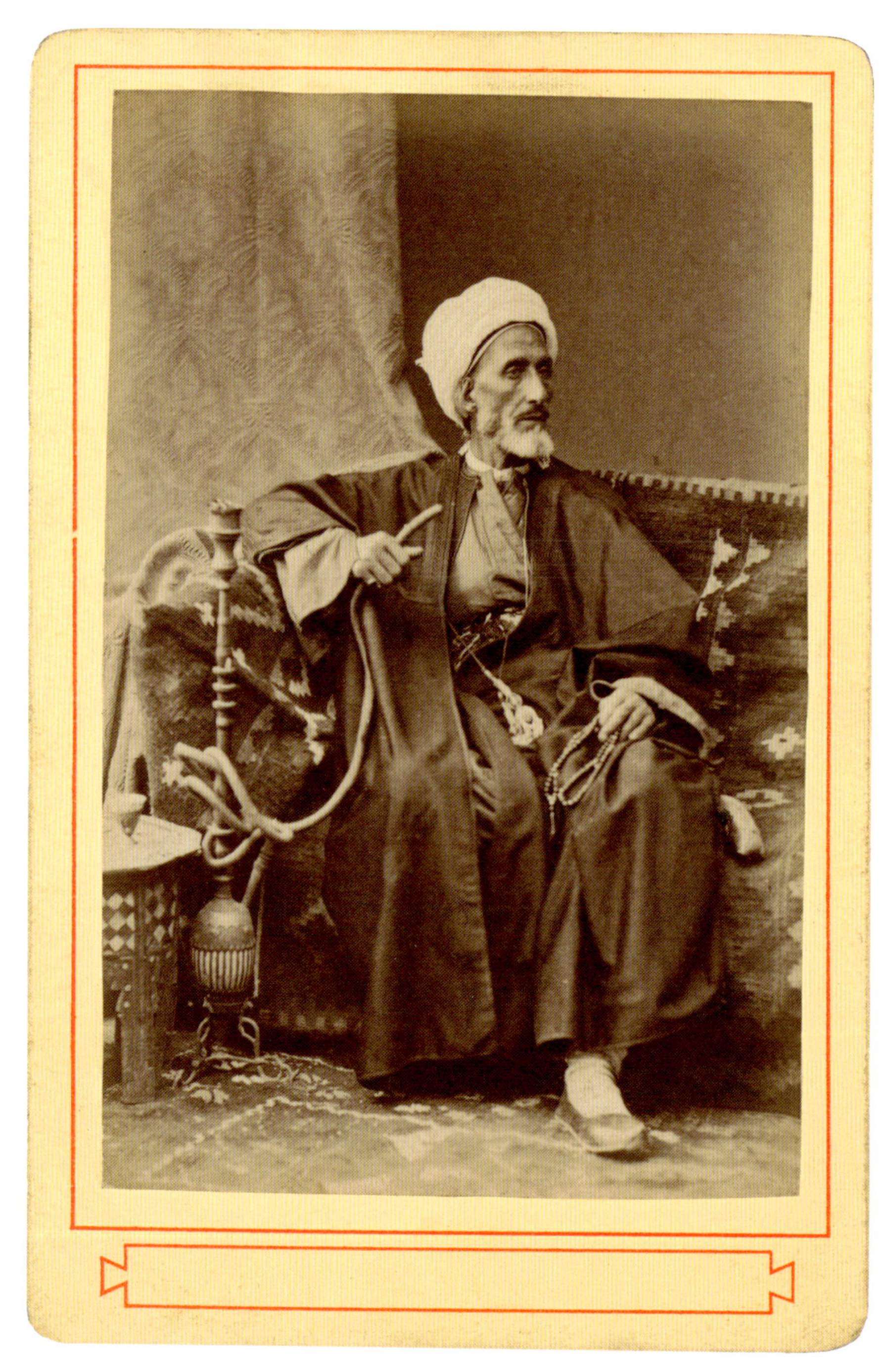

OTTO SCHOEFFT
Merchant with Narghile
mid-1860s

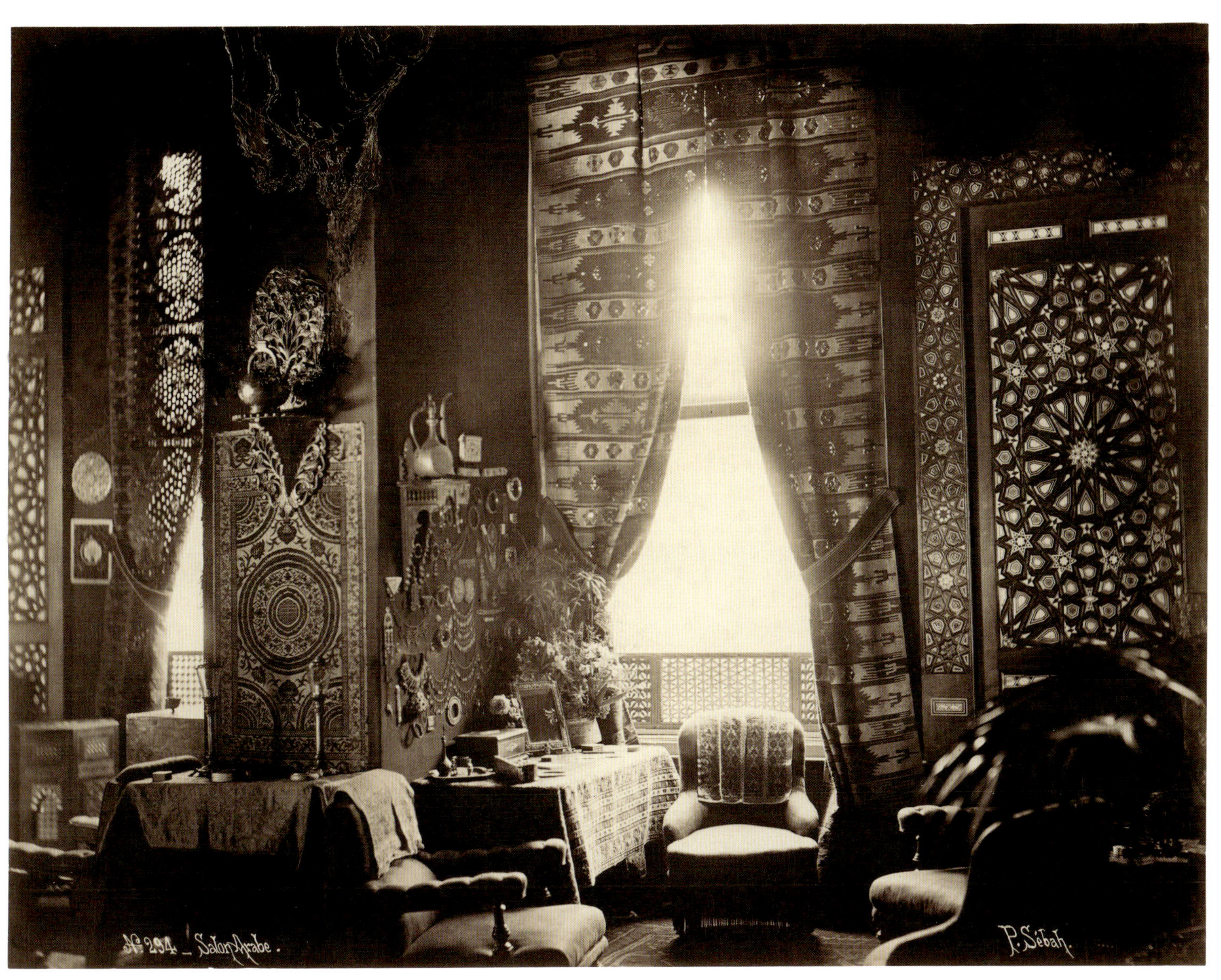

PASCAL SEBAH
Salon
Cairo, 1870s

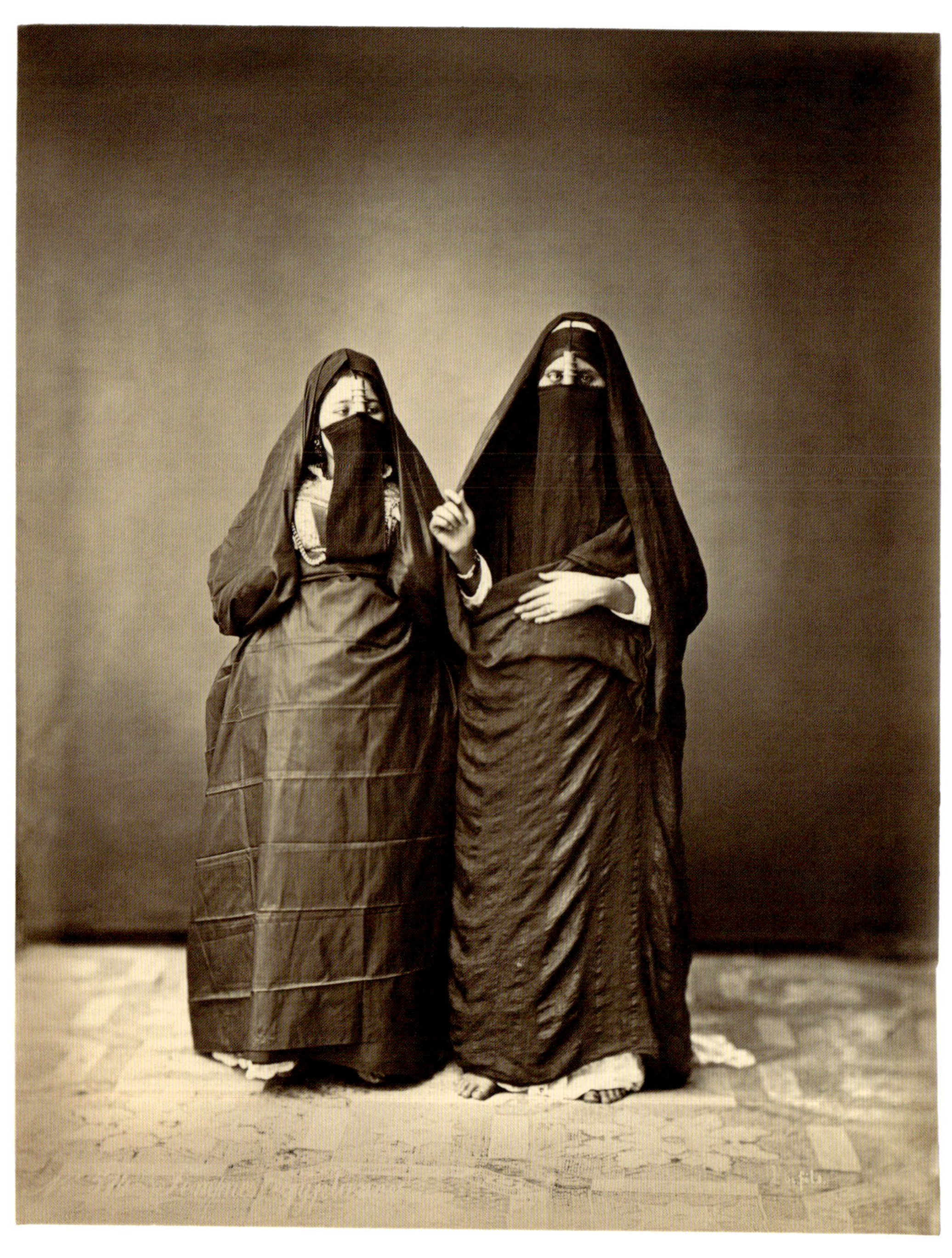

FÉLIX BONFILS
Two Women Wearing Face Masks
Cairo, 1860s

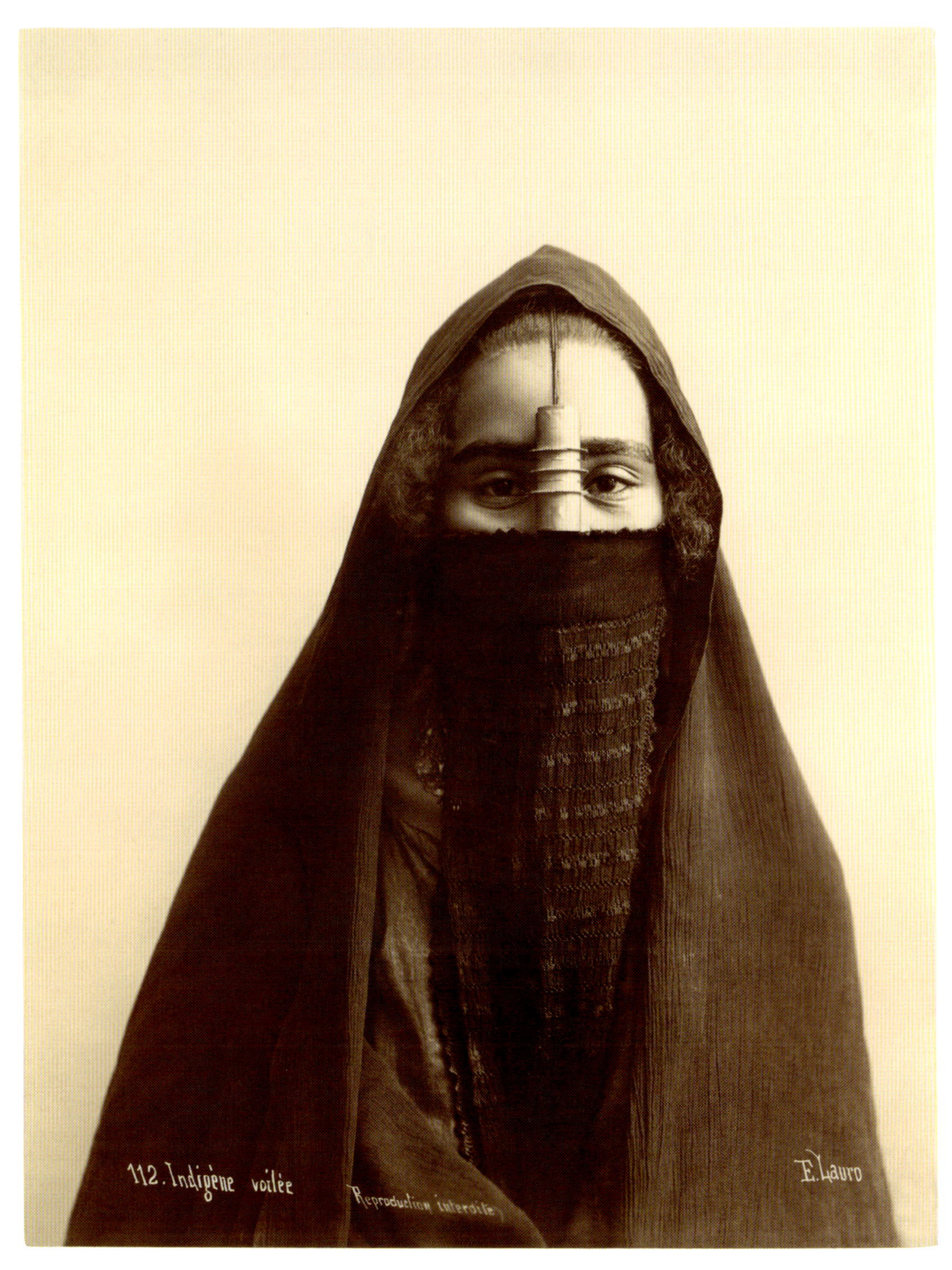

E. LAURO
Woman With Veil
Egypt, 1890s

FÉLIX BONFILS
Young Egyptian Woman Wearing a Face Mask
1860s

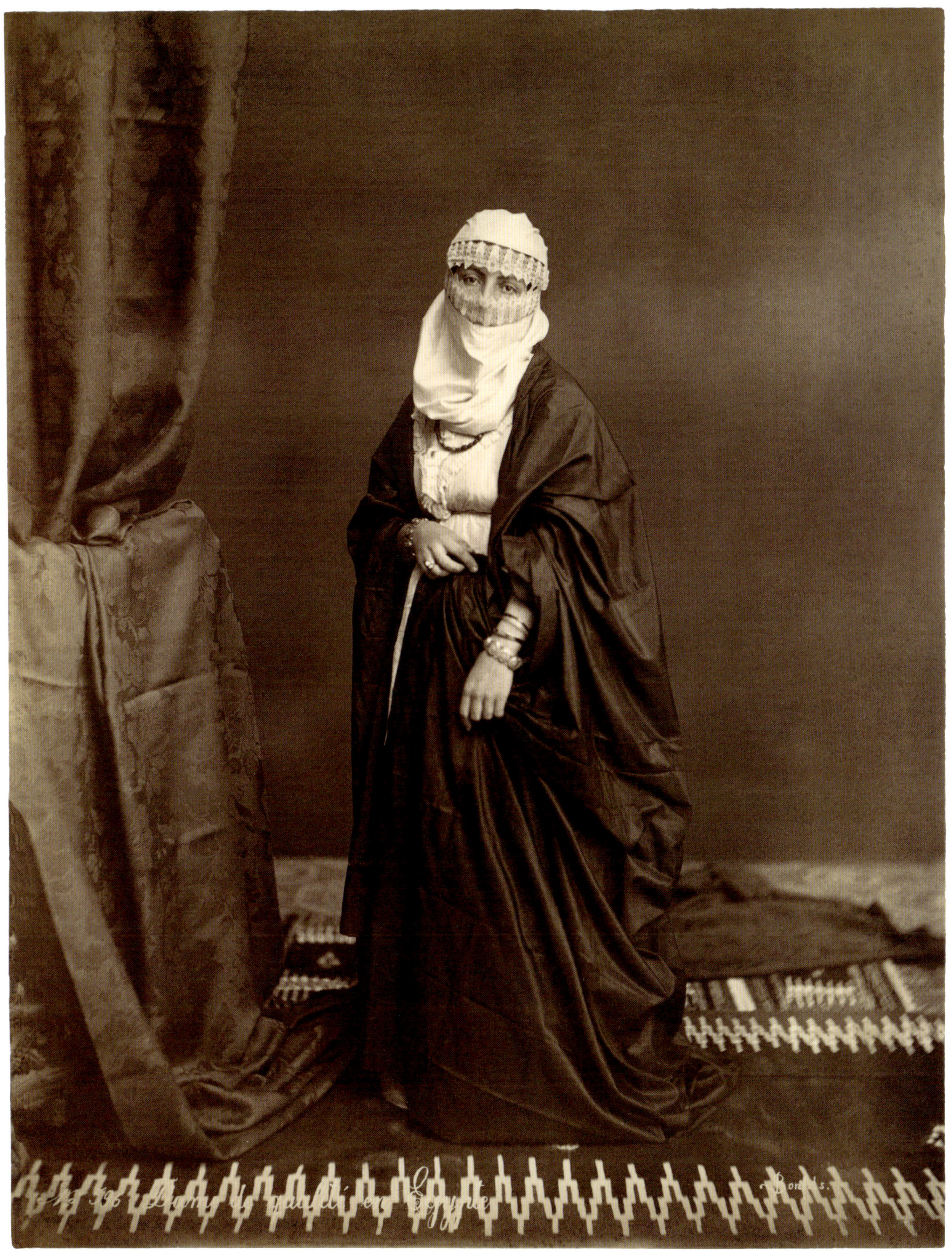

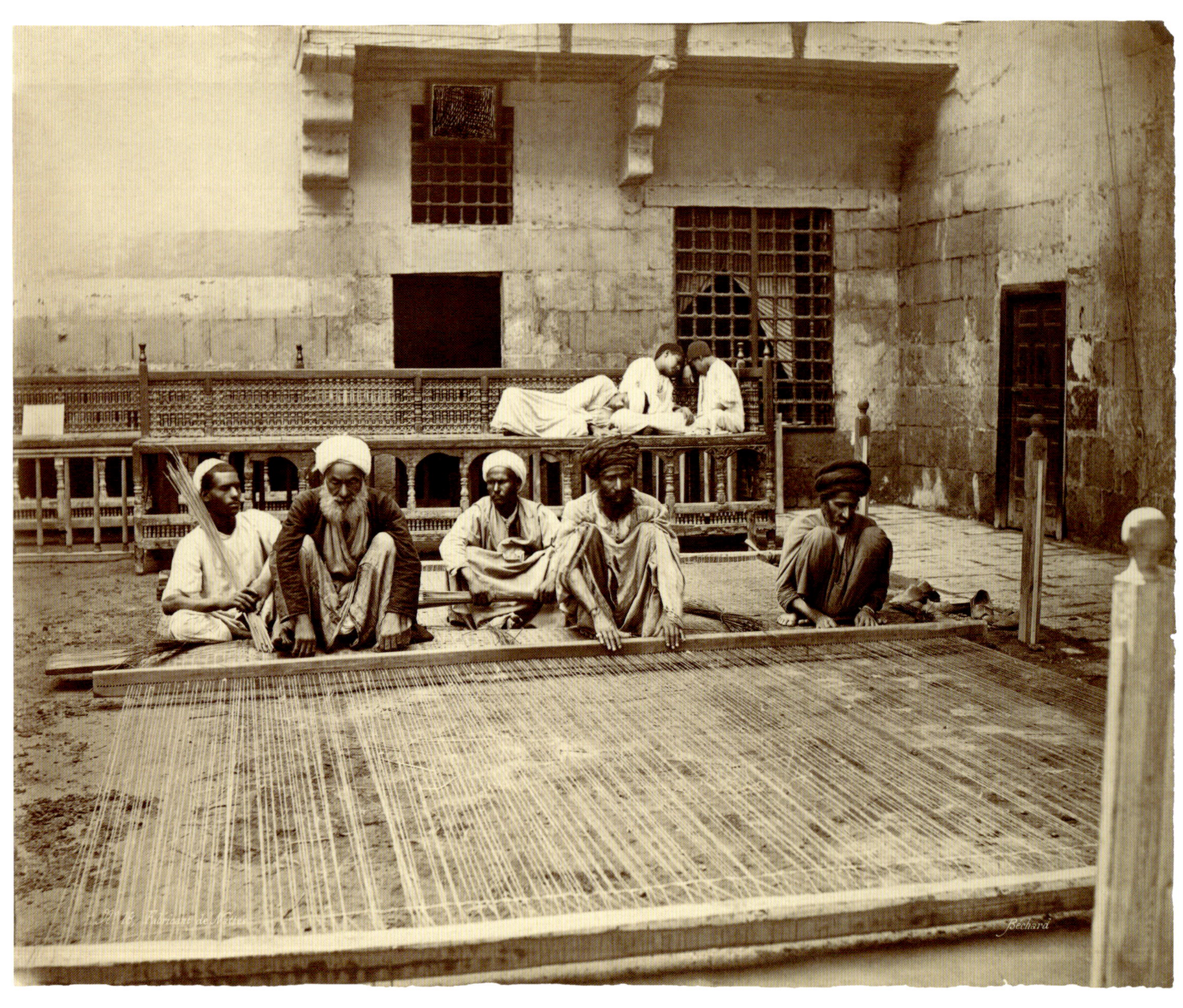

EMILE BÉCHARD
Carpet Weavers
Cairo, 1870s

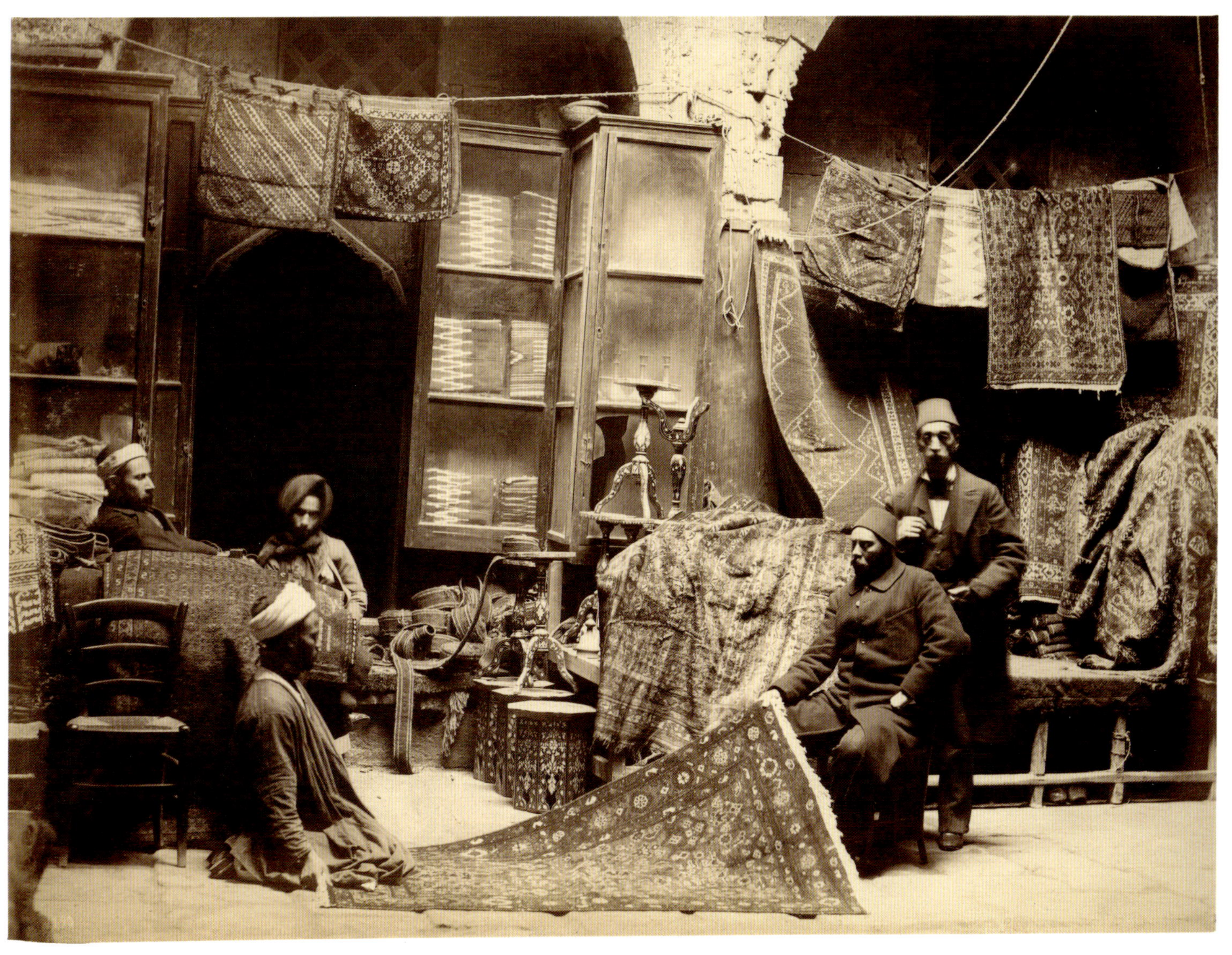

PASCAL SEBAH
Carpet Merchants
Cairo Bazaar, 1870s

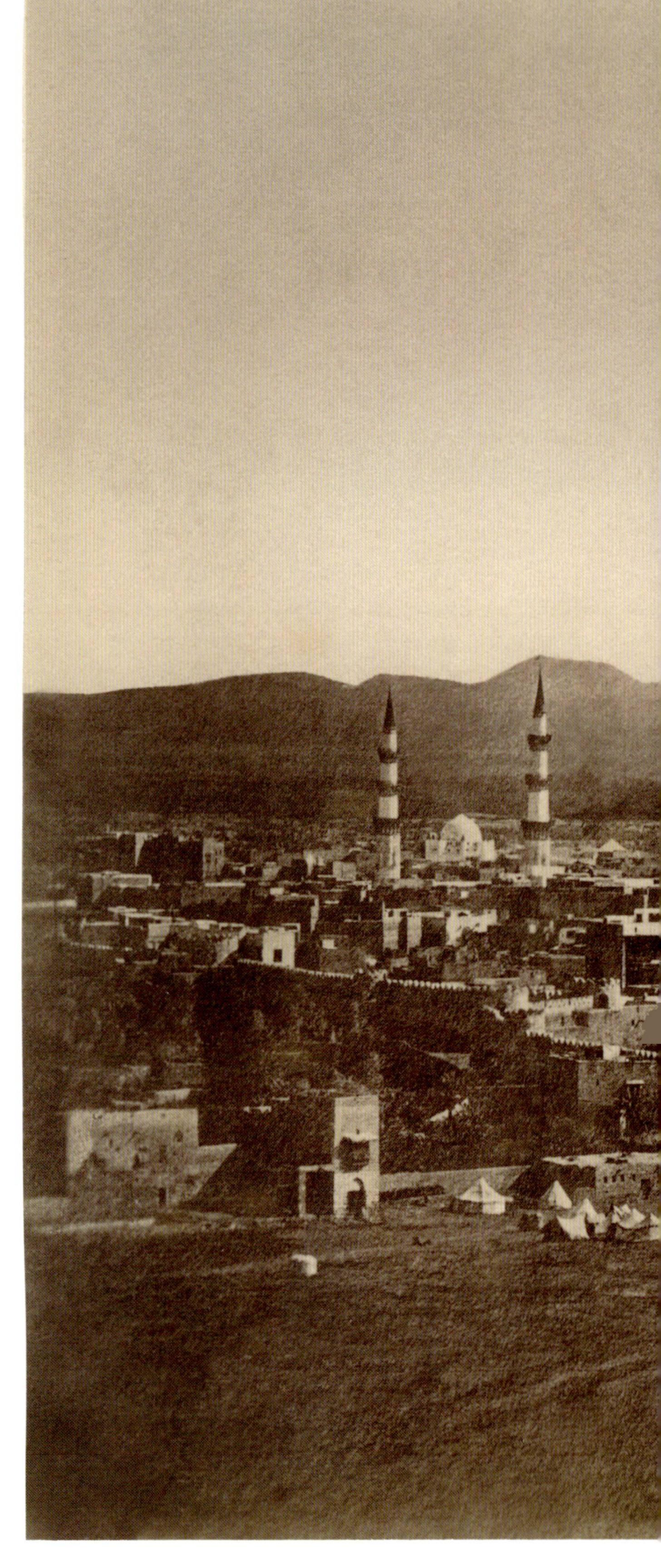

MUHAMMAD SADIQ (SULAYMAN AL-HAKIM)
The First Photograph of Medina from Bab al-Sham
c. 1890

Perhaps the scarcest pictures of the Middle East are photographs of Arabia and the holy cities of Mecca and Medina, circa 1880–86. The first photographer of Medina was Muhammad Sadiq, a colonel in the Egyptian service. Outside the city walls, Sadiq photographed the tents of the Turkish garrison, which one had to pass in order to enter the city. This print is a copy of Sadiq's original. It was made by the only known Arab photographer of the Middle East, Sulayman al-Hakim of Damascus, circa 1890.

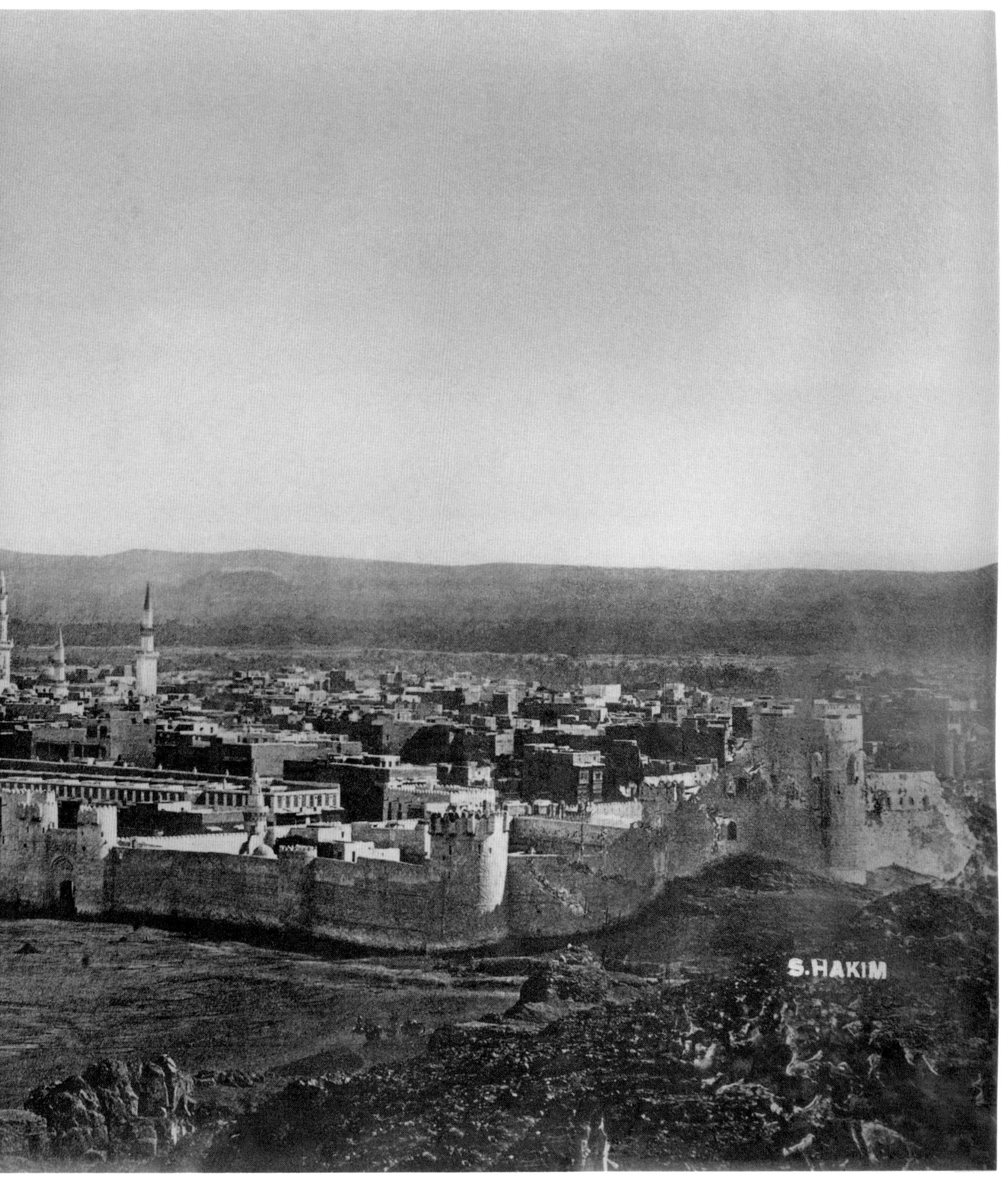
S.HAKIM

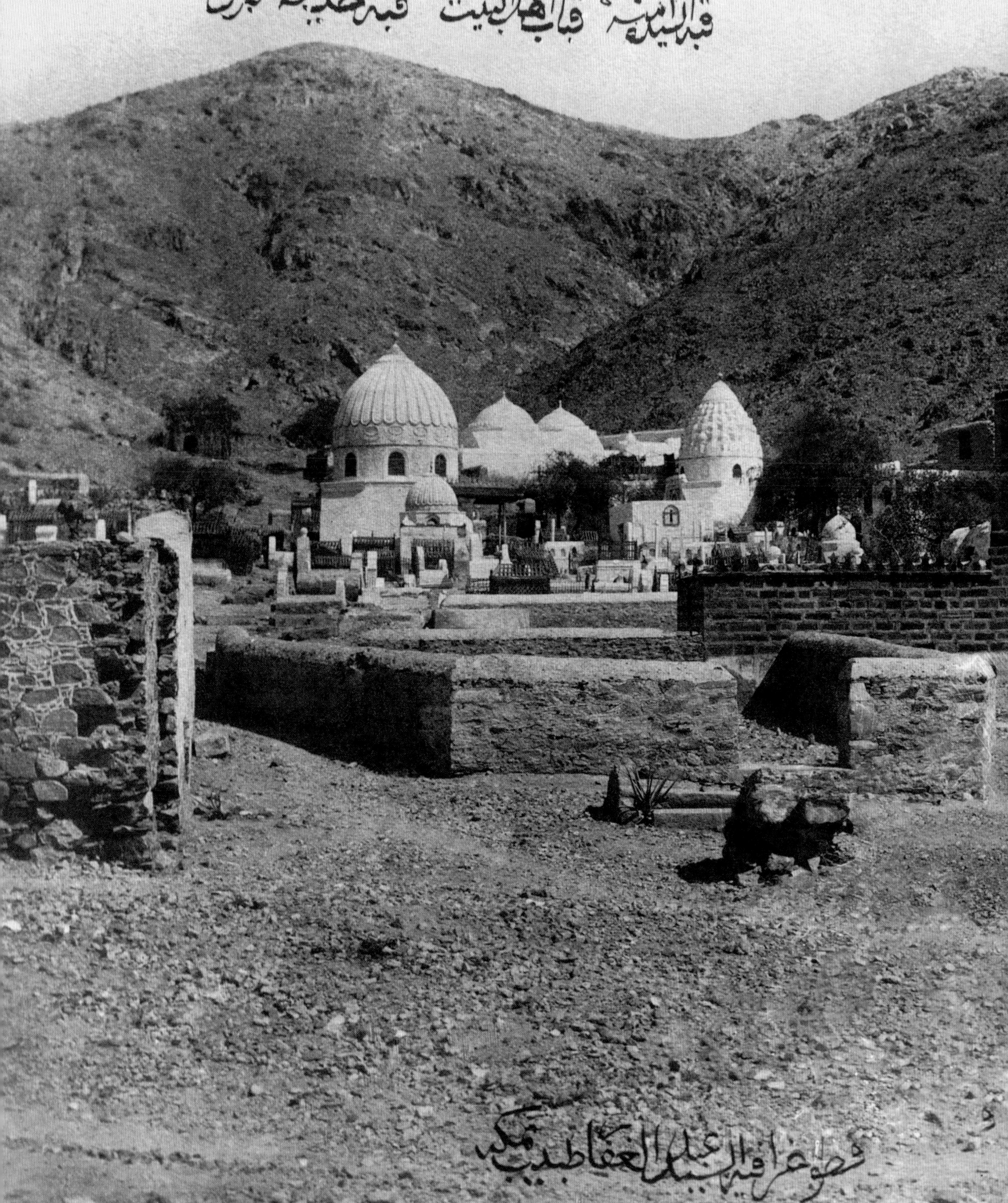
قبة السيدة آمنة
قباب أهل البيت
قبة خديجة الكبرى
فوطوغرافية السيد عبد الغفار طبيب بمكة

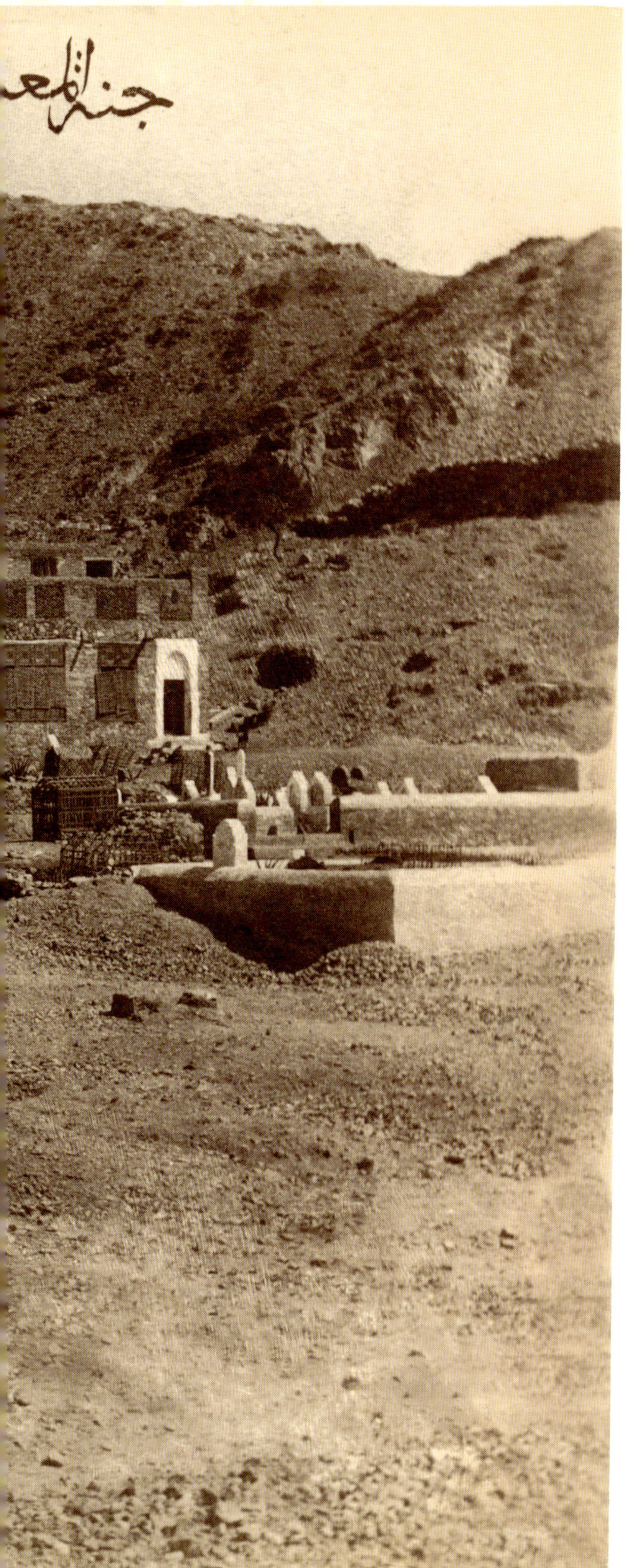

ABD AL-GHAFFAR
Garden of Mahalla, Tomb of the Prophet's Wife and Family
before 1889

The first resident photographer of Mecca was Sayyid Abd al-Ghaffar Tabeeb Makka (Doctor of Mecca). Signed Abd al-Ghaffar, prints of Mecca are exceedingly rare. The prints in this book were found in Hyderabad, India, in the 1970s. During the 1920s, religious fundamentalists tore down the tombs of the Prophet's wife and her family.

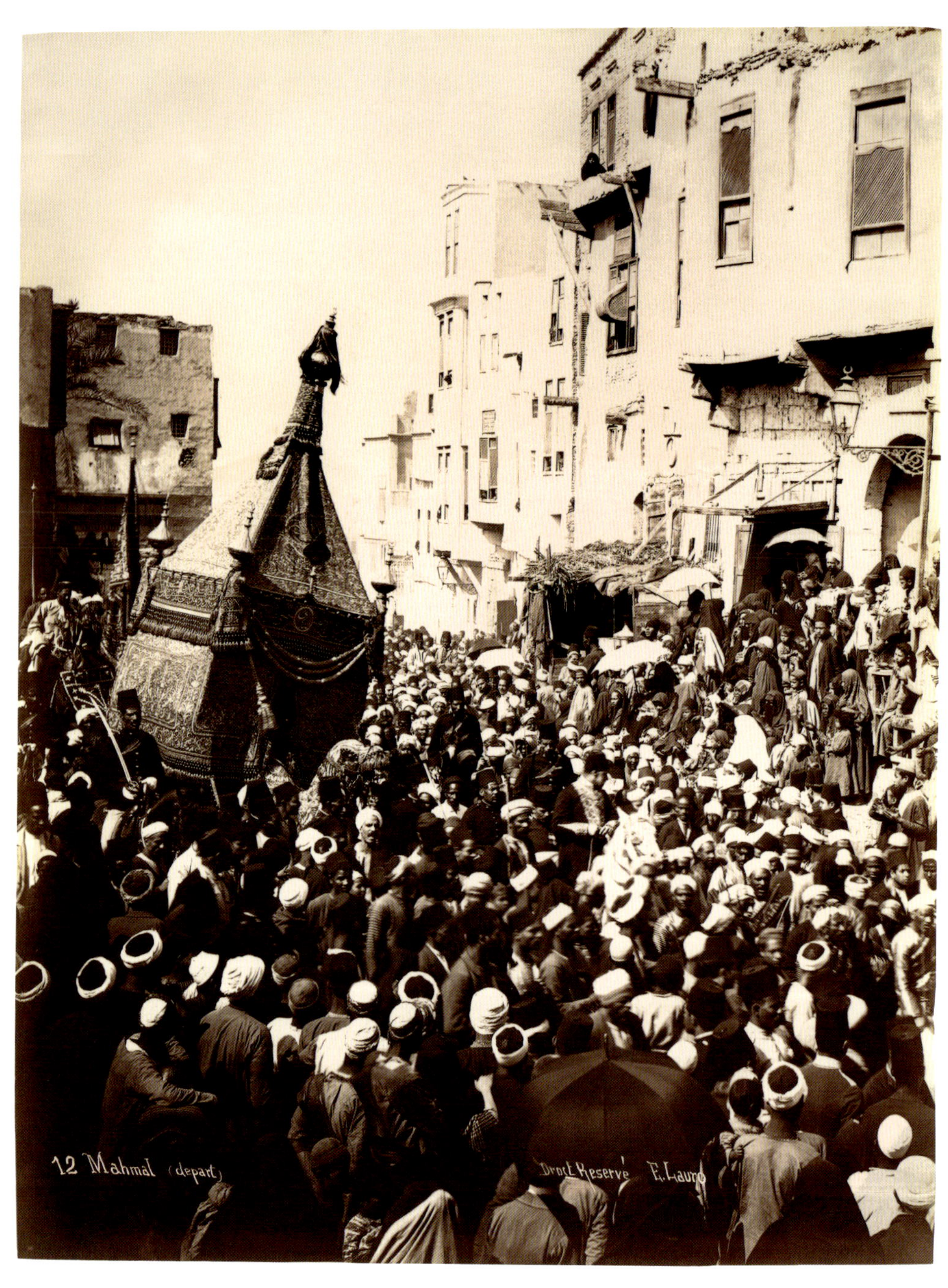

E. LAURO
The Mahmal *on the* Hajj *to Mecca*
Cairo, 1890s

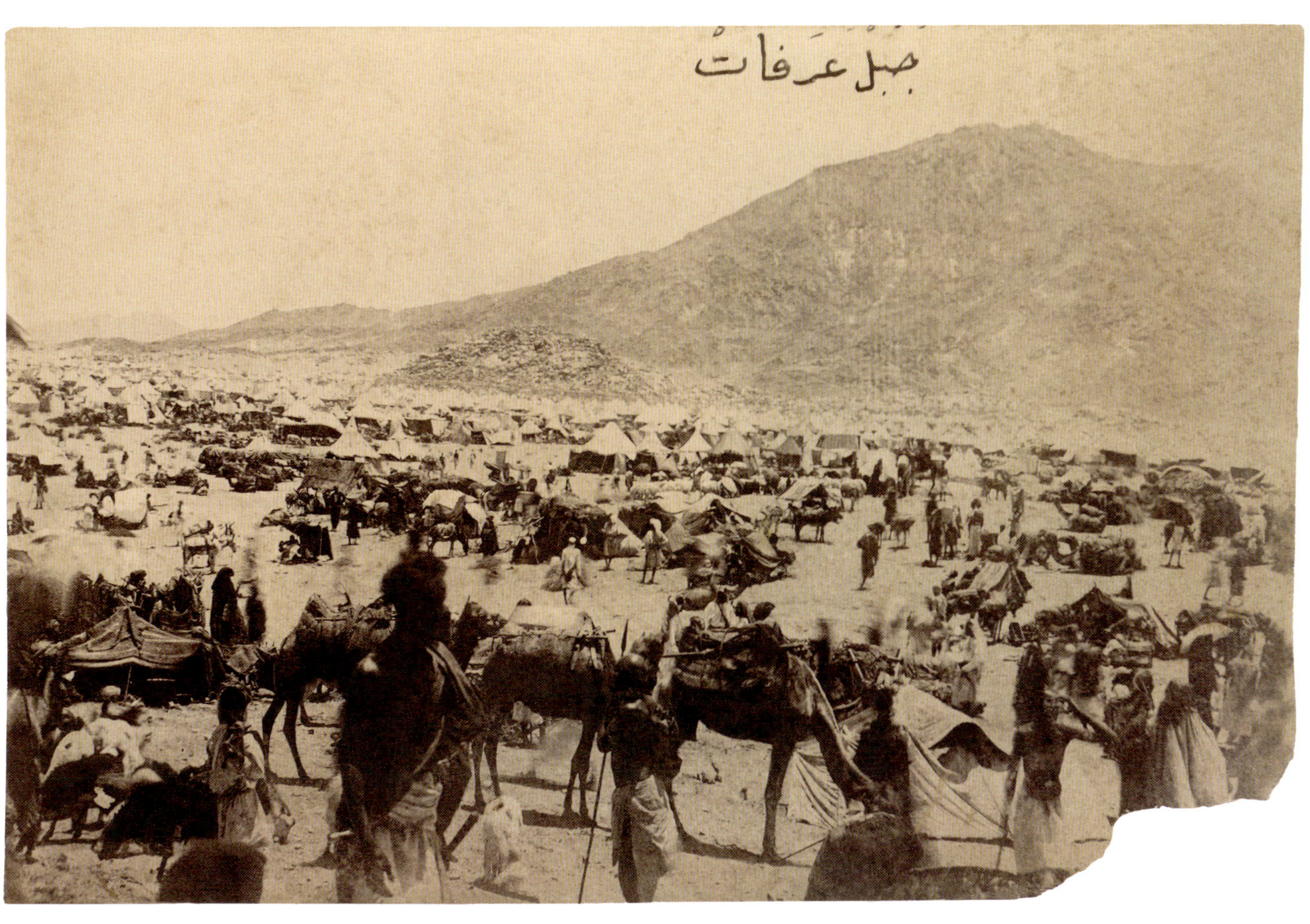

ABD AL-GHAFFAR
The Valley of Arafat, Pilgrim Encampment
Mecca, before 1889

Mount Arafat is where Muslims believe Muhammad delivered the Farewell Sermon to his followers, who had accompanied him for the *Hajj* towards the end of his life. The level area surrounding the hill is called the Plain of Arafat. It is a most important place in Islam because during the *Hajj* pilgrims spend the afternoon there on the ninth day of Dhu al-Hijjah. Failure to be present in the plain of Arafat on the required day invalidates the pilgrimage and pilgrims often spend all night here in vigil.

It has been already remarked, that the house of God is entirely covered on the outside with a large black cloth, called Tob el Kaaba, *or the Shirt of the Kaaba, suspended from the terrace, and fastened below by means of strings, which answer to the bronze rings that are fixed in the base. There is a new one brought every year from Cairo, as also a curtain to cover the door, which is truly magnificent, being entirely embroidered with gold and silver.*

Domingo Badía, *Travels of Ali Bey*, 1814

ABD AL-GHAFFAR AND PASCAL SEBAH
The Kaaba, Mecca
Istanbul, before 1889

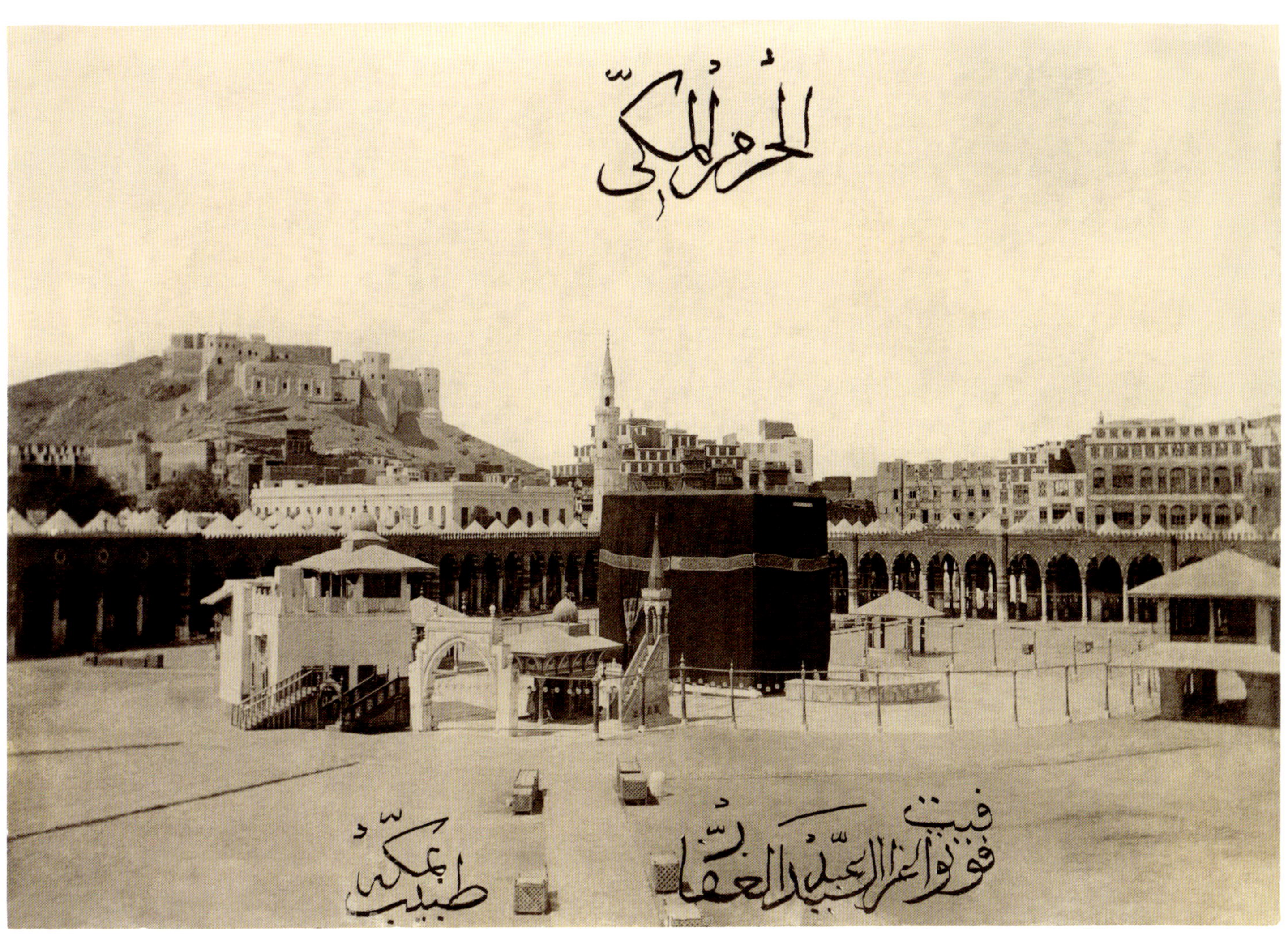
الحرم المكي
فوتوغراف السيد عبد الغفار
طبيب بمكة

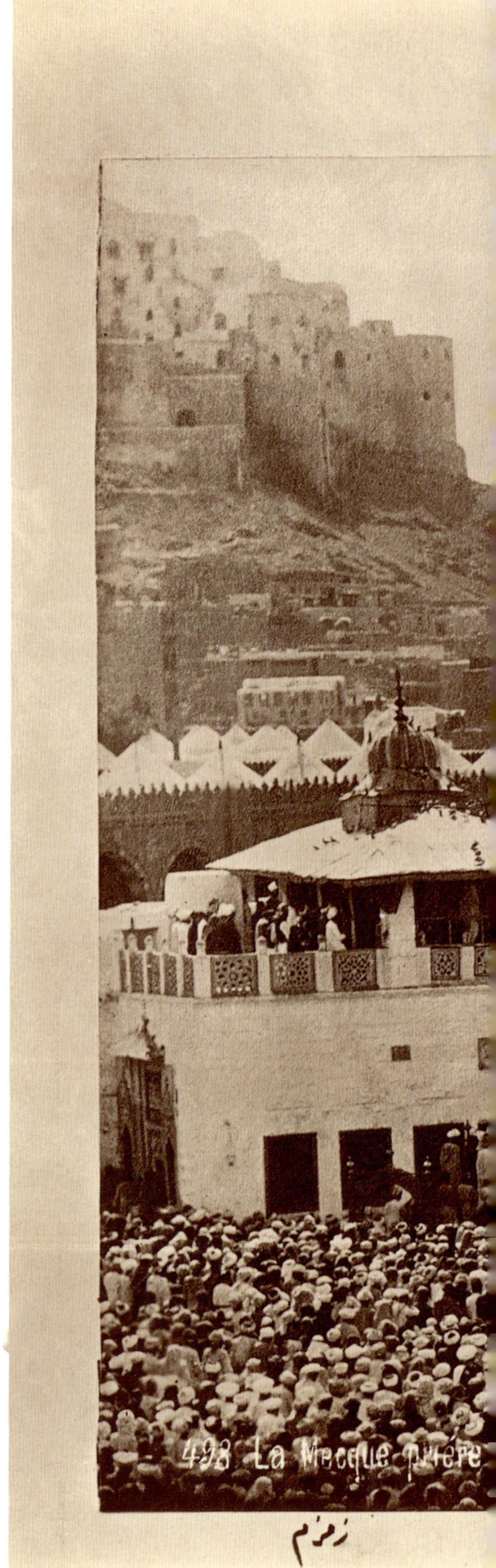

ABD AL-GHAFFAR
The Kaaba and Crowds of Worshippers of the Hajj
Mecca, before 1889

Islamic tradition says that the Kaaba was built by Ibrahim (Abraham) and that it 'reflects' a house in heaven called al-Bayt al-Ma'mur. One of the Five Pillars of Islam requires every capable Muslim to perform the *Hajj* pilgrimage at least once. Today, the most dramatic moment during the *Hajj* occurs when three million pilgrims simultaneously gather on the same day to circle the building.

Signed on the print: Abd al-Ghaffar. An 1880s copy print made of one of Abd al-Ghaffar's *Mecca of the Kaaba* pictures, and credited to Pascal Sebah (of Istanbul).

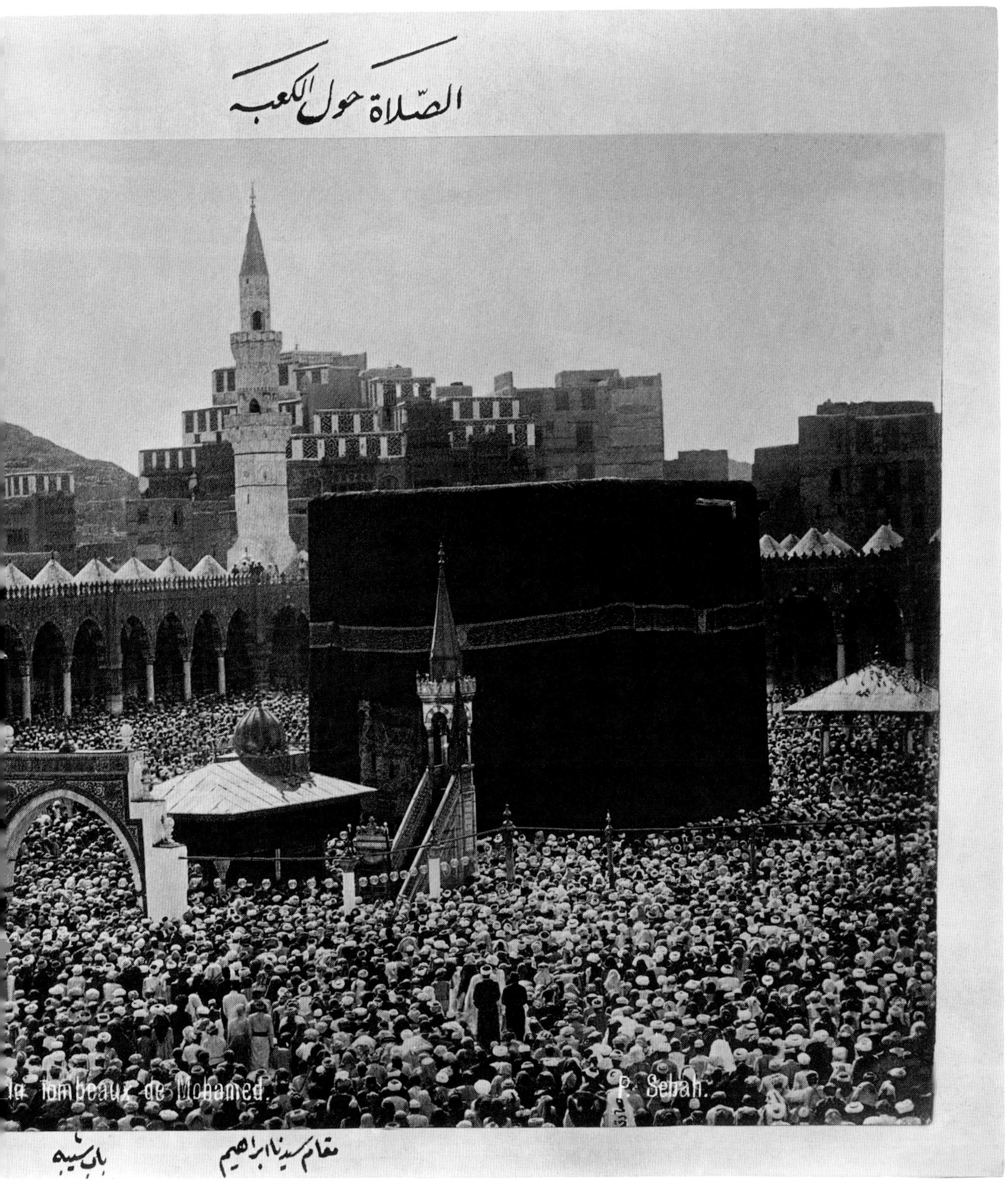
الصّلاة حول الكعبة
la Tombeaux de Mohamed.
P. Sebah.
مقام سيدنا ابراهيم
باب شيبه

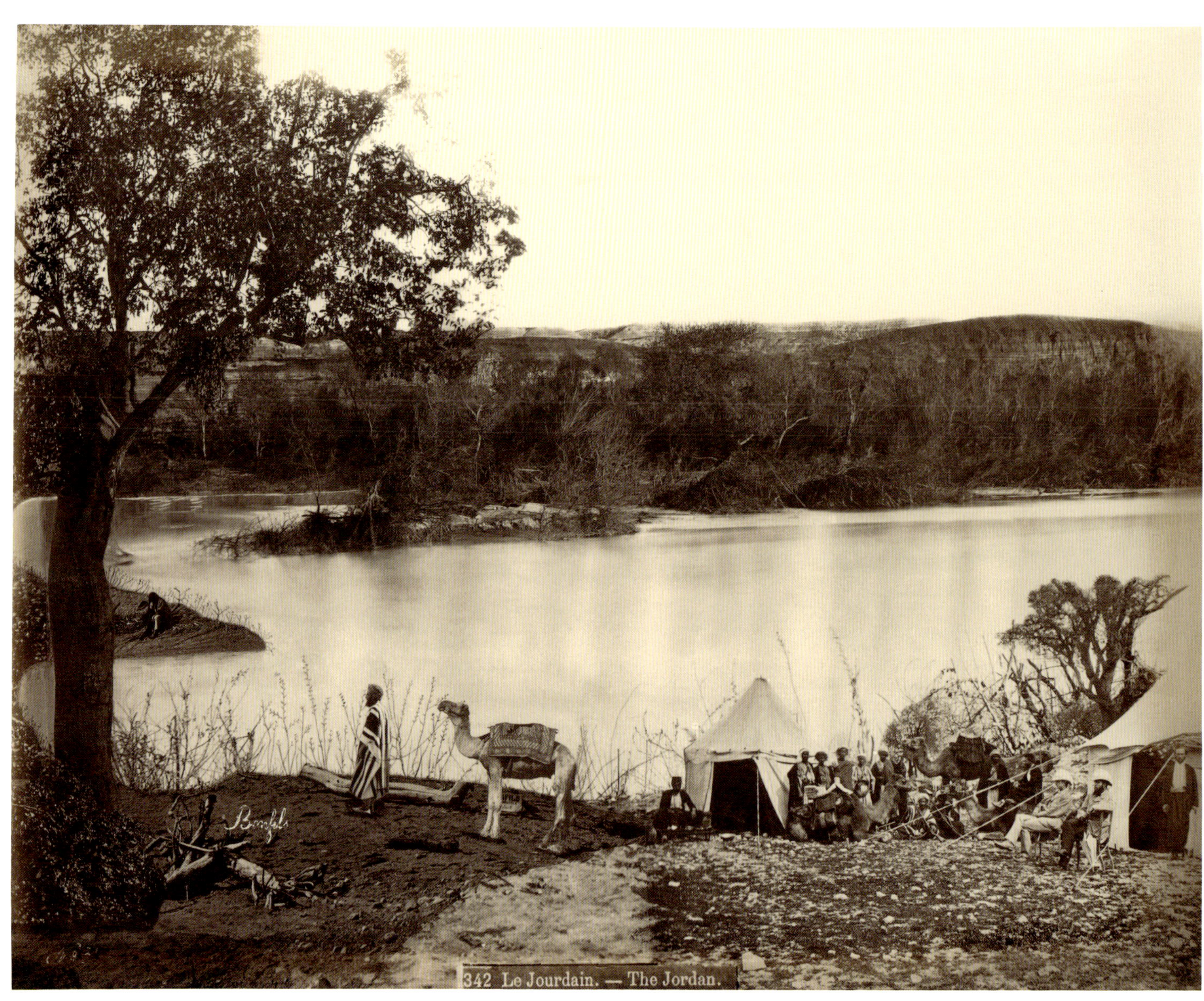

FÉLIX BONFILS
Camp on the Jordan River
1870s

A truly strange image by Bonfils, which upon closer inspection is a composite of several different photographs. Various elements in the picture (e.g., the camel and tent) are radically out of scale with the inhabitants of the scene.

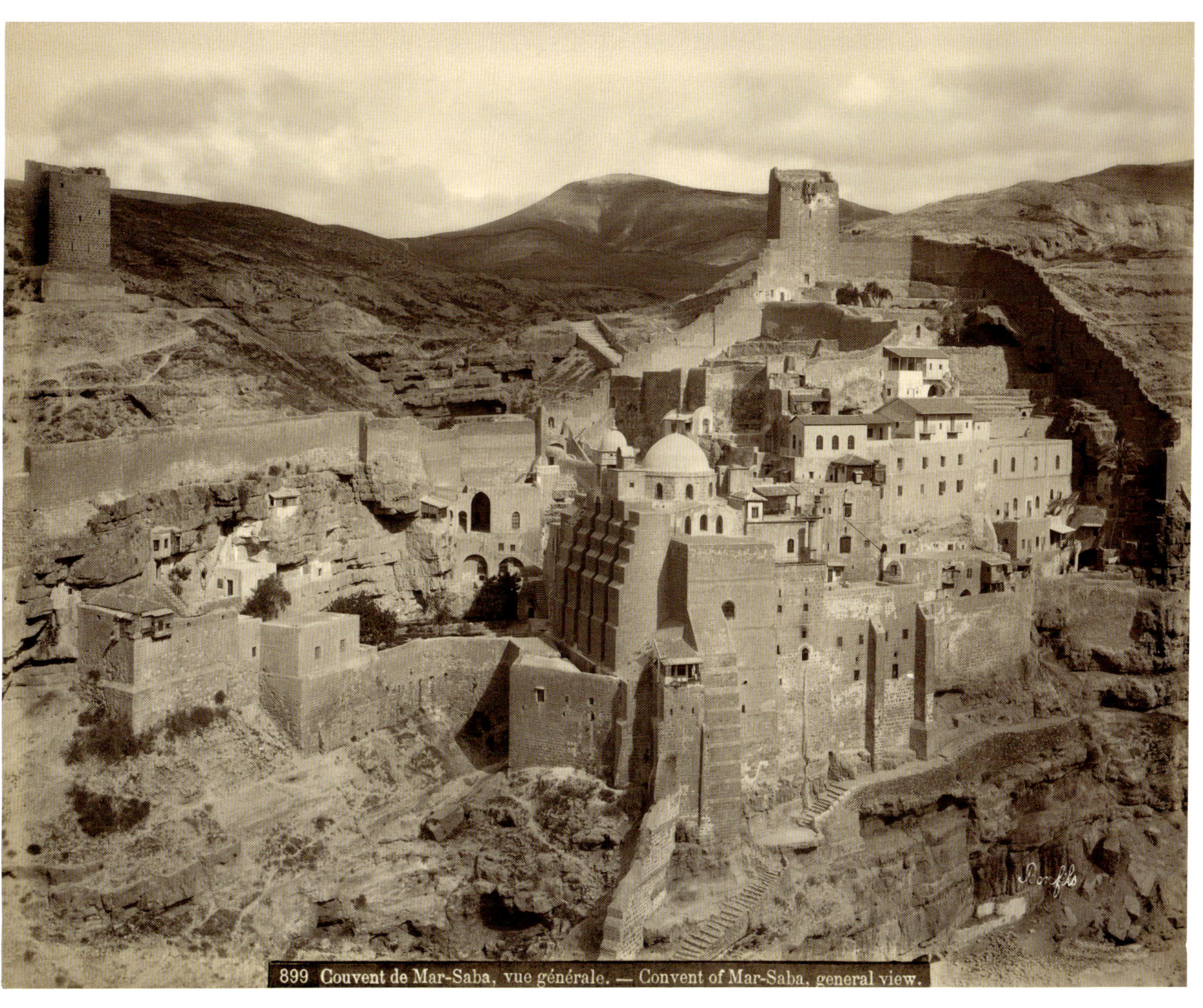

FÉLIX BONFILS
Convent of Mar Saba
Kidron Valley, 1870s

Mar Saba is a Greek Orthodox monastery overlooking the Kidron Valley, east of Bethlehem. Founded by Saint Sabas of Cappadocia in AD 439, it is considered to be one of the oldest inhabited monasteries in the world. Today it still maintains the ancient traditions of the Byzantine church.

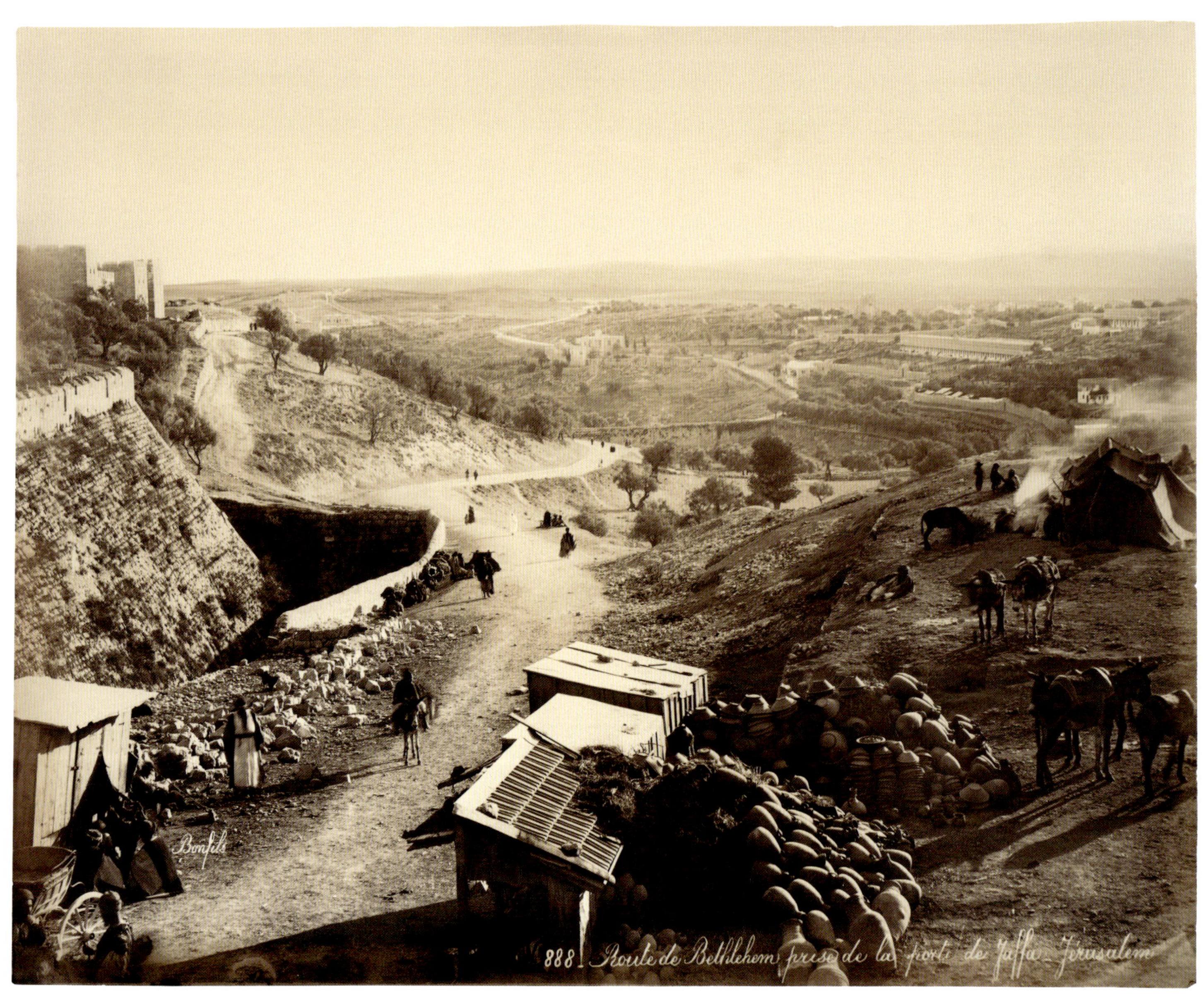

FÉLIX BONFILS
The Road to Jerusalem from Bethlehem
1870s

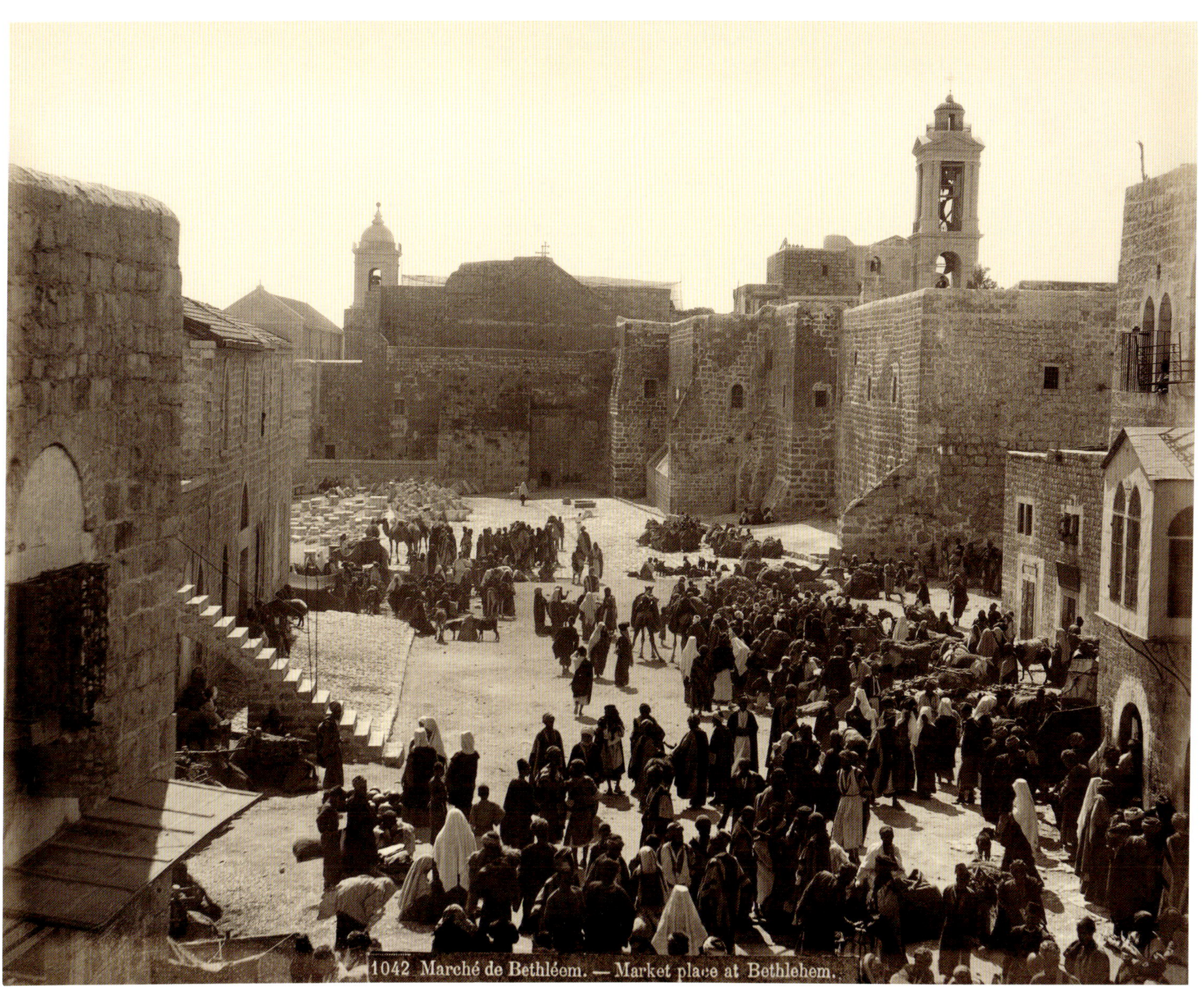

FÉLIX BONFILS
Marketplace at Bethlehem
1870s

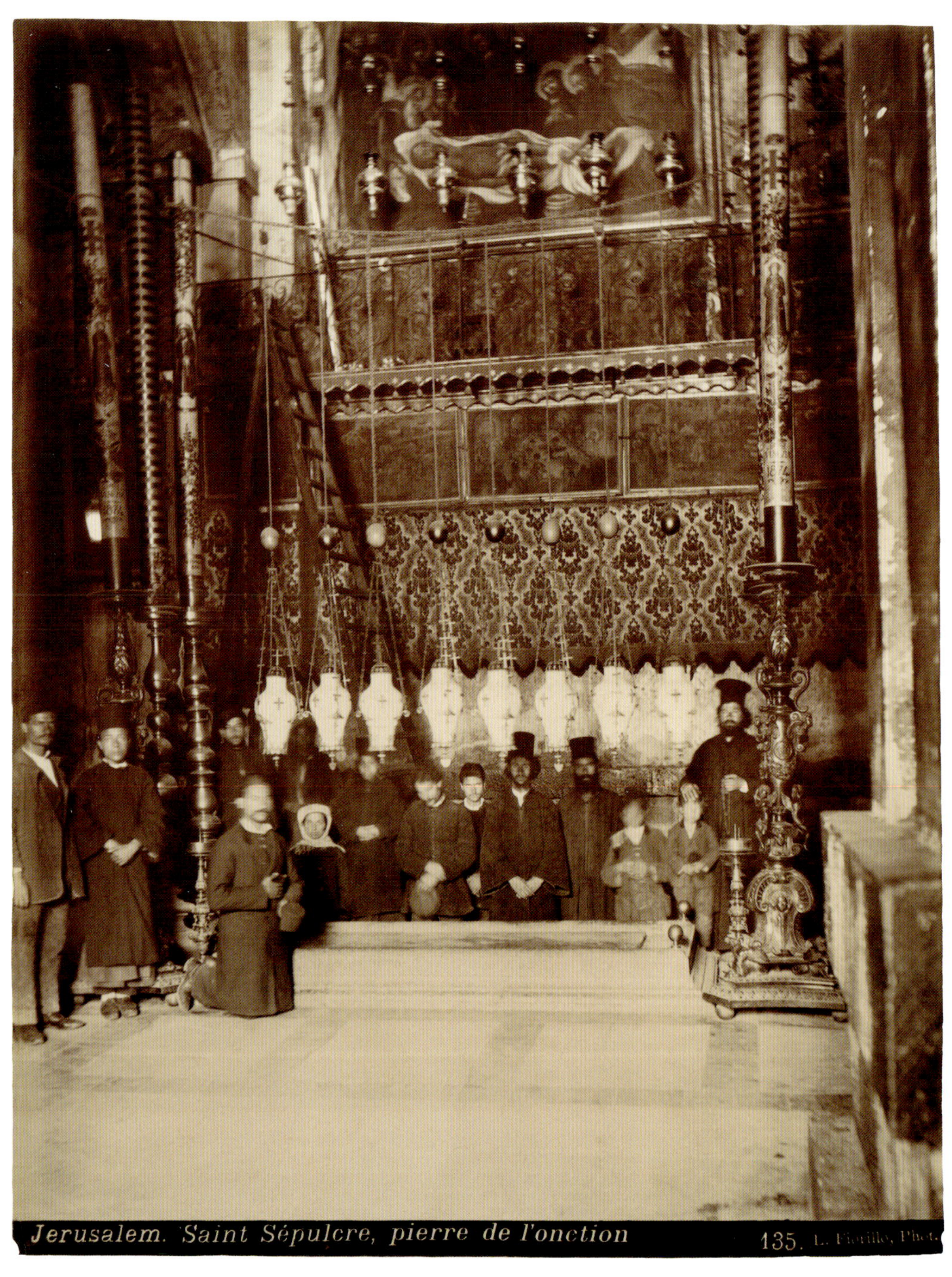

L. FIORILLO
Church of the Holy Sepulchre
Jerusalem, 1880s

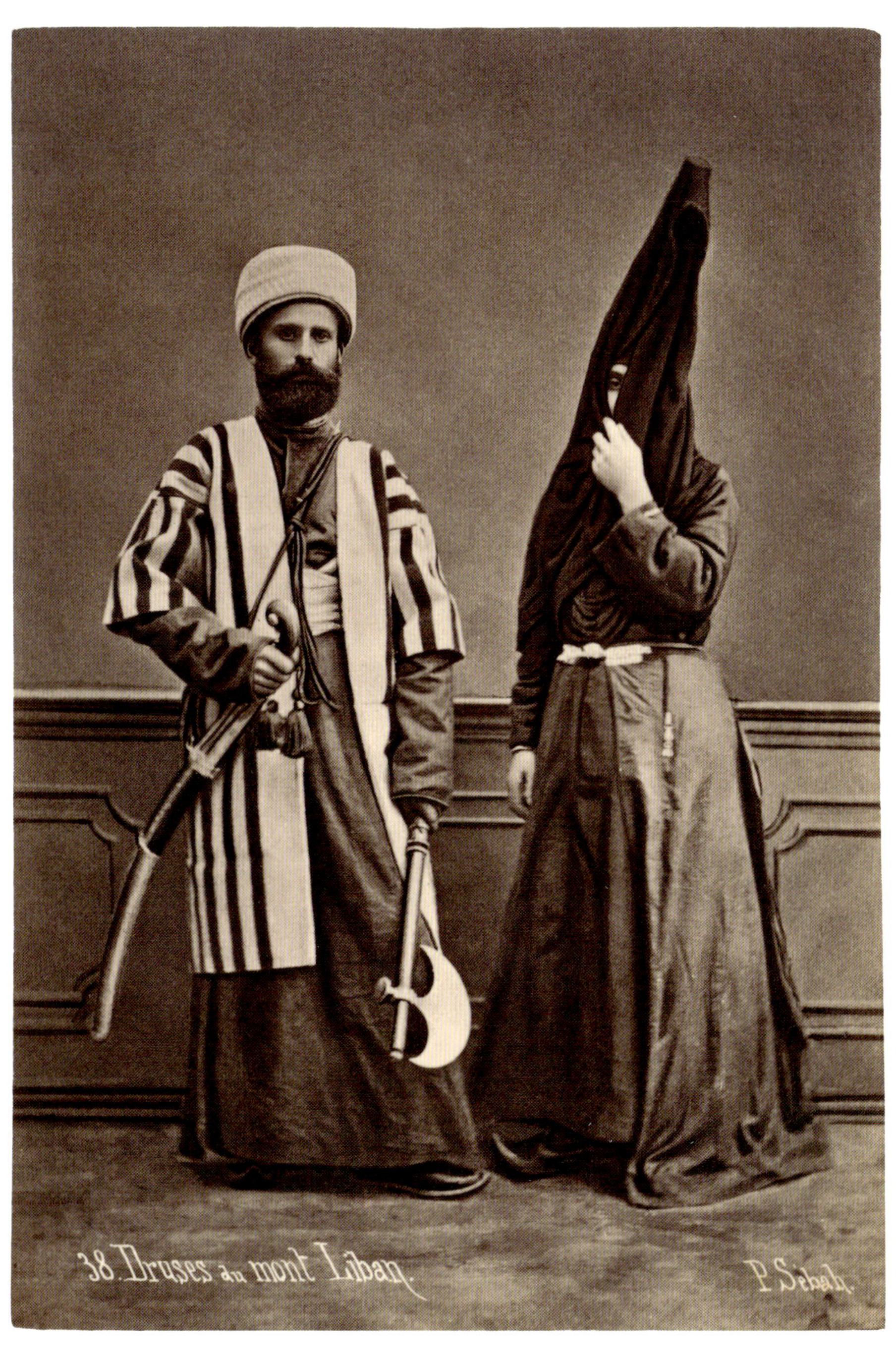

PASCAL SEBAH
Druze of the Mountains of Lebanon
1870s

The sect was founded by Hamza ibn Ali ibn Ahmad, a Persian Ismaili mystic and scholar, who moved to Egypt in 1014. In Cairo he assembled a group of scholars and leaders from across the Islamic world to form a new Unitarian Islamic movement. One night the Caliph al-Hakim, an early protector of the faith, vanished while on his evening ride, presumably assassinated. The Druze, however, believe he went into 'Occultation' with Hamza ibn Ali and three other prominent persecuted Druze preachers, leaving the care of the missionary movement in the hands of the faithful. Today the sect still survives in the mountains of Syria, Lebanon and Israel.

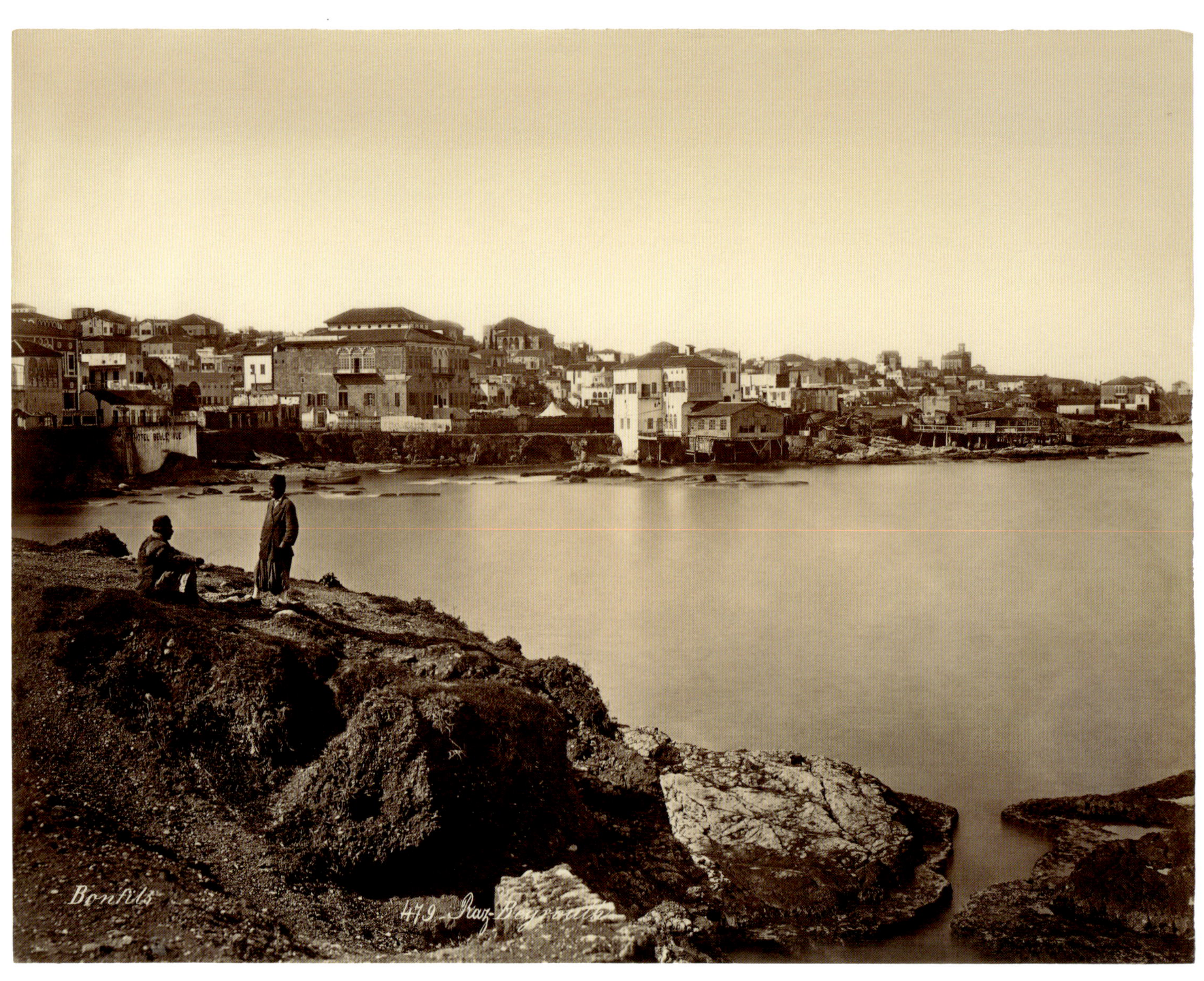

FÉLIX BONFILS
Beirut
1870s

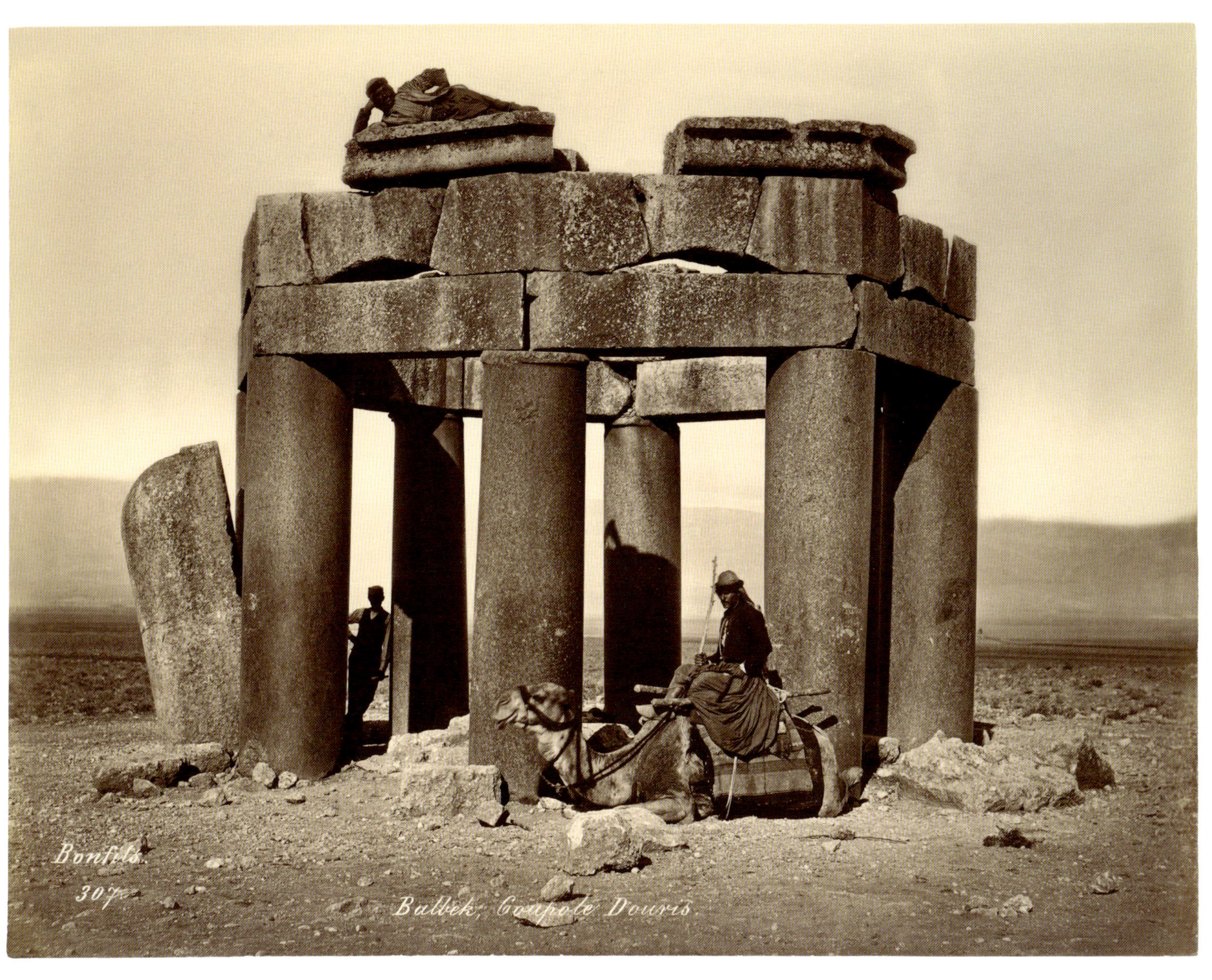

FÉLIX BONFILS
Dome of the Temple of Douris
Baalbek, 1870s

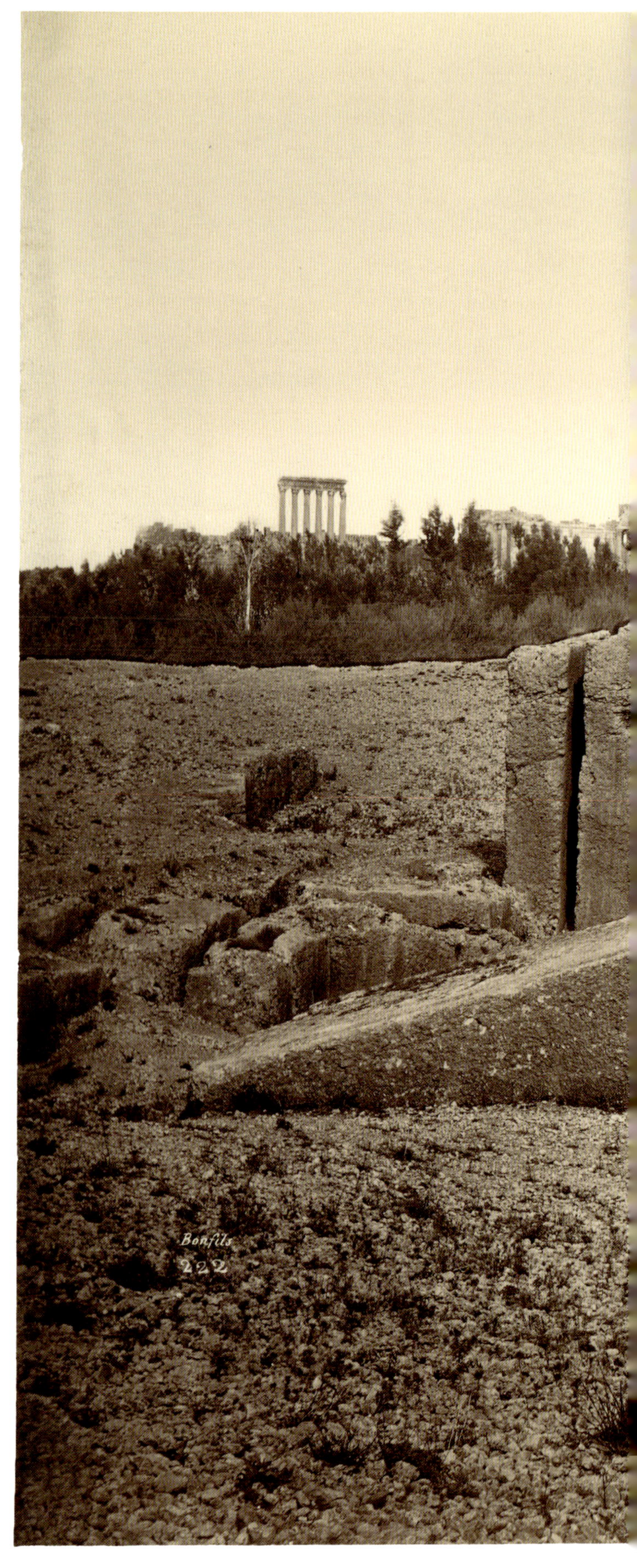

FÉLIX BONFILS
Stone Plinth
Baalbek, 1870s

'The stone of the south' (*al-Hajar al-Gubli*) was not used in the temple complex at Baalbek during its construction in the Roman period (15 BC – AD 68). Had it been freed from the quarry, the plinth would have been the largest stone ever moved. It is the largest known cut stone from the ancient world and is estimated to weigh 1,500 tons.

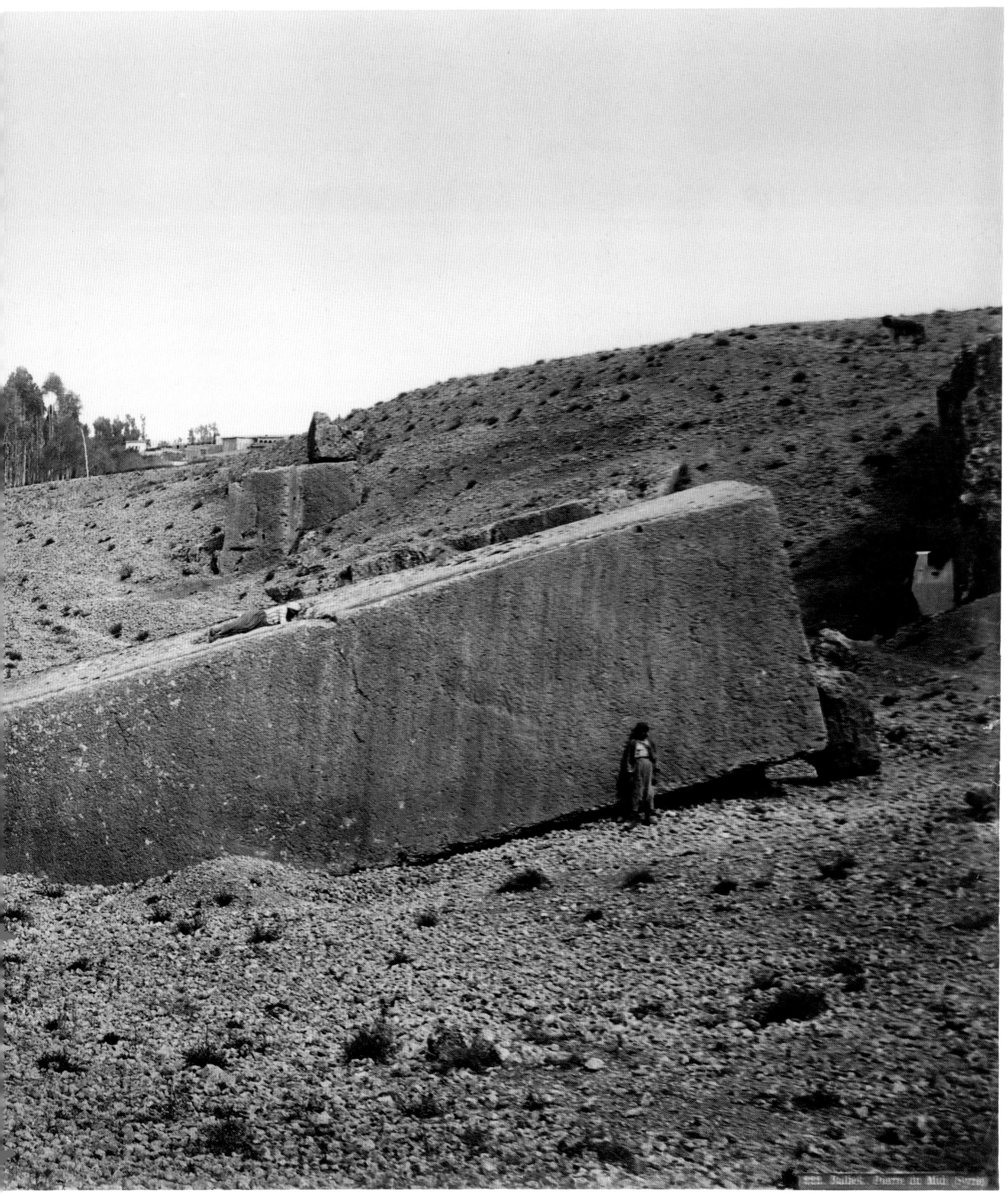

FÉLIX BONFILS
Temple of Jupiter, Columns and Man
Baalbek, 1870s

The history of Baalbek dates to the Early Bronze Age (2900–2300 BC). The Phoenicians settled as early as 2000 BC and built their first temple here dedicated to Baal, the sun god. Work on the religious complex during Roman times was never completed, though today the ruins indicate that Baalbek contained the largest religious buildings constructed in the entire Roman Empire. Of the massive Temple of Jupiter, today only these six Corinthian columns remain standing. Eight more were disassembled and shipped to Constantinople under Justinian's orders for his basilica, the Hagia Sophia.

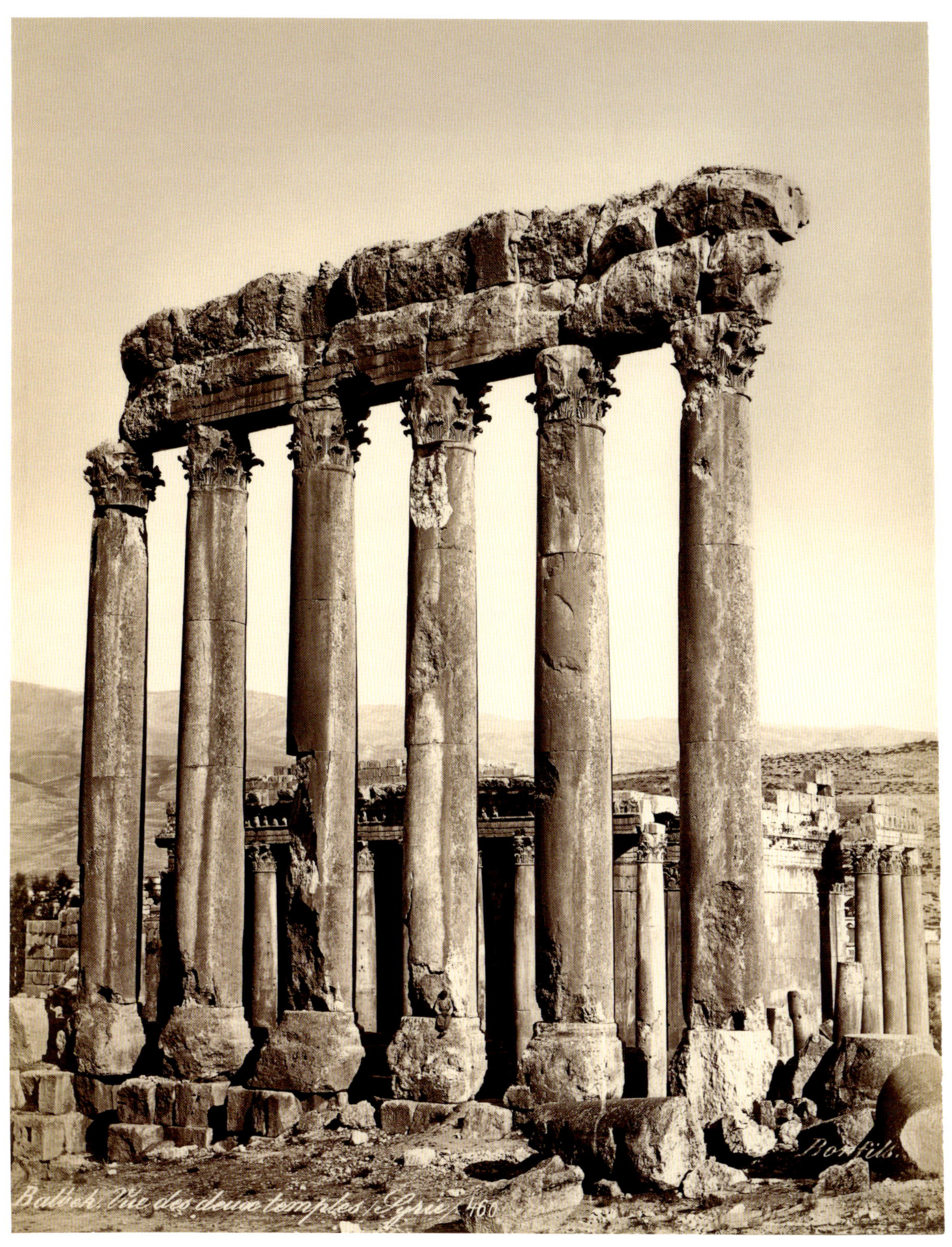
Bonfils.
Balbek. Vue des deux temples. Syrie. 460

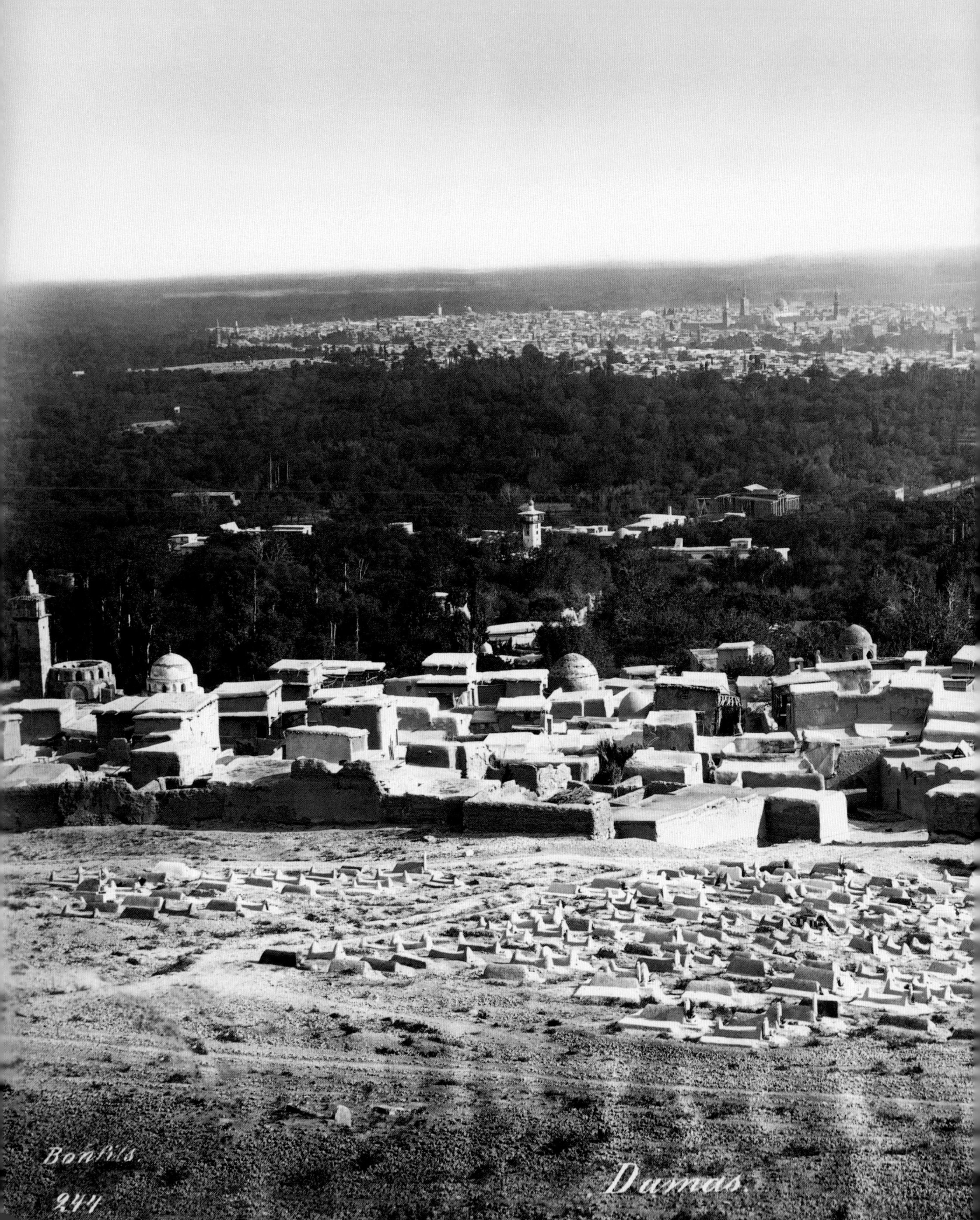
Bonfils.
244
Damas.

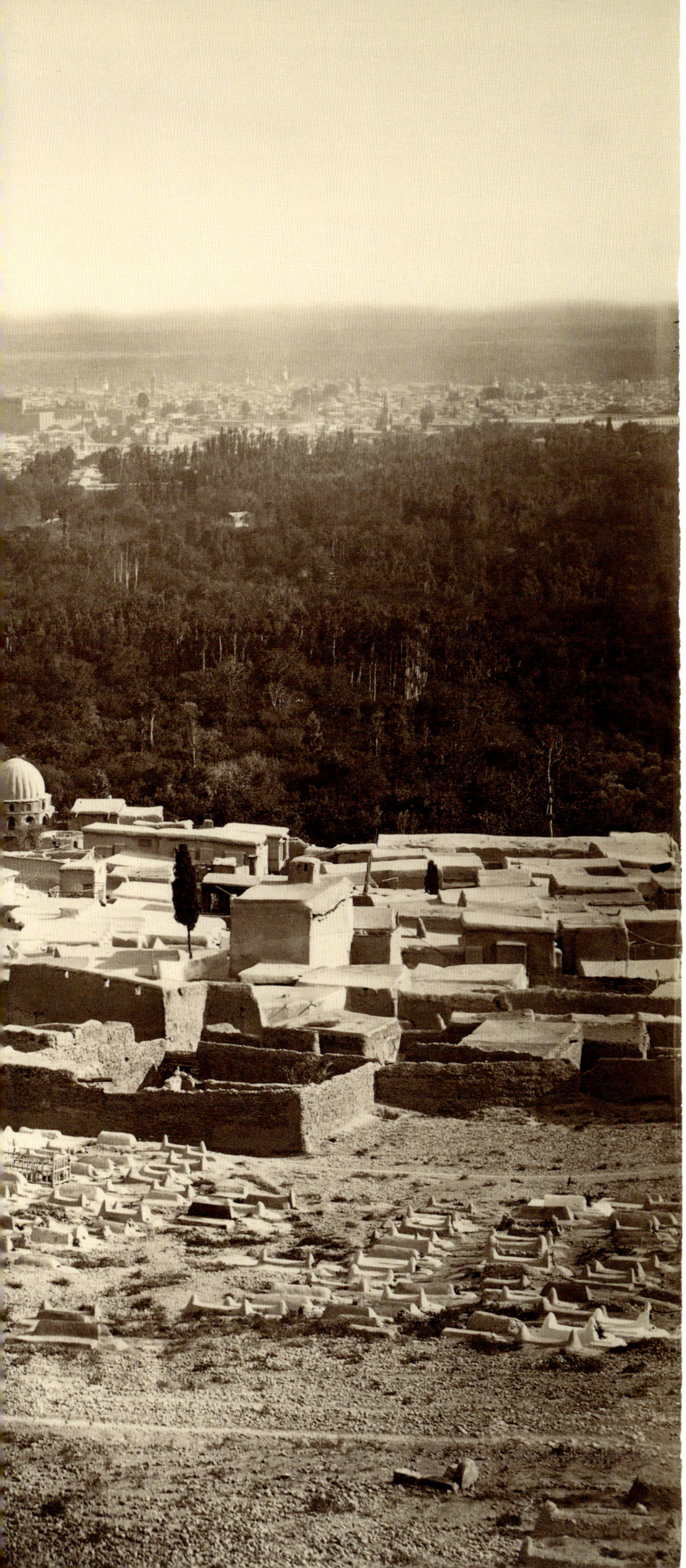

FÉLIX BONFILS
Damascus, A View from the Hills
1870s

Occupied since the second half of the seventh millennium BC – though with evidence of settlement dating to 9000 BC – Damascus is the oldest continually inhabited city in the world. It first came under Western control during the campaigns of Alexander. During the Roman period, the area of present day Syria became the granary of Rome. In the Arab period, the Umayyad Caliphate (AD 661) established Damascus as their capital and the empire of the Caliphate stretched from Spain to India.

On entering the houses of some important Armenian merchants, I was struck by the richness and elegance of their rooms. Having gone through the door and along a dark corridor, we arrived at a courtyard decorated with superb gushing fountains and shaded by one or two sycamores, or Persian willows. The courtyard is paved with large slabs of polished stone or marble; the walls, made of black and white marble, are covered in vines. Five or six doors, with marble architraves and sculpted with arabesques, introduce us into so many rooms or salons where the men and women of the family gather.

Alphonse de Lamartine, *Voyage en Orient*, 1835

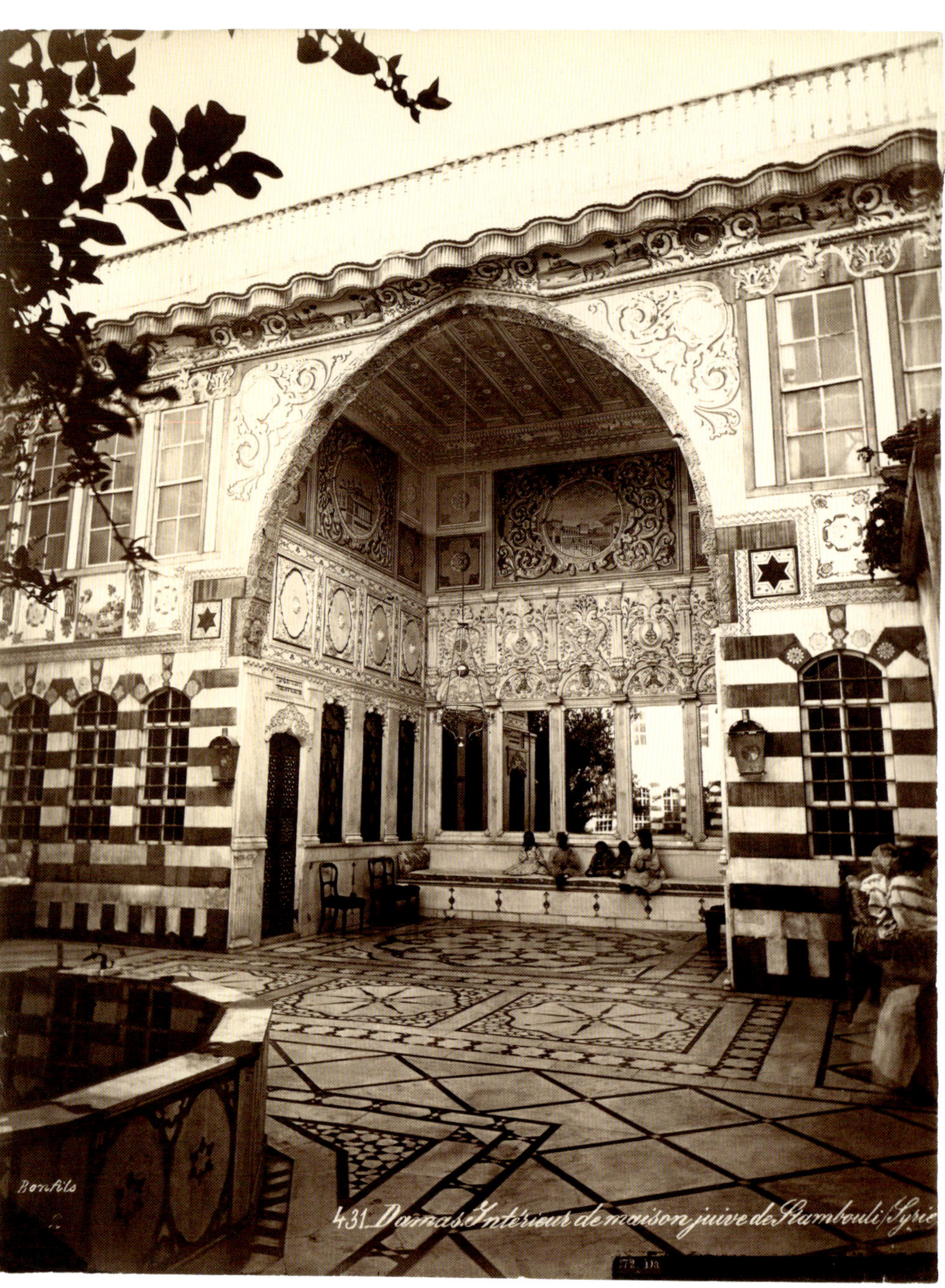

FÉLIX BONFILS
The Stambouli House, Damascus Interior Courtyard
1870s

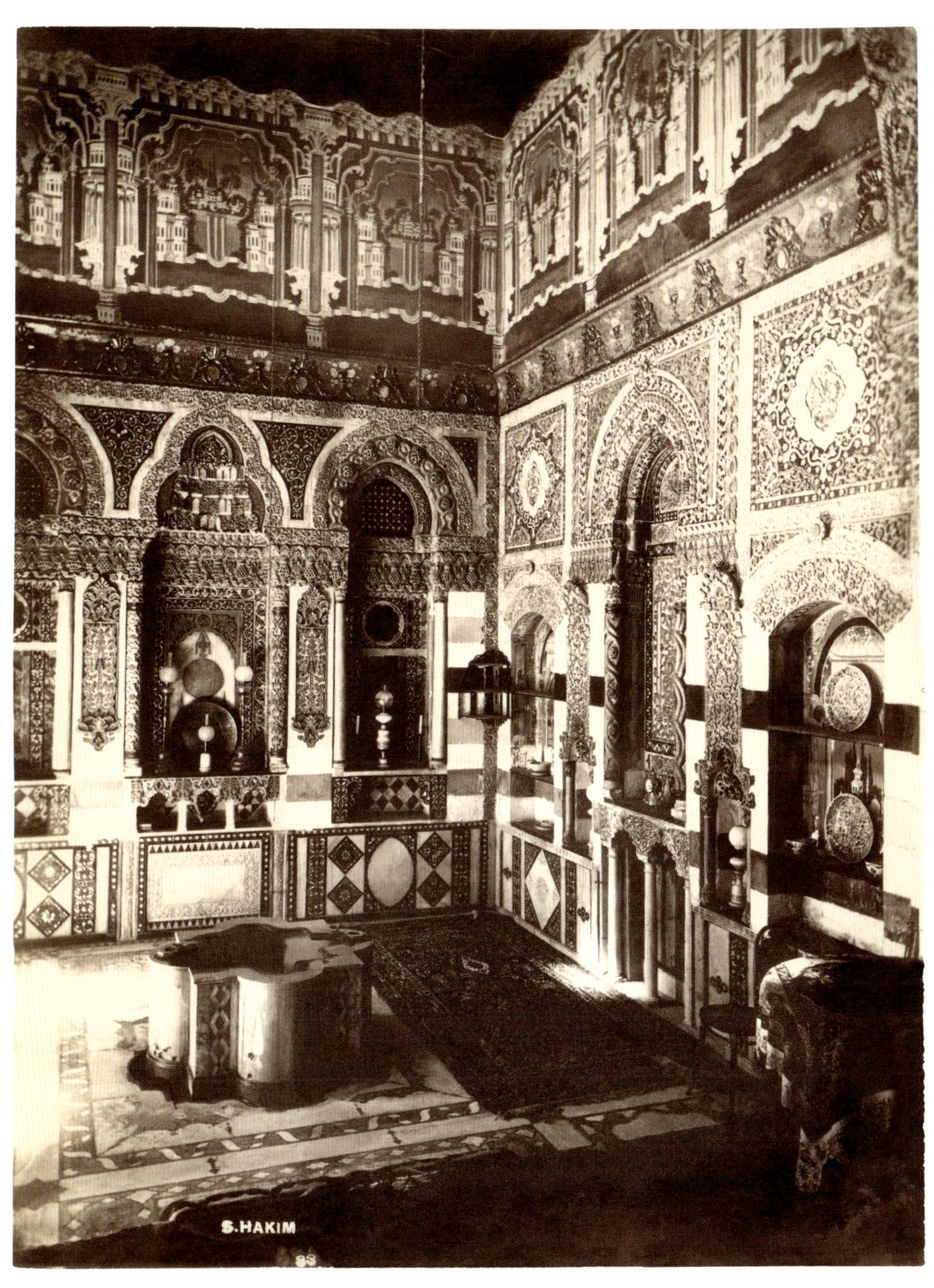

SULAYMAN AL-HAKIM
The Stambouli House, Damascus Interior
1890s

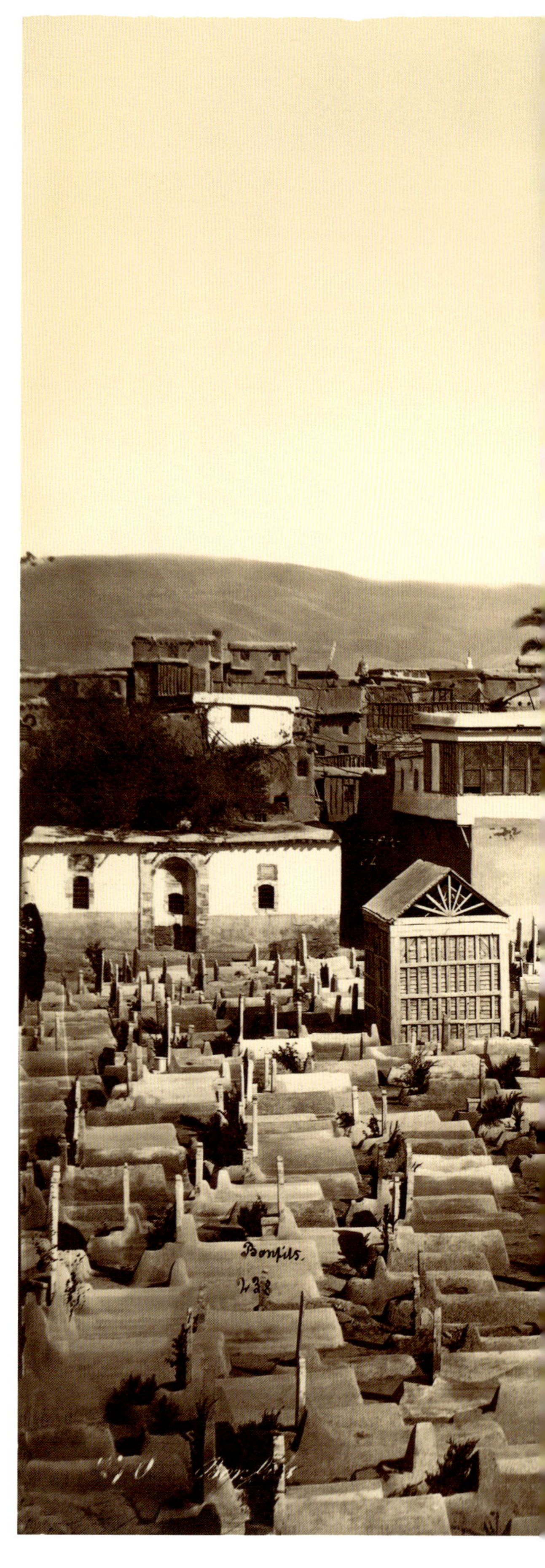

FÉLIX BONFILS
Muslim Family Graveyard
Damascus, 1870s

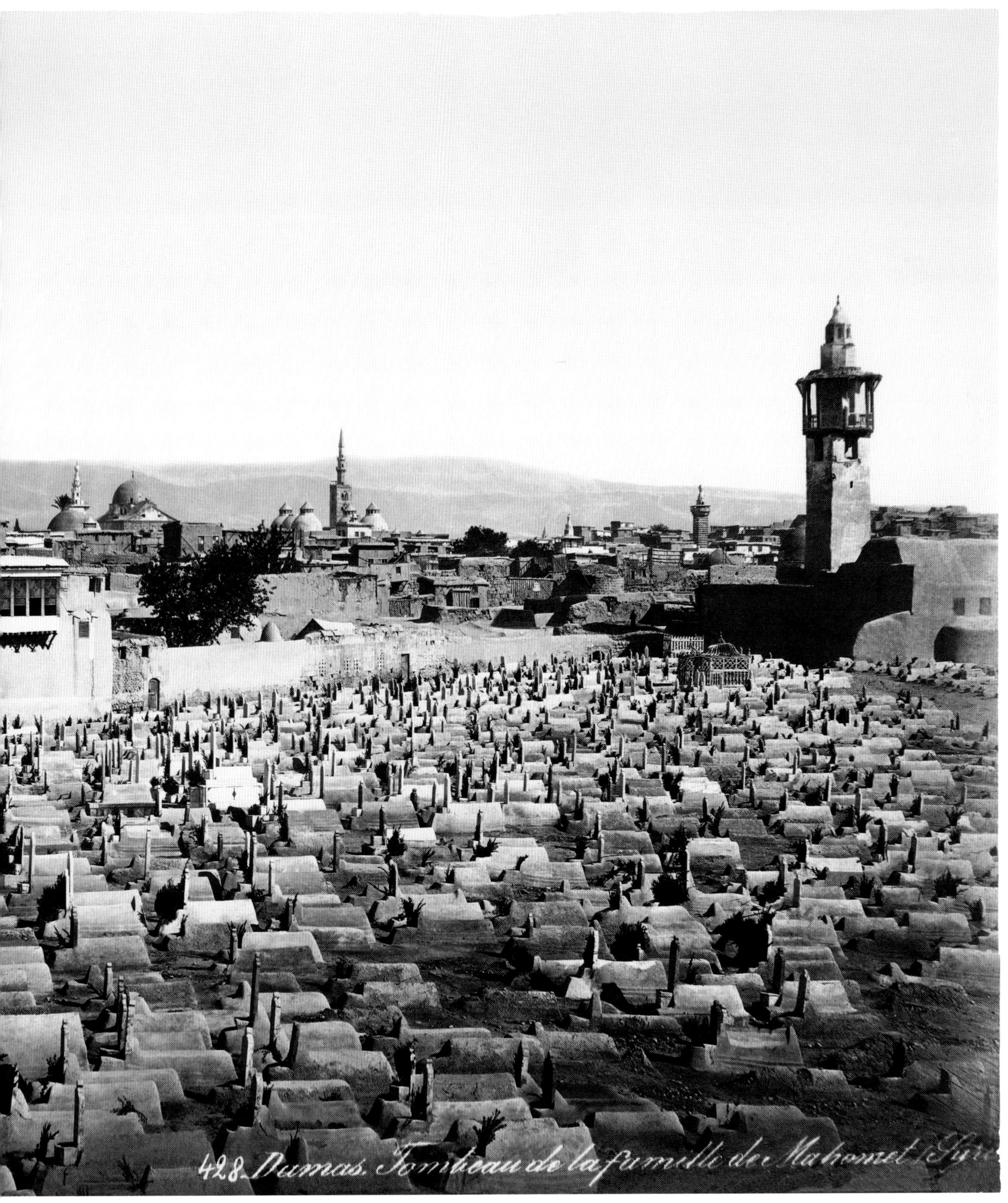
428. Damas. Tombeau de la famille de Mahomet (Syr

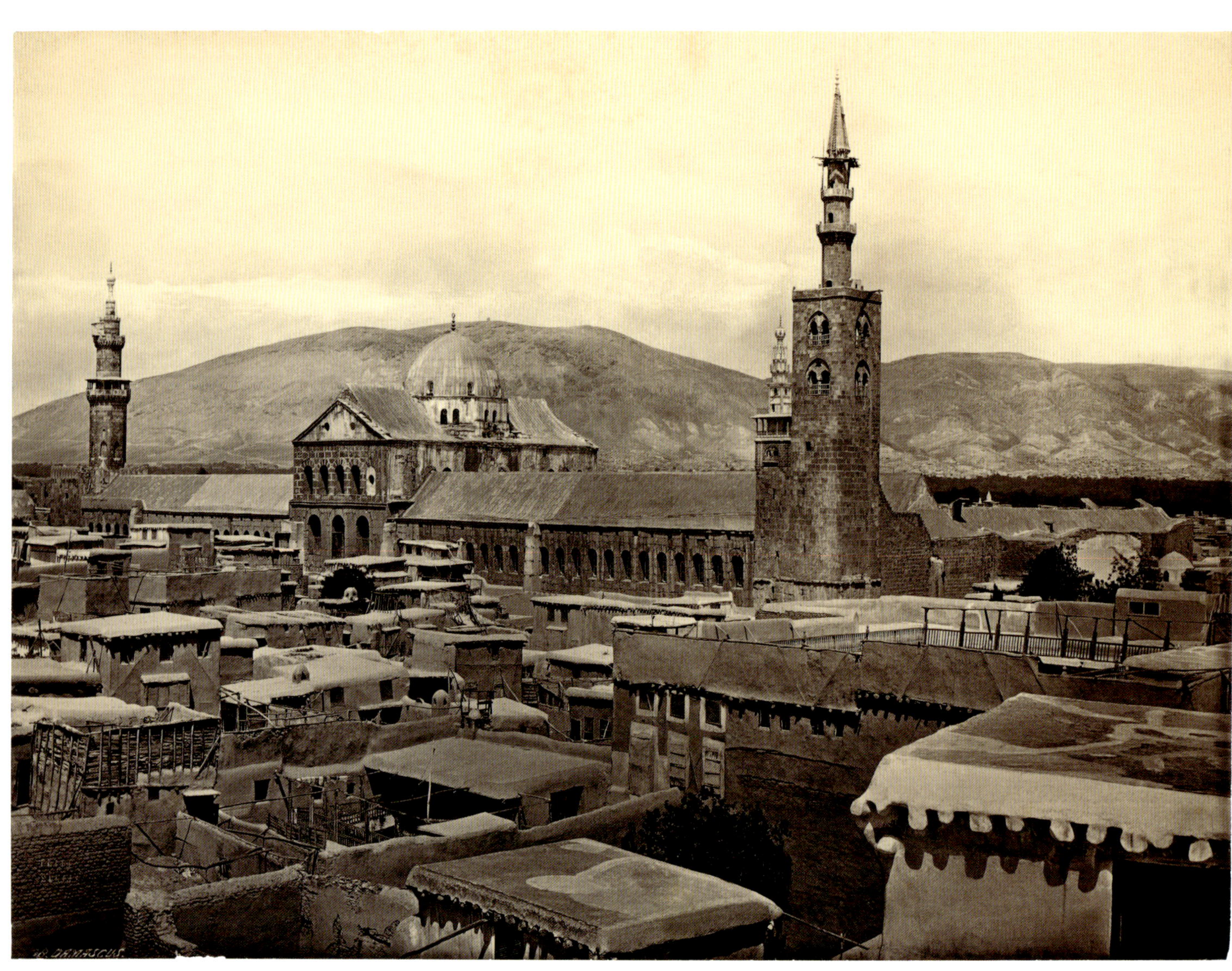

FRANK MASON GOOD
Umayyad Mosque
Damascus, 1870

The Umayyad Mosque, also known as the Grand Mosque of Damascus, is one of the largest and oldest in the world. Just outside is the tomb of Saladin, located in a small garden adjoining the north wall. Architecturally, the mosque was designed in part in the Byzantine style and contained some of the most impressive Byzantine mosaics, which survived into the nineteenth century.

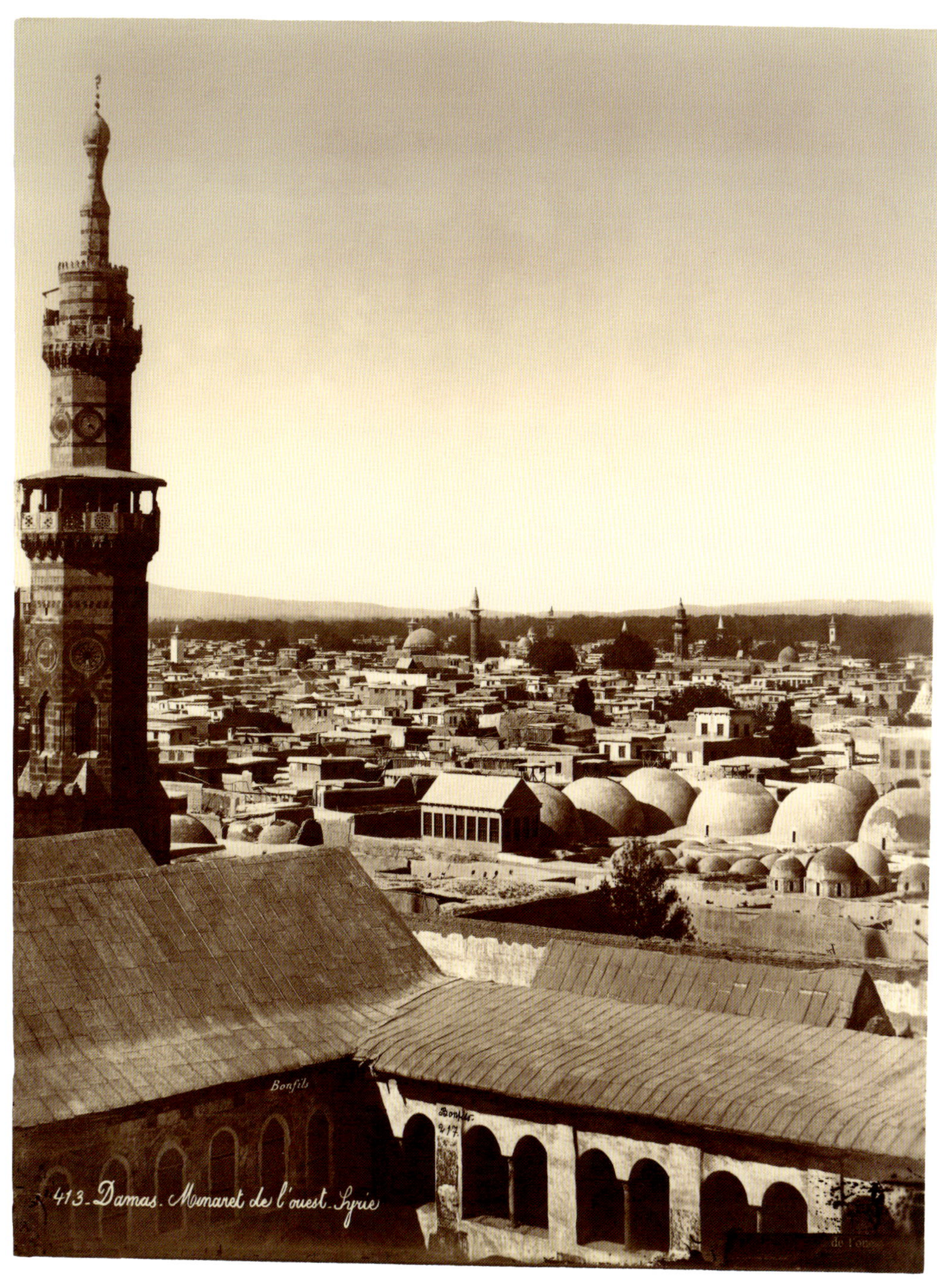

FÉLIX BONFILS
Minaret from the East, the Grand Umayyad Mosque
Damascus, 1870s

The minaret in the southeast corner of the mosque is the Minaret of Jesus. Many Muslims believe it is here that Jesus will appear at the End of the World. Over the rooftops is a view of the then unchanged medieval city of Damascus.

FÉLIX BONFILS
Courtyard of the Grand Umayyad Mosque
Damascus, 1870s

Built between 706 and 715 under the Umayyad Caliph al-Walid I, this mosque has been shared by both Muslim and Christian worshippers. The Umayyad Caliph borrowed two hundred skilled workers from the Byzantine Emperor to construct and decorate the mosque. The interior walls of the building were covered with fine mosaics depicting paradise.

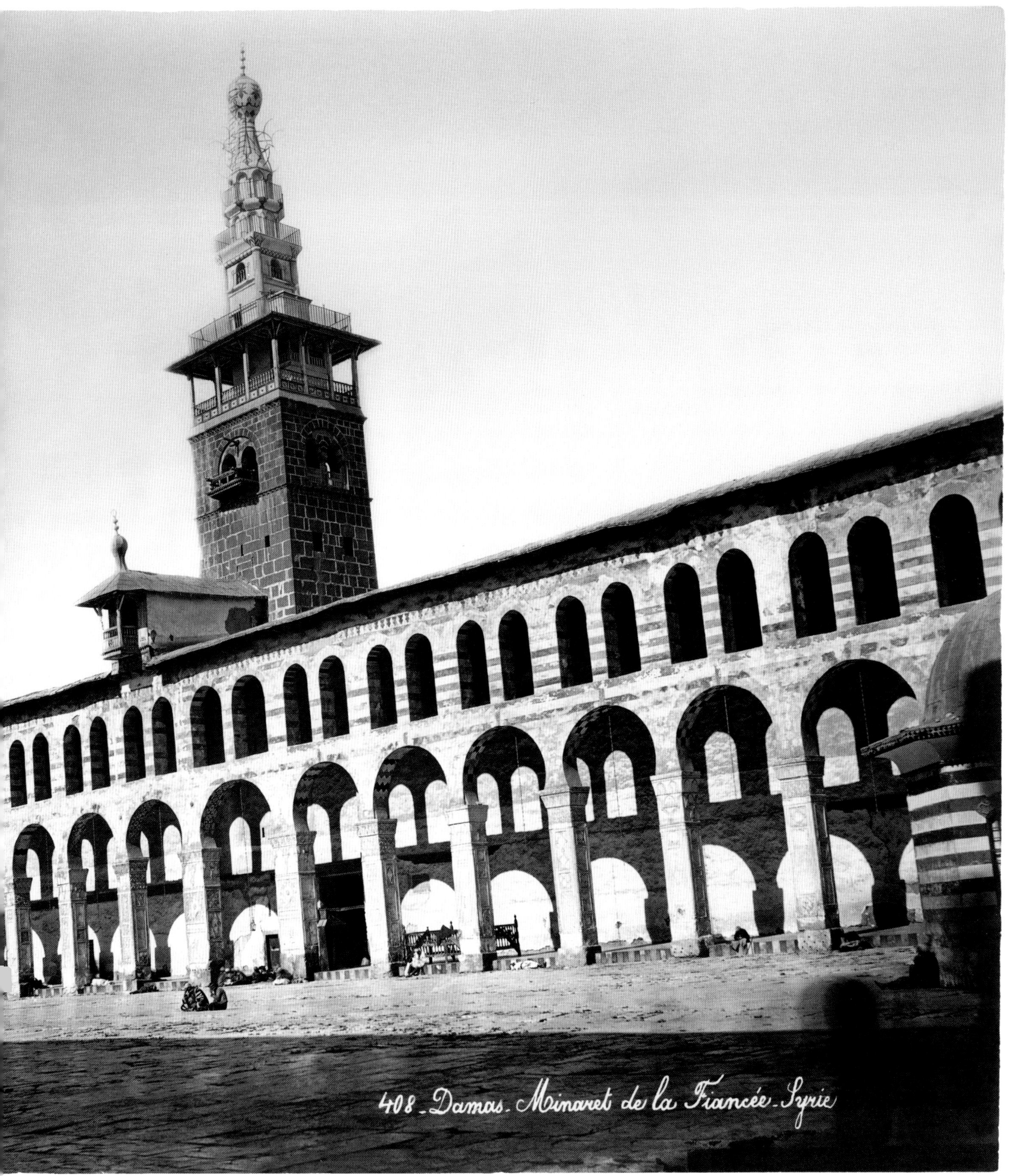
408 _ Damas _ Minaret de la Fiancée _ Syrie

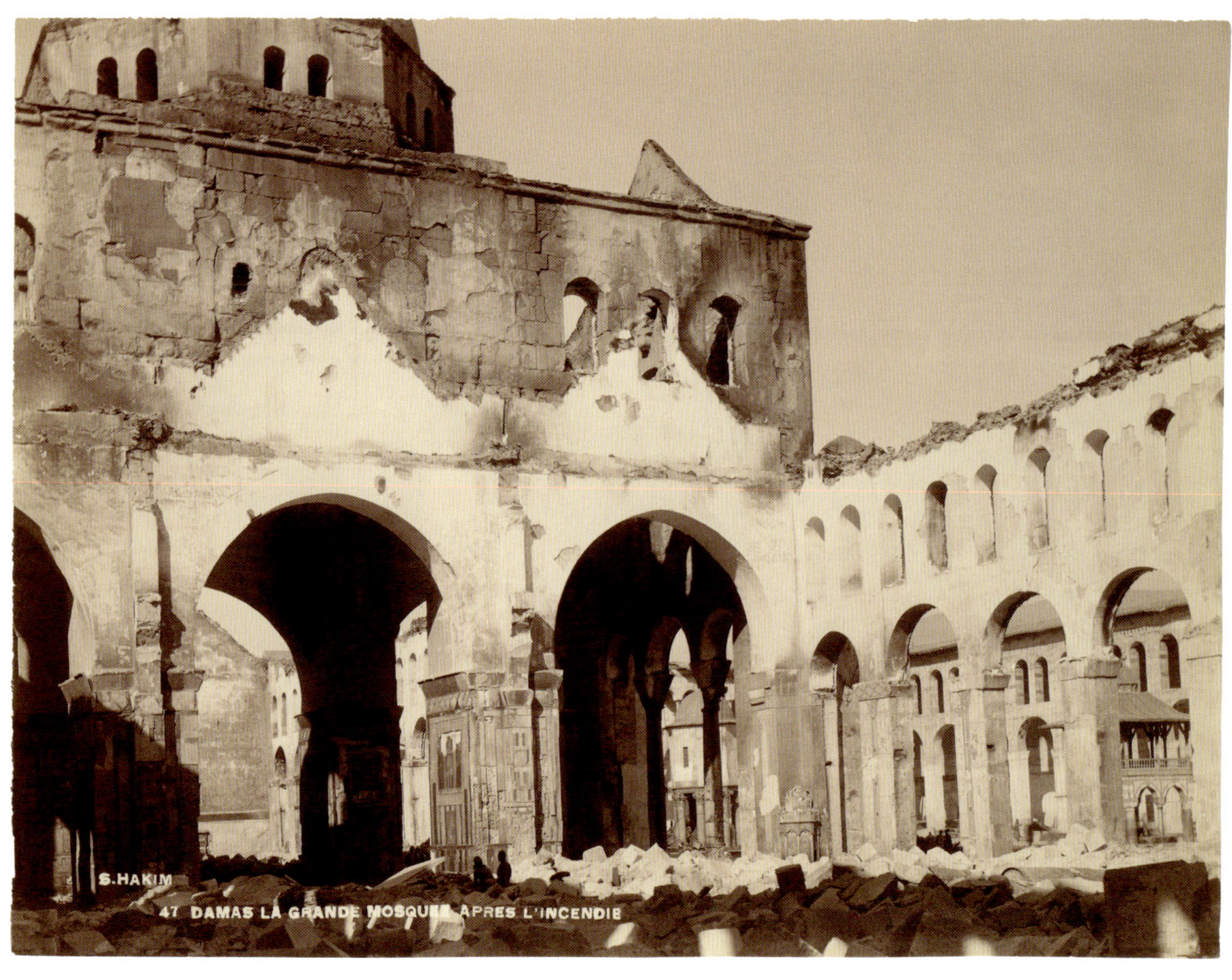

SULAYMAN AL-HAKIM
Ruins after the 1893 Fire, Umayyad Mosque
Damascus, 1893

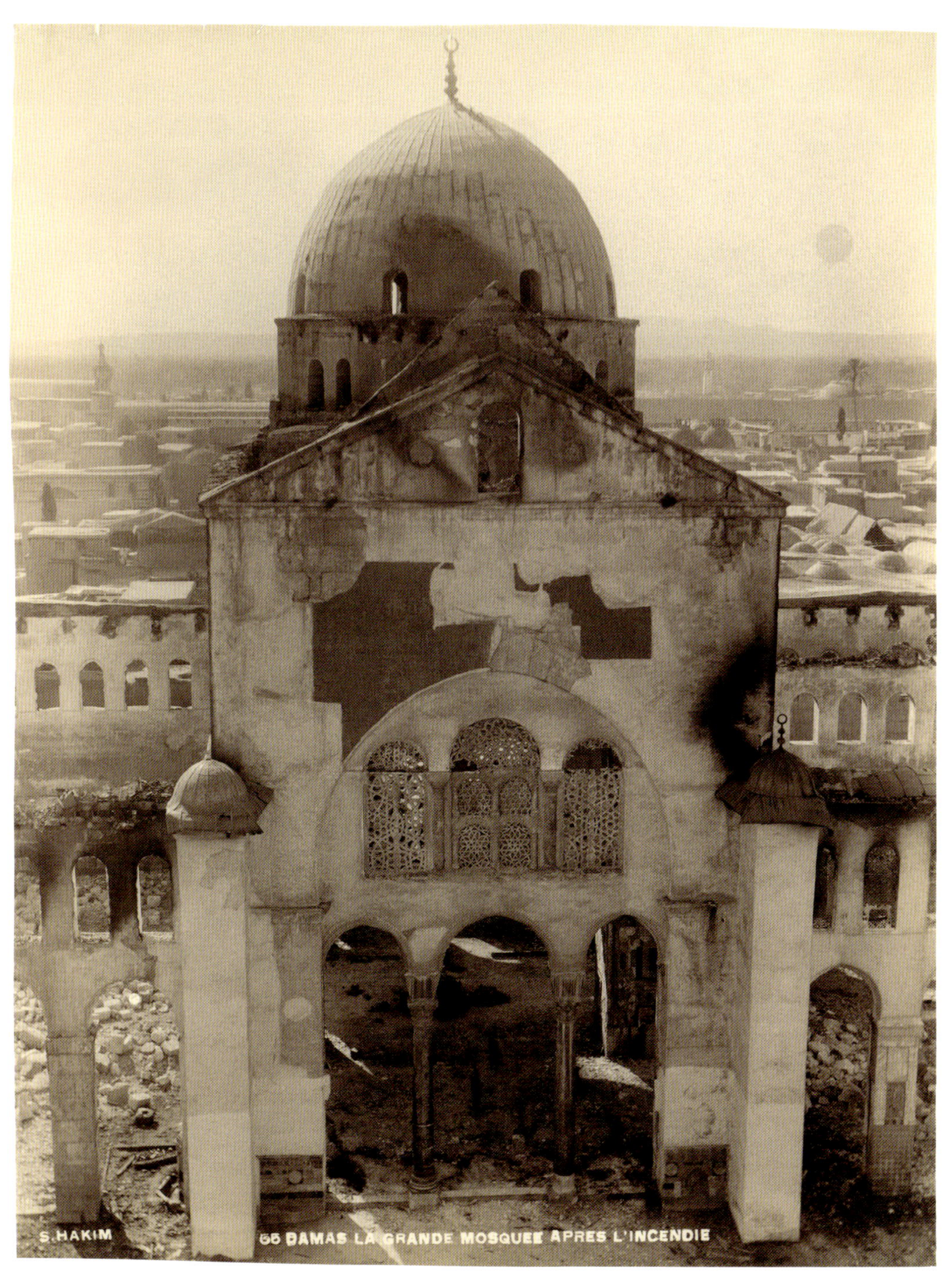

SULAYMAN AL-HAKIM
Ruins after the 1893 Fire, Umayyad Mosque
Damascus, 1893

There is a small wooden house upon the right of the central nave, adorned with blinds, gilding, ornaments of gold, and arabesque paintings; it encloses the sepulchre of the prophet John, the son of Zachariah. There are a number of iron and wooden frames in the form of cages suspended from all parts of the roof of the mosque, which are destined to hold small lamps during the illumination nights.

Domingo Badía, *Travels of Ali Bey*, 1814

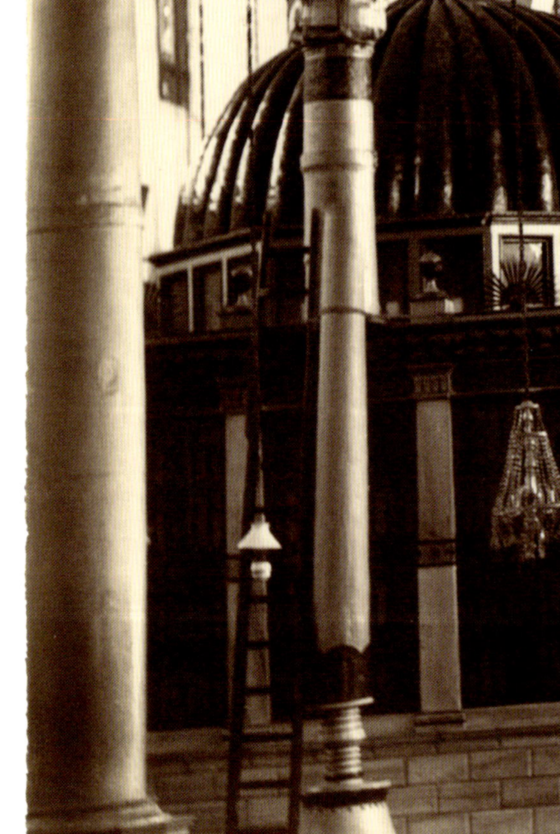

SULAYMAN AL-HAKIM
Tomb of St John, Umayyad Mosque
Damascus, 1893

Inside the great Umayyad mosque of Damascus is a shrine said to contain the head of John the Baptist (Yahya), honoured as a prophet by Christians and Muslims alike.

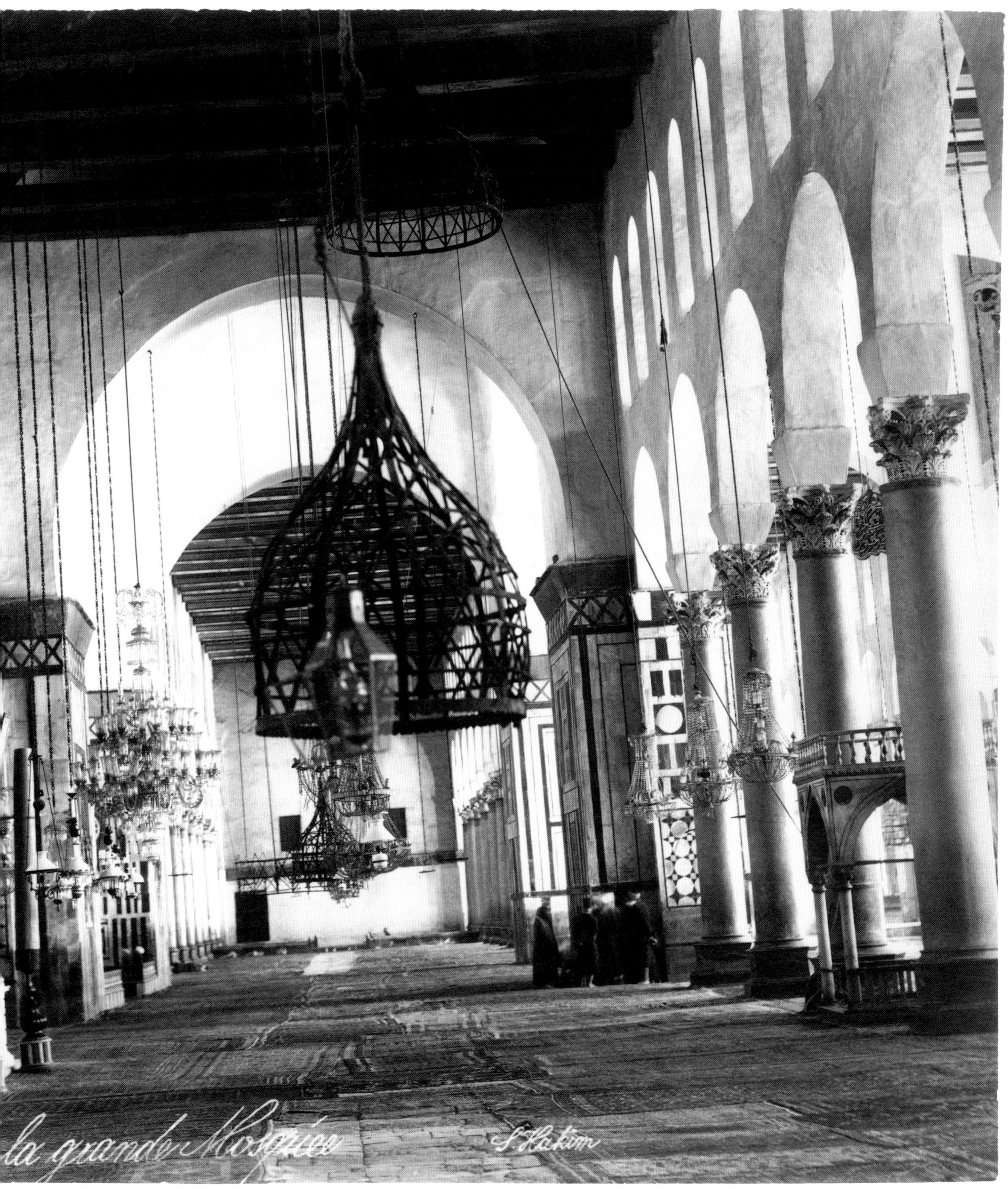
la grande Mosquée
S. Hakim

SEBAH AND JOAILLIER
Ancient Steps
Galata, Istanbul, 1880s

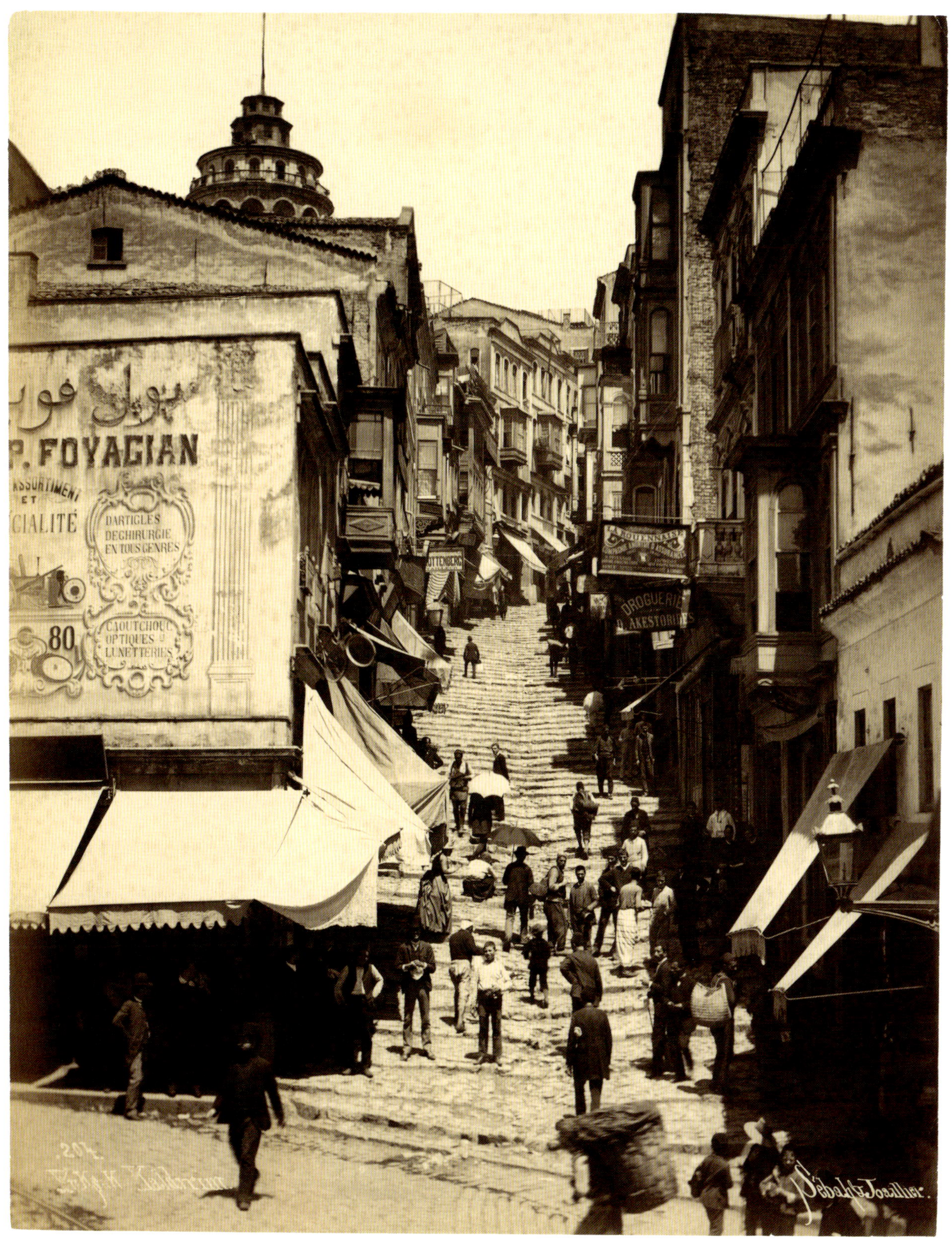
P. FOYAGIAN
ASSORTIMENT
ET
CIALITÉ
DARTICLES
DECHIRURGIE
EN TOUS GENRES
80
CAOUTCHOUC
OPTIQUES
LUNETTERIES
DROGUERIE
D. AKESTORIDES
Sébah & Joaillier.

The headdress of these Muslim monks consists of a thick felt bonnet, of a reddish or brown colour, which is most like a flower pot put on upside down. A white vest and jacket, a great plaited skirt of the same colour, like the Greek fustanella, *and tight white trousers down to their ankles, make up their costume, which has nothing monkish according to our view, but which does not lack certain elegance. At first I could only get a glimpse of it, for the Dervishes came disguised under a type of coat or cloak which was green, blue, the colour of Greek raisins, cinnamon or any other nuance, but which was not part of their uniform, and which they only took off before they began waltzing, to resume them again when sinking, exhausted, streaming with perspiration, and overcome with ecstasy and fatigue.*

Théophile Gautier, *Constantinople*, 1853

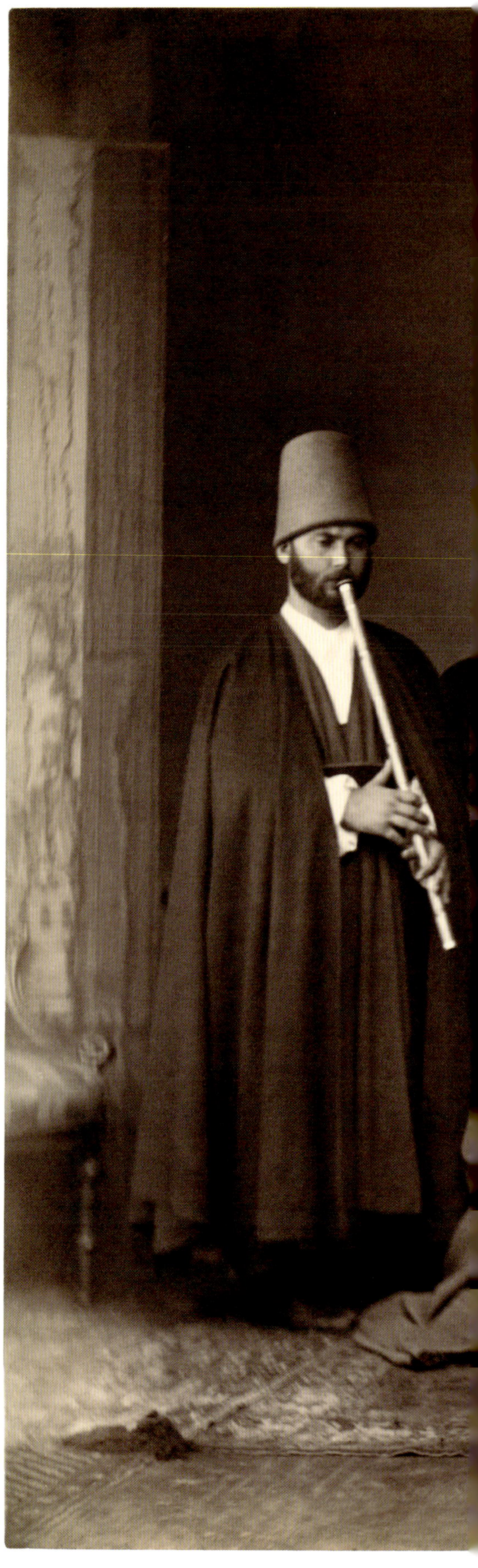

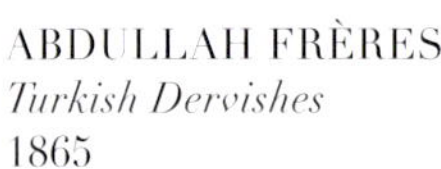

ABDULLAH FRÈRES
Turkish Dervishes
1865

The Mevlevi Sheikhs (seated) and their Dervish followers. A Dervish (Persian *Darvīsh*) is a soul who walks a Sufi Muslim ascetic path. Known for their extreme poverty and/or acts of austerity, the Dervishes are similar to the mendicant friars in Christianity, or the Hindu/Buddhist/Jain sadhus. In Persian, *Dar* means 'a door'. Dervish literally means 'one who opens doors'.

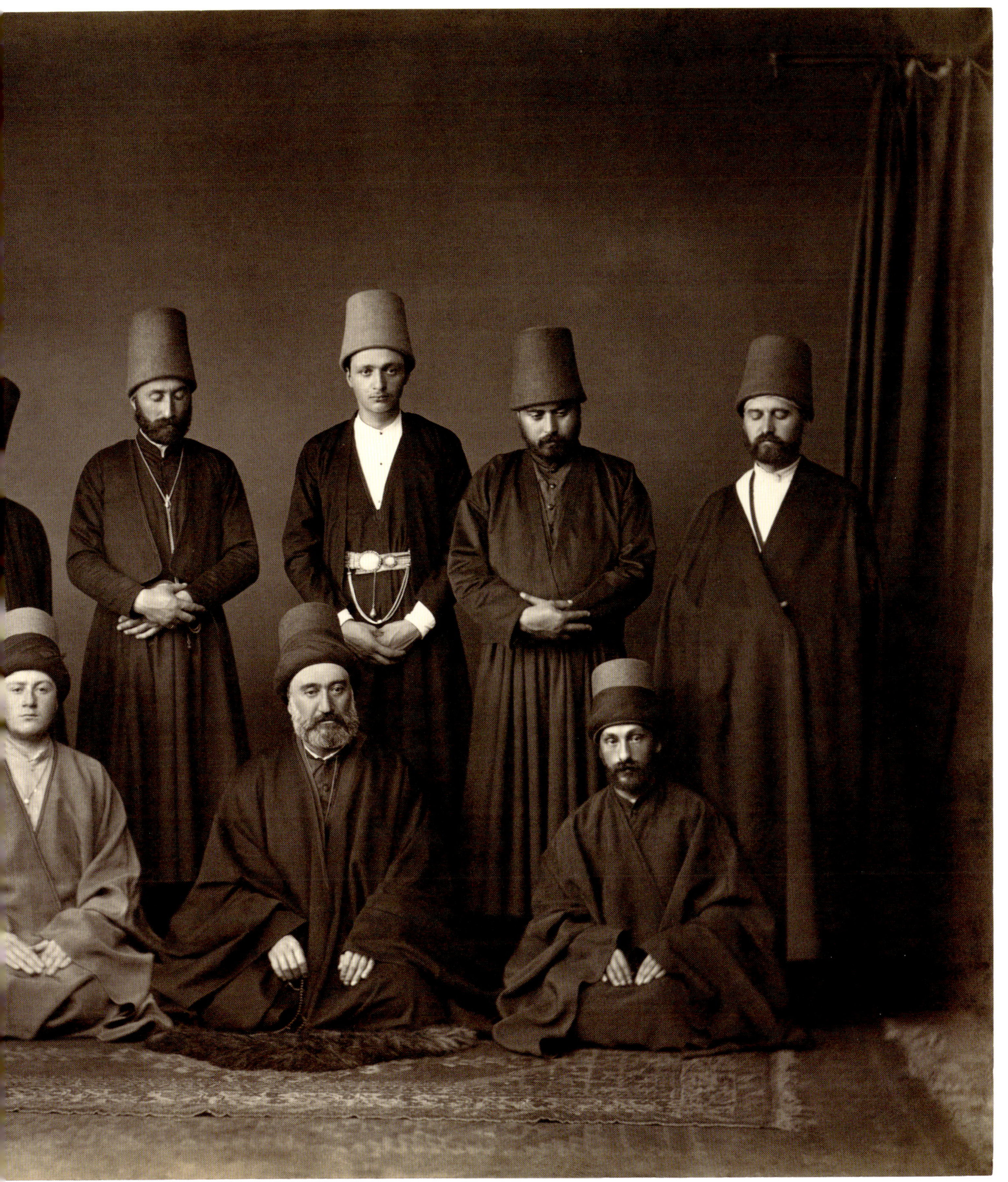

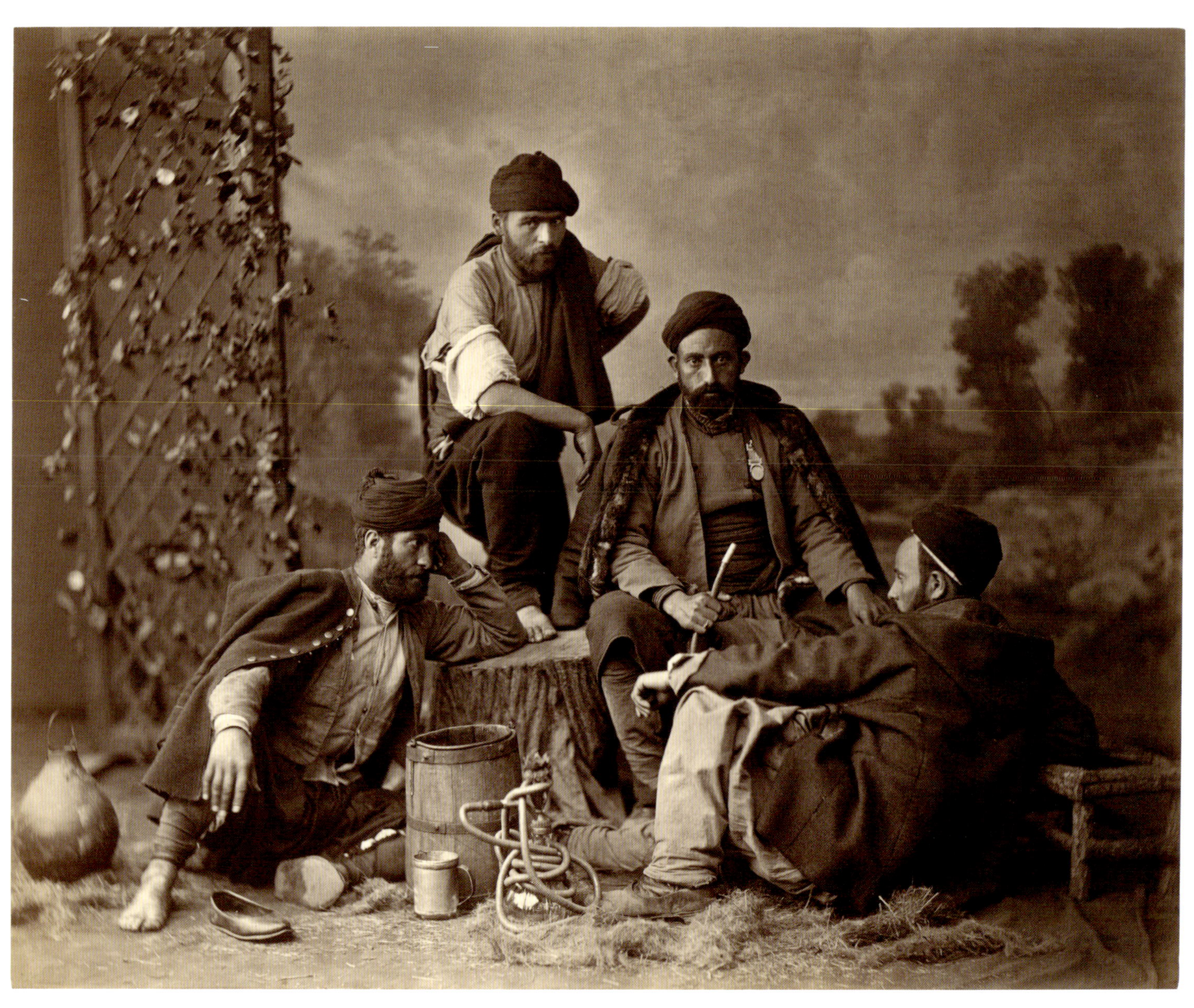

ABDULLAH FRÈRES
Village Porters
Turkey, 1865

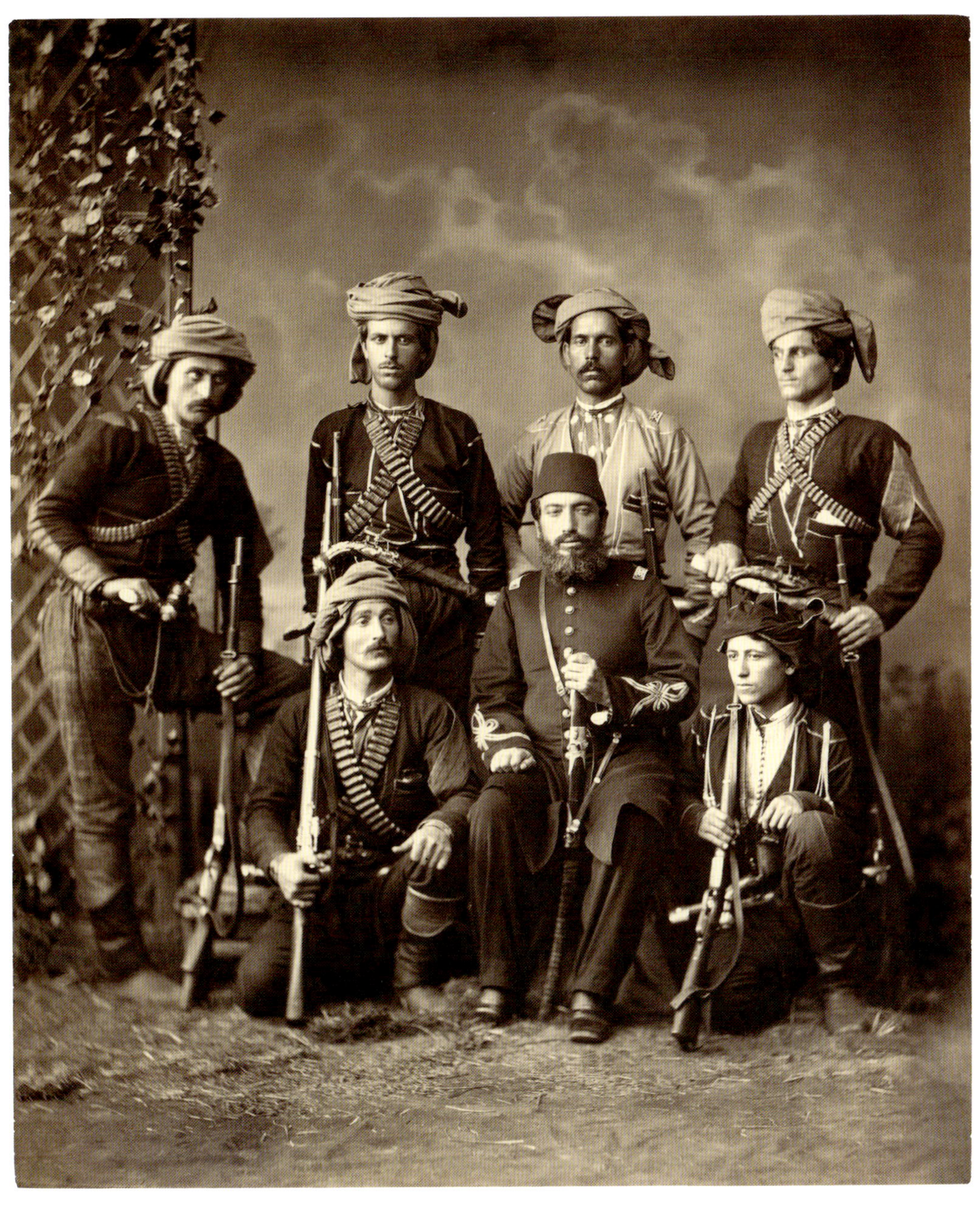

ABDULLAH FRÈRES
Georgian Bashi-Bazouks
1865

During the period of the Turkish Empire, the *Bashi-Bazouks* (irregular soldiers) were used to suppress revolts from the Euphrates to the Danube. Originally, Zeibecks were mountain Turkish warriors of western Anatolia. During the thirteenth to nineteenth centuries they acted as protectors of their villages against landlords, bandits and tax collectors. During the nineteenth century the firm of Abdullah Frères photographed a series that documented *Bashi-Bazouks*: the mountain warriors of Circassia, soldiers from the warlike Caucasus and the Zeibeck tribes around Smyrna.

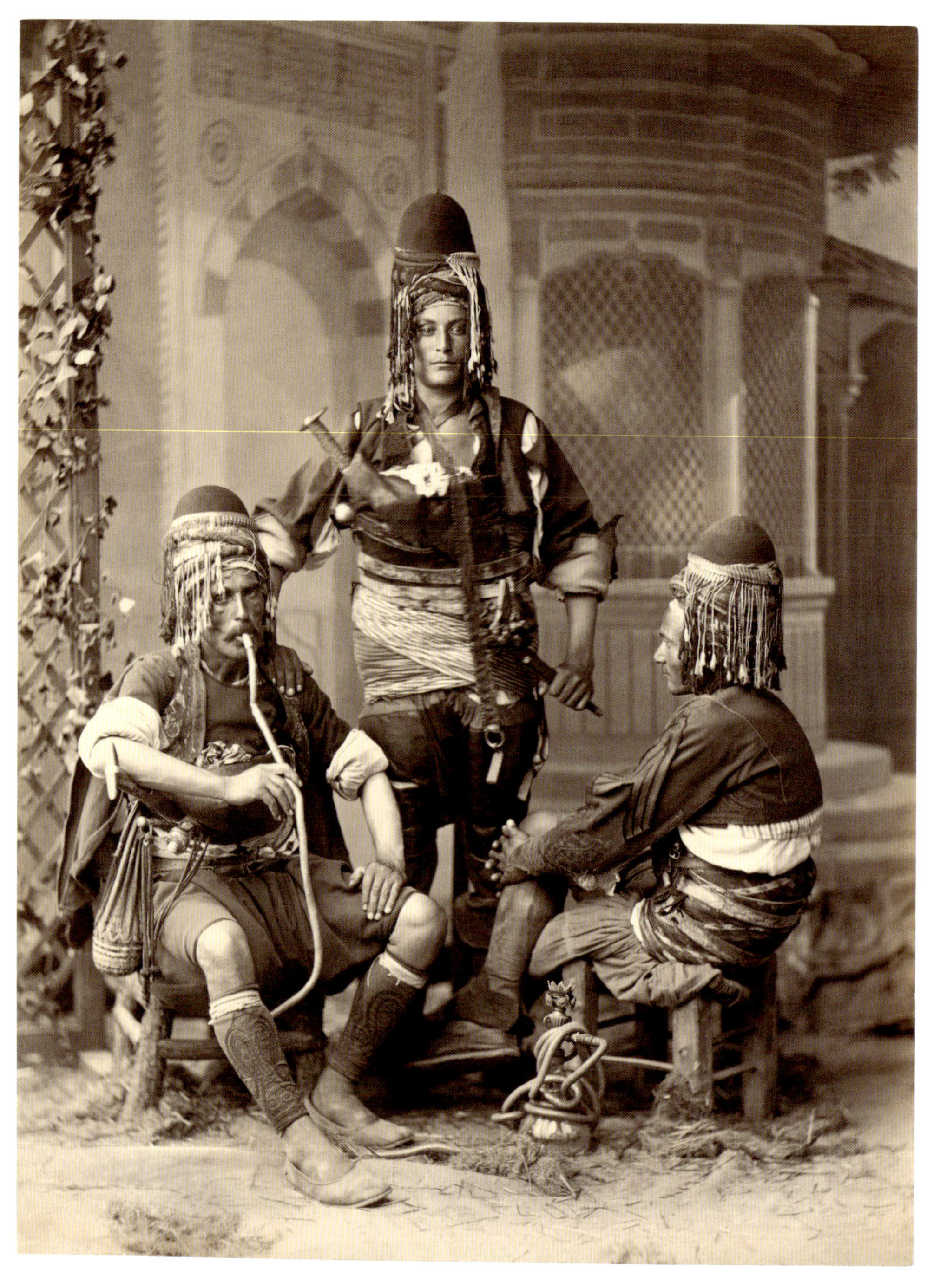

ABDULLAH FRÈRES
Zeibeck Bashi-Bazouks
1865

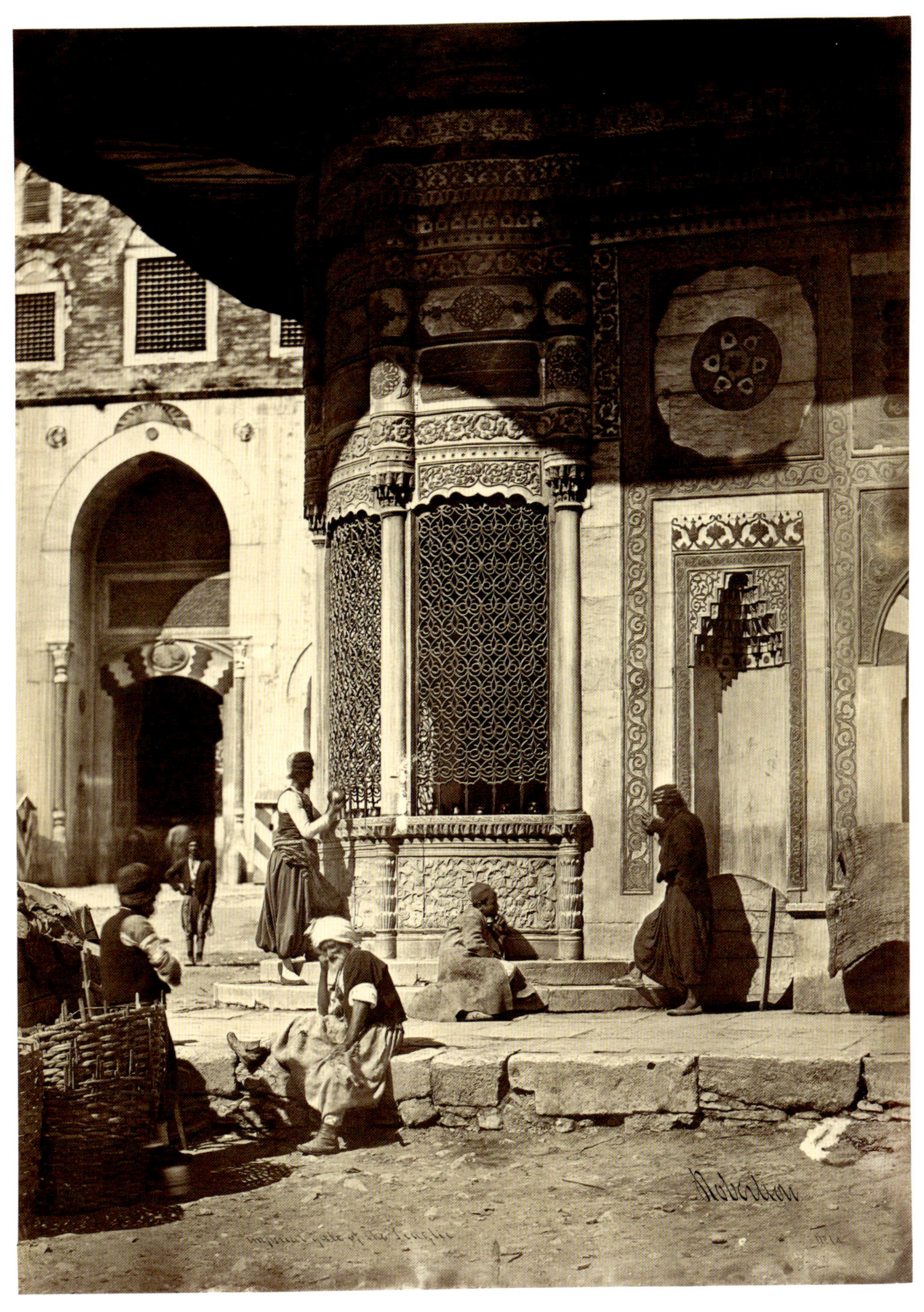

JAMES ROBERTSON
Entrance to the Seraglio
Istanbul, 1853

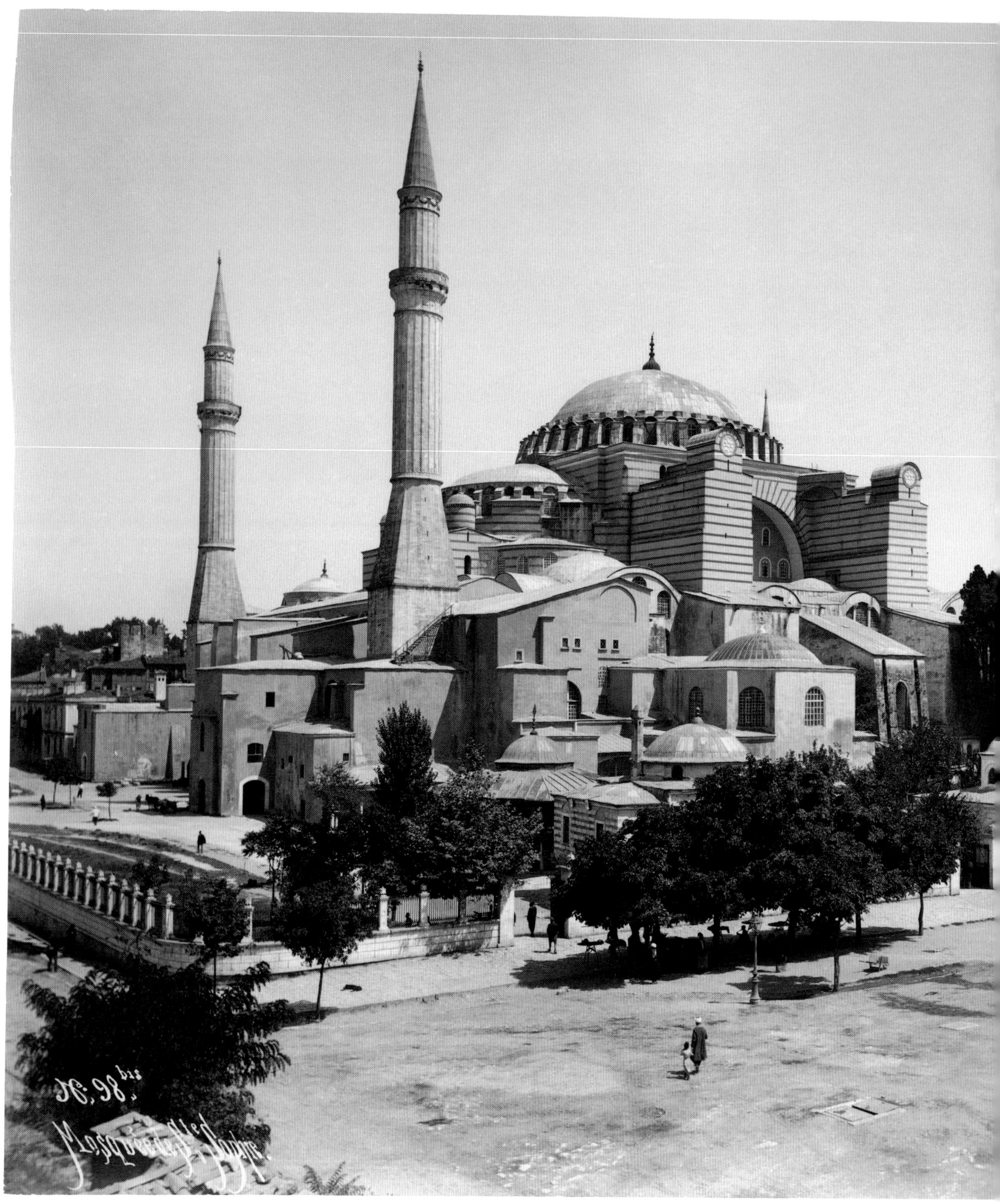
N. 98 bis
Mosquée de Ste Sophie.

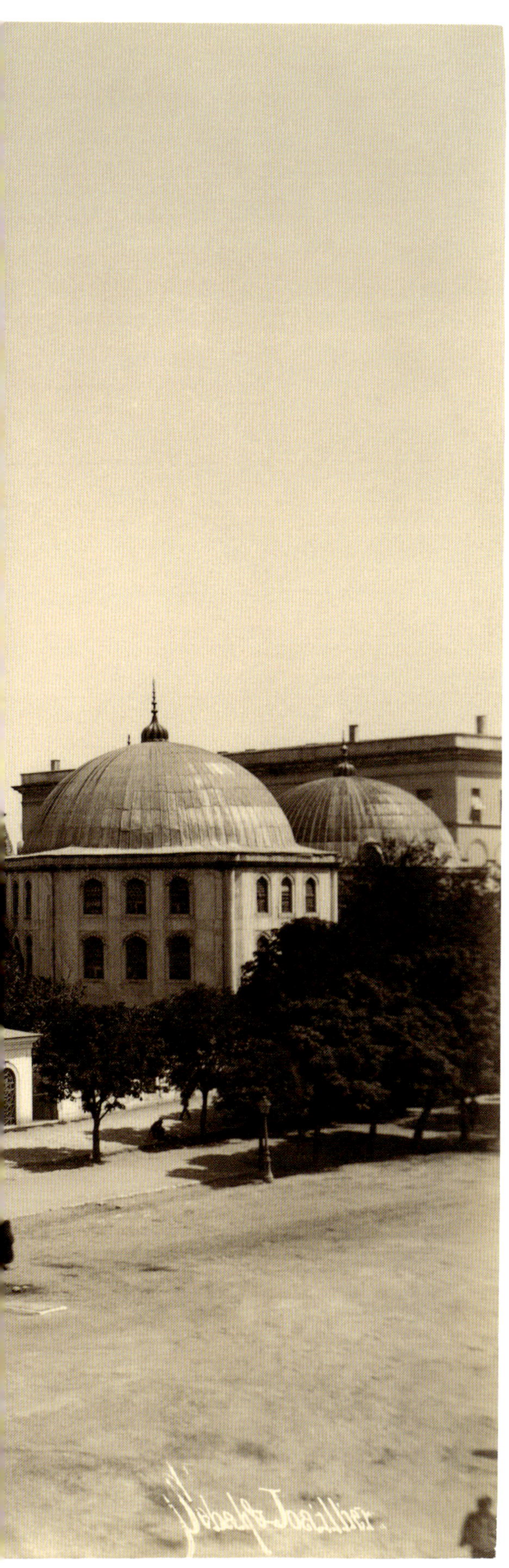

PASCAL SEBAH
Exterior, Hagia Sophia
Istanbul, 1870s

The Hagia Sophia was constructed between AD 532 and 537 on the orders of the Byzantine Emperor Justinian. Considered the epitome of the Byzantine style and to have changed the history of architecture, the building was the largest cathedral in the world for nearly a thousand years, until the completion of the Cathedral of Seville, Spain, in 1520.

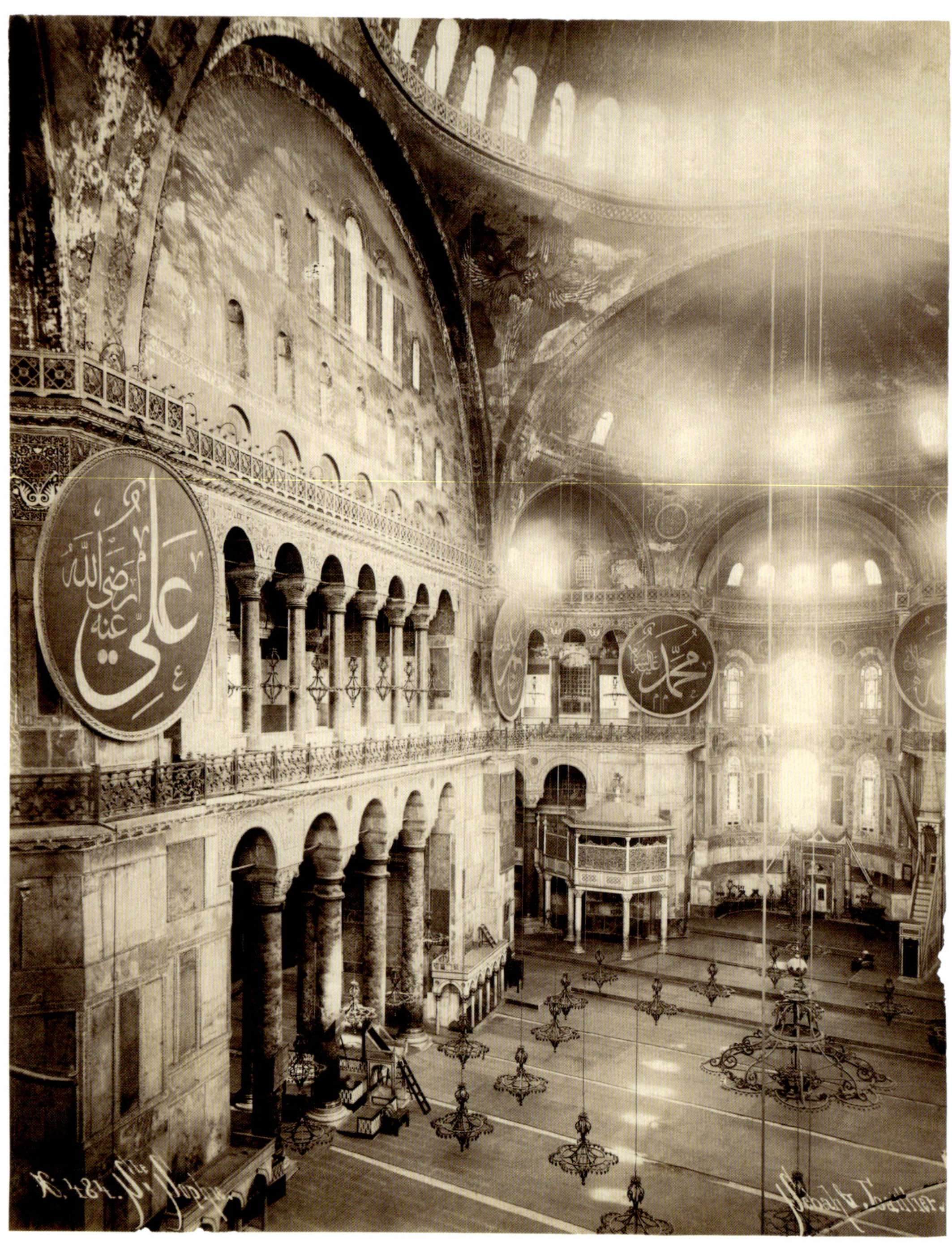

SEBAH AND JOAILLIER
Interior, Hagia Sophia
Istanbul, 1880s

The Hagia Sophia was the Cathedral of Constantinople and the centre of the Eastern Christian Empire (Byzantium). In the last 1450 years, the building has been a patriarchal basilica, a mosque and is now a museum. It remains one of the grandest, most famous buildings in the world.

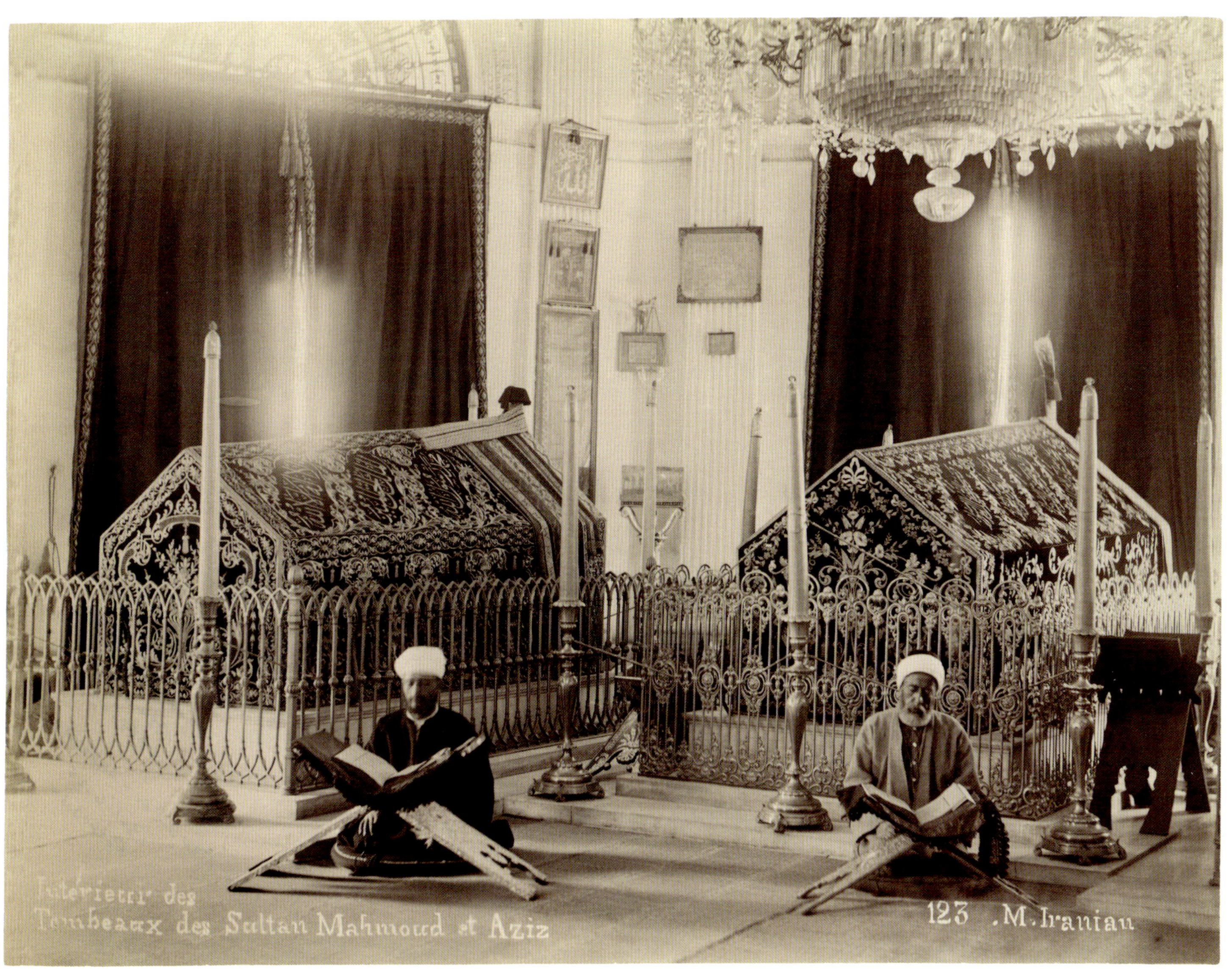

M. IRANIAN
Tombs of the Turkish Sultans
Mahmud and Aziz
1880

After the fall of Constantinople in 1453, the Ottoman Empire controlled a vast area, extending from present day Qatar to Algeria; from the shores of the Caspian Sea to the gates of Vienna; and from what is now Southern Russia to the Arabian Sea (including all of the Red Sea). At the height of its power in the sixteenth and seventeenth centuries, the Ottoman Empire spanned three continents and controlled much of Western Asia, Eastern and Southeastern Europe, the Caucasus and North Africa.

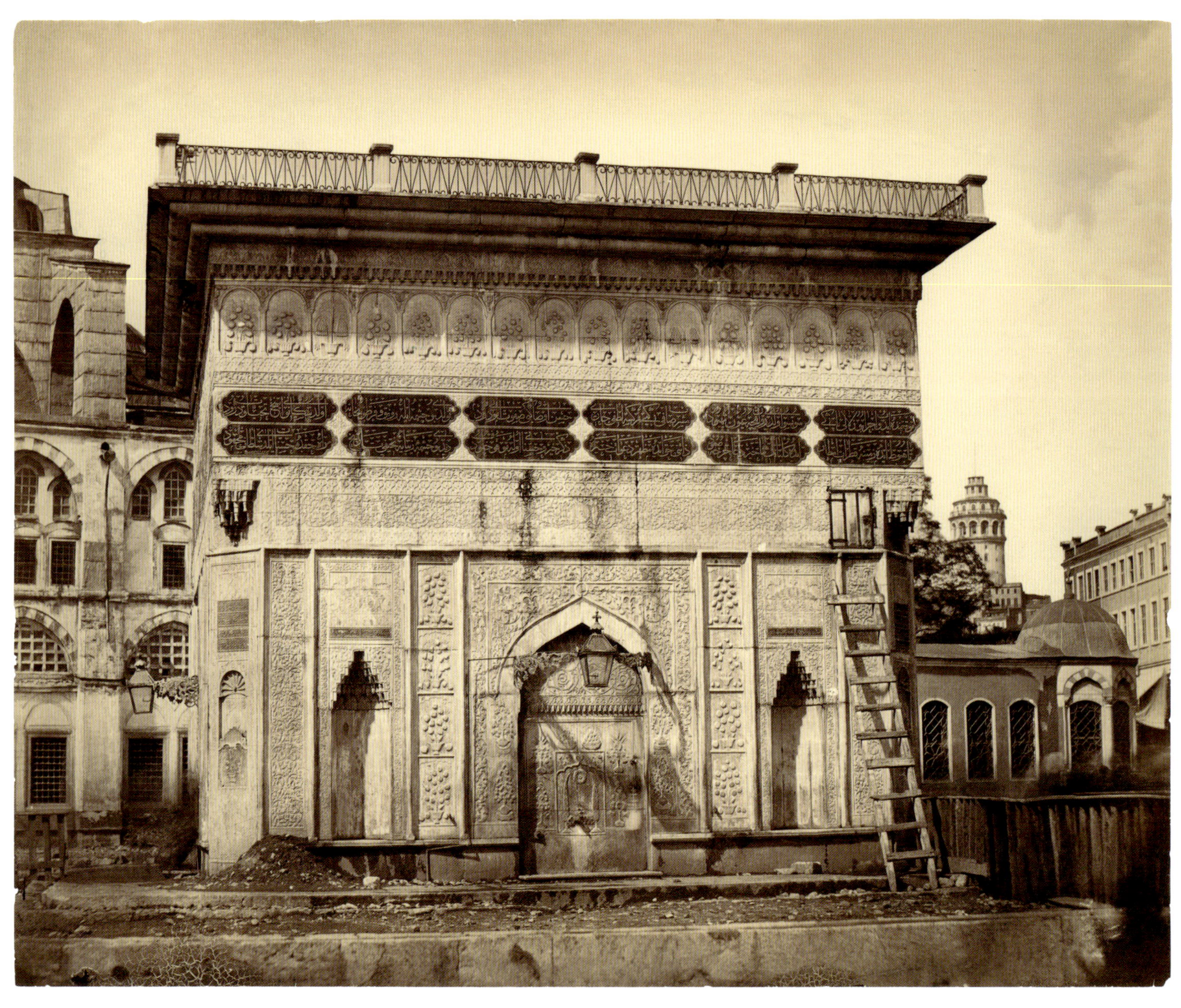

GUILLAUME BERGGREN
Fountain at Tophane
Istanbul, 1870s

At last, we have arrived. With great difficulty we managed to avoid, in the streets of Galata, the small donkeys dragging long wooden beams, and the porters, prompt and nimble under piles of bundles that would break more than one back in Europe. As you approach Istanbul, the activity increases: barrels are rolled over the bridge and along the quays, foreign wood is piled up, parcels are pushed, things are numbered and registered; shovelfuls of coal are thrown into the hold of ships and the sea disappears under the traffic of boats crossing in all directions.

Countess of Gasparin, *Constantinople*, 1867

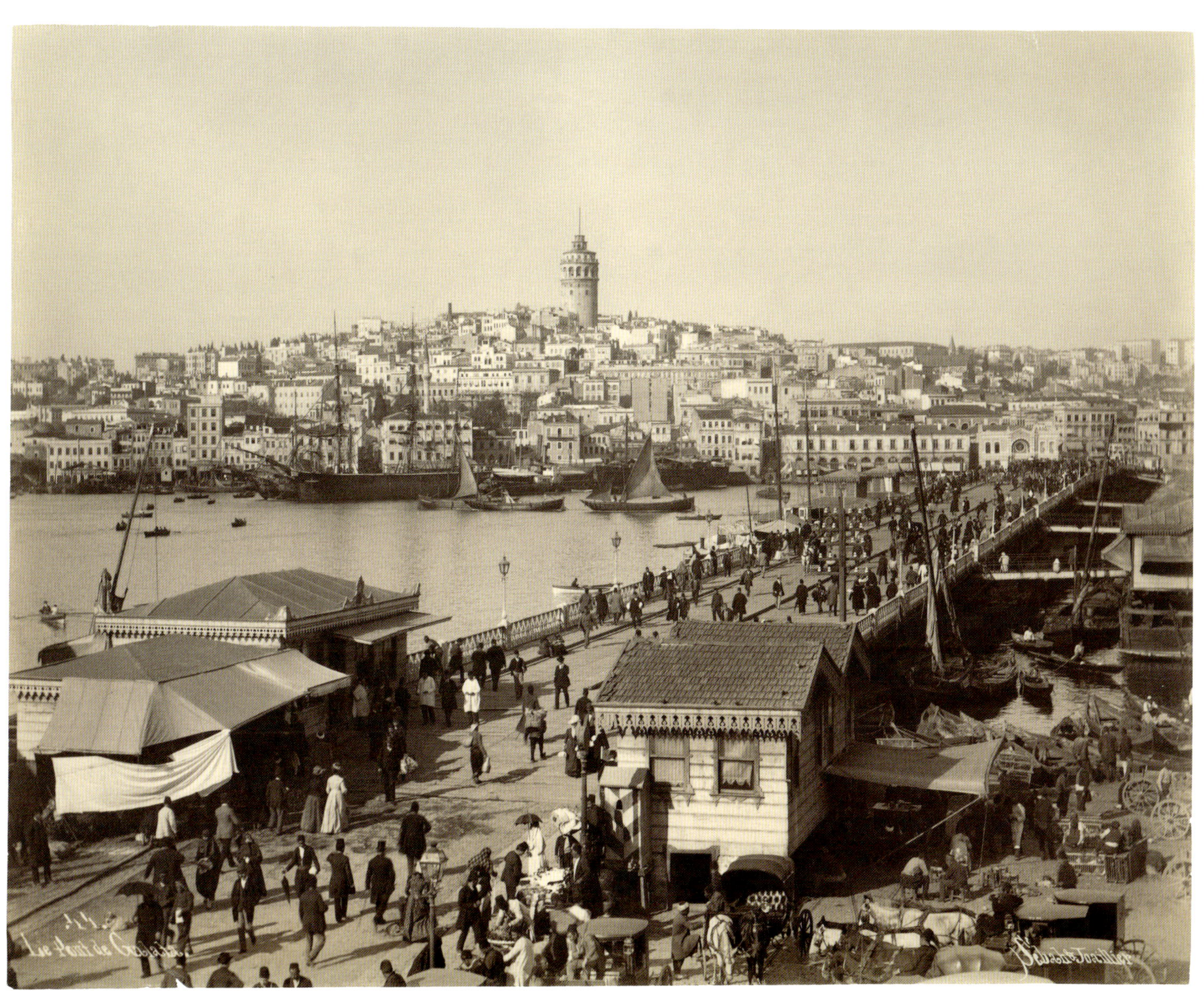

SEBAH AND JOAILLIER
Galata Bridge and the Galata Tower
Istanbul, 1880

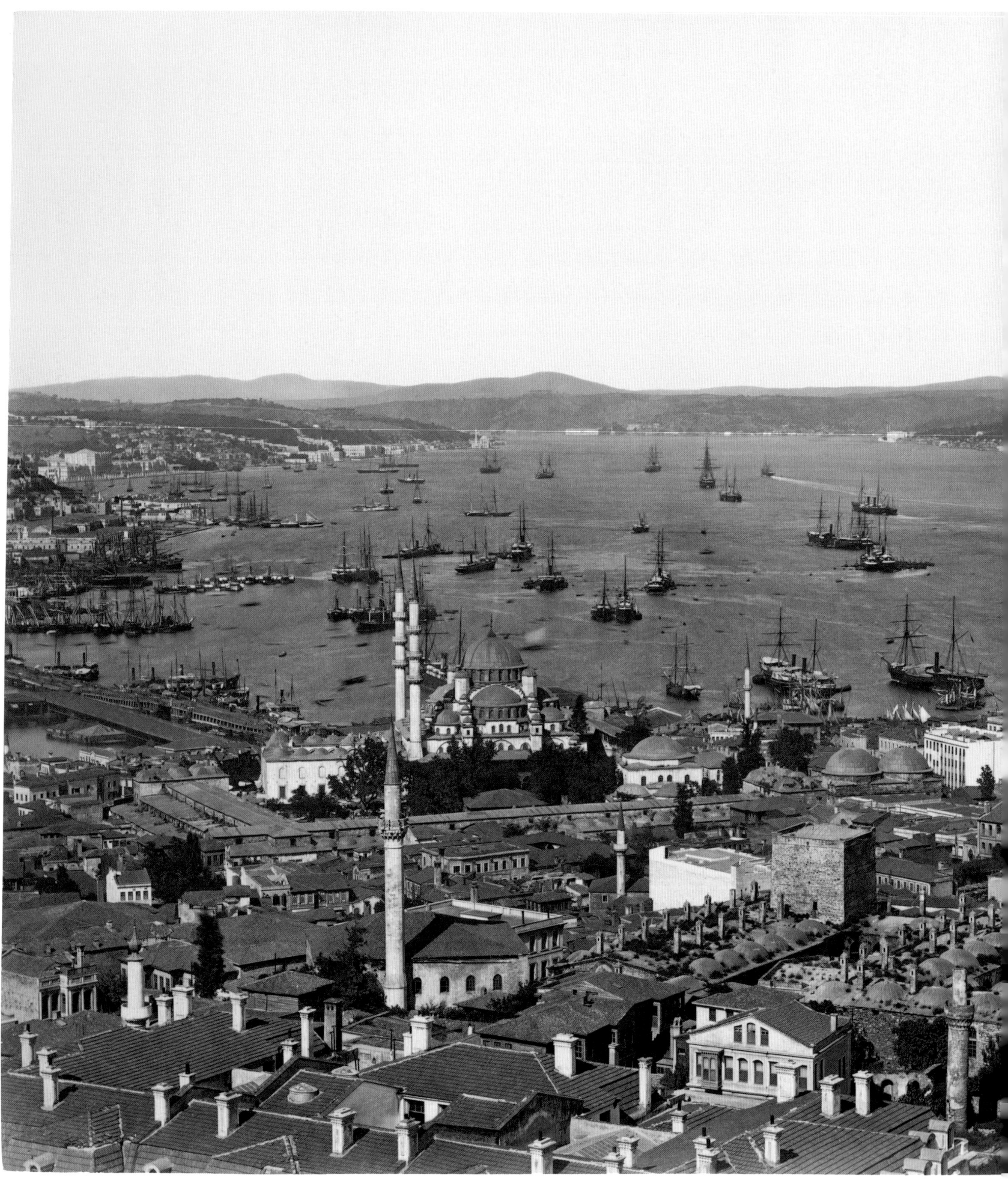

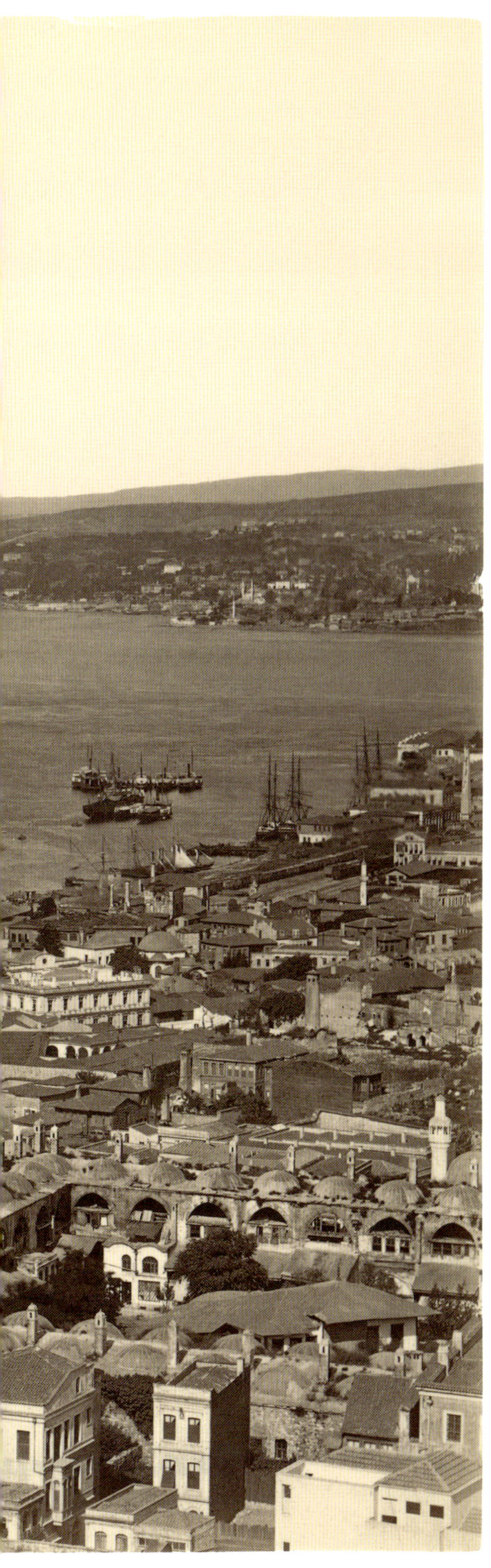

A few strokes took us to the exact point in the Golden Horn from where it is possible to enjoy a view of the Bosphorus, the Sea of Marmara and finally the whole harbour, or rather the inland sea of Constantinople. There we forgot Marmara, the Asian coast and the Bosphorus, to contemplate the valley of the Golden Horn and the seven towns suspended upon the seven hills of Constantinople, converging on the peninsula that forms this unique and incomparable city, at once city, countryside, sea, harbour, shore of rivers, gardens, wooded mountains, deep valleys, sea of houses, swarm of ships and streets, tranquil lakes and charming solitudes: a view that no brush can render except in detail and where each stroke of the oar carries the eye and the soul to opposing aspects and impressions.

Alphonse de Lamartine, *Voyage en Orient*, 1835

GUILLAUME BERGGREN
The Bosphorus from Istanbul
1870s

A Short Biographical Index of Commercial Photographers Active in the Middle East in the Nineteenth Century

Clark Worswick

The following biographical index is drawn primarily from two sources: Nissan Perez, *Focus East, Early Photography in the Near East (1839–1885)*, New York: Harry Abrams, 1988; and Ken Jacobson, *Odalisques & Arabesques: Orientalist Photography 1839–1925*, London: Bernard Quaritch, 2007. In a field beset by ever-evolving biographical work on nineteenth-century photographers of the Middle East, Ken Jacobson's work is the most current study available. Importantly, each biographical entry in the reference pages of the book is heavily annotated with bibliographic information that is sourced to the period of its publication.

It is personally interesting to note – in a conversation that has lasted for three and half decades – that against the then prevailing opinion of the 1970s, and the now current opinion of the first decade of the twenty-first century, both Ken Jacobson and myself have held a firm opinion about nineteenth-century Middle Eastern commercial photographic work. Against a host of amateur photographers active in the 1850s, against officially sponsored, government photographic surveys, and in counterpoint to hoards of casual photographers, the pictures of the nineteenth-century commercial photographers of the Middle East rose to remarkable heights of quality.

This opinion is still firmly held by both of us. It was the opinion we held in 1975. It is our opinion today. Few people in the photography field, however, appear to agree with us and this book I hope is a vindication of our belief.

Abd al-Ghaffar

(Active in Mecca, circa 1885)

There is a great mystery concerning Sayyid Abd al-Ghaffar Tabeeb Makka (Doctor of Mecca), believed to be of Indian or Malay birth, whose work documenting the holy city in the mid-1880s is almost never seen and is difficult to find. At this point, despite two generations of scholarly research, Abd al-Ghaffar and his biography remain opaque. Apart from inscriptions upon his photographs in Arabic, which credit the picture to 'Sayyid Abd al-Ghaffar Tabeeb Makka (Doctor of Mecca)' nothing else is known about Abd al-Ghaffar. His photographs of the holy city and the Hajj are the second known group of pictures made in Mecca, the first being by Colonel Sadiq Bey (aka, Muhammad Sadek) in 1880.

Abdullah Frères

(Active in Turkey and Egypt, 1861–99)

Of Armenian descent, the Abdullah brothers – Vichen, Hovsep and Kevork – established one of the longest lived and most respected photographic firms in Istanbul, and later in Cairo. In the nineteenth century, the firm held the Royal Patent of *Abdullah, Photographes du Sultan*, and the brothers received regular Royal Patronage. In addition to views of the city, the firm also created an early body of work in the 1860s documenting 'types of the Empire', which included fine figure studies such as the photographs in the present work titled *Dervishes, Circassians and Bashi-Bazouks*. In 1899, the firm was purchased by Johannes Sebah of Cairo, thus ending a thirty-year commercial rivalry between the Sebah and Abdullah firms.

Al-Hakim, Sulayman
(Active in Damascus, 1880s–90s)

Sulayman al-Hakim is possibly the only known Arab photographer of the Middle East during the nineteenth century. A resident of Damascus in the Asruniya section of the city, the photographer took pictures of the architecture and the domestic interiors of Damascus, as well as documenting religious festivals. After a catastrophic fire in the great Umayyad Mosque in Damascus, during 1893 al-Hakim made a memorable series of photographs that detailed the extensive destruction of the nearly thousand-year-old mosque. Additionally, in the late 1880s al-Hakim reprinted under his own name Colonel Sadiq Bey's 1880 photograph of the holy city of Medina, the first known photograph of the city.

Béchard, Emile
(Active in Egypt, 1870s–80s)

Initially in partnership with Hippolyte Délié in the early 1870s, Béchard's studio was in the Ezbekiya Gardens, Cairo. For over a decade Béchard was one of the most accomplished commercial photographers in Egypt. His photographs are carefully composed and show a great psychological understanding of his sitters. He created well-composed landscapes, a series of scenes of Egyptian life and carefully observed views of Egyptian archaeological sites.

Berggren, Maison: Guillaume, Hilda Ullin *(niece)*
and David Joseph *(former assistant)*
(Active in Istanbul, 1866–1916)

Originally from Stockholm, Guillaume Berggren trained as a photographer in Germany in 1859 and arrived in Turkey in 1866. His Istanbul studios were in Pera and the photographer centred his long-lived business on tourists. The studio specialised in 'native types of Turkey', as well as the sites of the city. The photographs of Berggren are usually well composed and carefully thought out. In 1916 he sold much of his archive to the Germany Embassy, which in turn deposited his photographs in the Germany Archaeological Institute, Istanbul.

Bonfils, Maison: Félix (1831–1885), **Marie-Lydie** (1837–1918)
and Adrien Bonfils (1861–1929)
(Active in Egypt, Palestine, Syria, etc., 1867–1939)

One of the most successful commercial photographic establishments in the world, Maison Bonfils, a French family firm, was first set up in Beirut in 1867. In the late 1860s Félix Bonfils made a series of notable Egyptian photographs that included a section of 'Egyptian types' that became a hallmark of the firm. In the same period Bonfils created a series of distinguished archaeological and urban 'views' in the areas surrounding Cairo. By the early 1870s it was reported that the Bonfils had 15,000 prints and 9,000 stereoscopic views in stock. Notably, in 1873 Bonfils began producing series of photographs of the Roman city of Baalbek and he created a now scarce series of large and magnificent 30 x 40 cm views of the ruins. In 1876 the company issued its first *Catalogue des vues photographiques de l'Orient*, which, by 1901, came to include photographs of most of the Middle East, the Islands of Crete and Rhodes, Anatolia and Upper Egypt, in addition to listing '300 Costumes, Scenes et Types d'Egypt, de Palestine et de Syrie'.

Fiorillo, L.
(Active in Alexandria and Palestine, 1870s–98)

Listed in the commercial directories of Egypt between 1873 and 1898, Fiorillo produced a stock of photographs for tourists that included Egypt and Jerusalem.

Frith, Francis Jr. (1822–1898)
(Active in Egypt, Sinai, Palestine and Syria, 1856–59)

One of the earliest and perhaps the most successful commercial photographers of the Middle East, Francis Frith came eventually to produce seven books on the subject, illustrated by his photographs. The result of three gruelling journeys throughout the Middle East, when they were exhibited in London his Egyptian photographs caused a sensation. In the early 1860s, the photographer established the firm of Francis Frith & Co. (of Reigate, outside London). By 1892, the firm was represented by an inventory of commercially available 'world-wide views' with a stock of a million prints. During the period 1866–75, Francis Frith & Co. dispatched photographer Frank Mason Good to the Middle East. Once there, and later in India and the Far East (China and Japan), Good created a selection of photographs marketed as *Frith's Universal Series*. The Good-Frith photographs are of a very accomplished, high order.

Garrigues, Maison
(Active in Tunisia, 1870s–1911)

Advertising itself as *'Photographe de S. A. Le Bey de Tunis'*, in the late 1870s the firm first produced what appear to be scarce views of the streets, markets and mosques of Kairouan and Tunis. Garrigues was also adept at producing a series of studio portraits of local people and 'native types'.

Good, Frank Mason
(Active in Egypt, Sinai, Palestine and Syria, 1866–75)

Between 1866 and 1875, Good was employed first by Francis Frith & Co. and then by both the Autotype Co. and Mansell & Co. (of London). Over a nine-year period, from the age of twenty-seven Good travelled throughout the Middle East making a now forgotten series of photographs. Working in a smallish format – 155 x 210 cm (6 x 8 inches) – and published as *Frith's Universal Series*, these photographs are amongst the most distinguished collections of 'views' executed in the area during the nineteenth century. Good's work appeared at an unpropitious moment, as it coincided with a worldwide recession (1873–79). Judging by the numbers of these photographs that have appeared on the photography market in the last forty years, few of the *Frith's Universal Series* were printed. Even fewer were sold. Yet today the pictures remain startling in their artistic clarity of purpose.

Hammerschmidt, Wilhelm
(Active in Egypt, Syria and Jerusalem, 1860–65)

In Egyptian photography of the early 1860s, Wilhelm Hammerschmidt, formerly of Berlin, was an artist of immense talent. Shortly after arriving in Cairo he set up a photographic business in the bazaar area of Mouski. In addition to full-plate views of Egyptian monuments and scenes of Cairo (which appear in rare coloured versions), the photographer sold reduced-sized pictures, termed cartes de visite, of Egyptian 'types' and 'trades'. Working in the then antique Taupenot process, which was six-times slower than Archer's wet plate process used by Frith, Hammerschmidt's early photographs of Egypt have an almost unearthly chiaroscuro. His early Egyptian pictures have the bite and look, the lights and darks, of a ravishing mid-1850s picture. Very few of Hammerschmidt's pictures appear on the market because of the brevity and the difficulties of his career in Cairo, which only lasted a few short years. A man of presumably dreamy, artistic temperament with an inability to listen to advice, he photographed a pilgrim party. He was severely wounded for his efforts and retired shortly after.

Lehnert & Landrock: Rudolf Franz Lehnert (1878–1948)
and Ernst Heinrich Landrock (1878–1966)
(Active in Tunis, Cairo and Palestine, 1904–?)

As Ken Jacobson notes: 'The photographs of Lehnert & Landrock are probably the most ubiquitous surviving Orientalist imagery of North Africa in the early twentieth century. They present a highly idealised vision of [a] romantic Orientalism.' It appears that the Swedish Landrock was the businessman while Lehnert, born in Bohemia, was the photographer, but both lived in Arab palaces and devoted themselves to the milieu that they documented. The intent of their work was 'to create artistic images of views and people of the Orient'. As a result, their work was and is distinct from any other commercial Middle Eastern firm presented in this book.

Quarelli, F.
(Active in Beirut, 1870s–90s)

An interesting photographer of Middle Eastern 'types' who was resident in Beirut. Today, Quarelli's work is virtually unknown and few of his prints survive. In the 1894 Baedeker's guide, Quarelli's work, as well as that of Félix Bonfils, is acknowledged.

Schoefft, Otto
(Active in Alexandria and Cairo, 1860s–80s)

Listing himself on the back of his photographs as *'O. Schoefft, Photographe de la cour d'Egypte'*, Schoefft's early work in the 1860s is virtually impossible to find today. The German photographer is now recognised by only a few surviving photographs but his work created an almost literary, heroic vision of his Egyptian and Bedouin subjects. In the late 1860s, Schoefft with another Austrian photographer named Schier formed the short-lived firm, Schier & Schoefft of Cairo.

Sebah & Joaillier: Pascal (1823–1886) **and Johannes Sebah** (1872–1947)
(Active in Istanbul, Cairo, Syria, Palestine, etc., 1856–1952)

Pascal Sebah was the fourth son of an Armenian mother and a Melchite Syrian Catholic father. Sebah opened his first studio in Istanbul during 1856. Sebah & Co. became one of the triumvirate gatherings of the greatest Middle Eastern photographers of the nineteenth century, which included Abdullah Frères, Bonfils and the Sebah firm. By 1875, Pascal Sebah had established a studio in Cairo and the firm offered views of Egypt, Greece, Istanbul and Nubia, as well as 'costumes and types' of Egypt and Turkey. Two years after Sebah's death in 1886, the studio was taken over by his sixteen year old son, Johannes. Variously, the firm's photographs are signed P. Sebah, P. Sebah Photo, Sebah & Joaillier, and finally, J.P. Sebah. In 1899, the Sebah firm bought out their rival, Abdullah Frères, including the stock and custom.

Zangaki Brothers: George and Constantine Zangaki
(Active in Egypt, 1886–1915)

In its earliest days, the firm of these Greek or Turkish photographers listed itself as *'Photographie Orientale: Zangaki frères, vues du Canal et d'Orient'*. As Ken Jacobson, in his irresistible manner, remarks about the firm, 'their photography consists of standard tourist views and ungainly portrait compositions, which are not ameliorated by their typical substandard printing. They specialised in studies of native groups in the studio, or the street but the people are often posed without either style or dignity.' As one can note, however, even a drudge can occasionally produce a great picture if you pursue this object for three decades. Witness the Zangaki's photograph *Pyramid, Camels and Photographer's Van* on page 28.

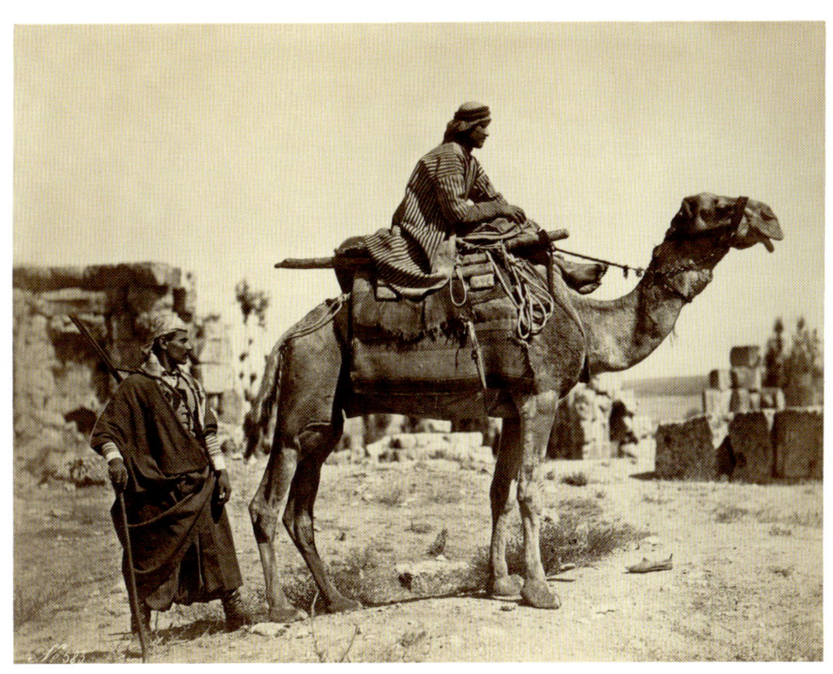

FÉLIX BONFILS
Ship of the Desert
1870s

ORIGINAL IDEA
canopia

EDITION
TURNER

TEXTS
Issam Nassar (essay)
Patricia Almárcegui (essay and quotes)
Clark Worswick (essay, captions and biographies)

PHOTOGRAPHS
All the photographs are from the Clark & Joan Worswick Collection except those on pages 46-47, 49 (private collection), and 38-39, 44 (Jorge Virgili Collection)

DESIGN
The Studio of Fernando Gutiérrez

TRANSLATION
Maite Lorés

COPYEDITING
Keith Patrick

COLOUR SEPARATION
Robert Hennessey
Juan Manuel Castro Prieto

PRINTING
Brizzolis

BINDING
Ramos

ISBN: 978-84-7506-898-5 (English)
978-84-7506-896-1 (Spanish)
D.L.: M-32373-2010

DISTRIBUTED IN THE UNITED STATES AND CANADA BY:
D.A.P. / Distributed Art Publishers
155 Sixth Avenue, 2nd floor
New York, NY 10013

DISTRIBUTED IN EUROPE BY:
Idea Books
Nieuwe Herengracht 11
Amsterdam 1011 Rd
The Netherlands

DISTRIBUTED IN THE UNITED KINGDOM BY:
Artdata
12 Bell Industrial Estate
50 Cunnington Street
London W4 5Hb
United Kingdom

SPANISH EDITION AVAILABLE
DISTRIBUTED IN SPAIN BY:
A. Machado Libros, S.A.
C/ Labradores, 15, 3–1
Pol. Ind. Prado del Espino
28660 Boadilla del Monte-Madrid
Spain

Les Punxes Distribuidora, S.L.
C/ Sardenya, 75–81
08018 Barcelona
Spain

DISTRIBUTED IN MEXICO AND LATINAMERICA BY:
Océano
Milanesat, 21–23
08017 Barcelona
Spain